THE PRACTICE OF FIELD INSTRUCTION IN SOCIAL WORK: THEORY AND PROCESS
Second Edition

This book is designed to guide social workers in their work as field instructors. It is unique in that it presents a conceptual system that unites social work theory taught in the classroom to actual practice in a variety of community settings. This system gives the field instructor a model to guide the student through a process that focuses attention on common elements of all social work practice situations. Many examples are presented to illustrate the application of this process.

In addition, the text incorporates current research and experience on pre-practicum preparation, the importance of the initial meeting with students, the relationship between field instructor and student, guidance and monitoring of the learning process, evaluation procedures, legal liability and ethical issues, and working with students where age, experience, gender, differing ethnicities, or the presence of a disability may need consideration. Field education is examined bearing in mind the multiple and rapidly changing contexts of social work and social welfare policies and practices, university and service organizations, and professional and legal requirements.

The Practice of Field Instruction in Social Work is an invaluable text for anyone preparing to become a field instructor, for current field instructors, and for faculty members responsible for field coordination. The information presented here is based on current research and teaching experience. The model presented in the book has been used with success in undergraduate and graduate programs throughout Canada and other countries.

MARION BOGO holds the Sandra Rotman Chair in Social Work and is former Acting Dean, Associate Dean, and Practicum Coordinator, Faculty of Social Work, University of Toronto.
ELAINE J. VAYDA is Professor Emeritus, School of Social Work, York University, where she was Practicum Coordinator for 18 years.

D1189442

MARION BOGO AND ELAINE VAYDA

The Practice of Field Instruction in Social Work: Theory and Process

Second Edition

Columbia University Press
New York

Columbia University Press
Publishers Since 1893
New York   Chichester, West Sussex

First published in 1998 by University of Toronto Press Incorporated in Canada

Library of Congress Cataloging-in-Publication Data

Bogo, Marion.
    The practice of field instruction in social work : theory and
process / Marion Bogo, Elaine Vayda. — 2nd ed.
        p.   cm.
    Originally published: Toronto ; Buffalo : University of Toronto
Press, 1987.
    Includes bibliographical references.
    ISBN 0-231-11319-6 (pbk. : alk. paper)
    1. Social work education—Canada.   2. Social work education—
Canada—Bibliography.   3. Social service—Field work—Study and
teaching—Canada.   4. Social service—Field work—Study and
teaching—Canada—Bibliography.   I. Vayda, Elaine J., 1927–   .
II. Title.
HV11.B595   1998
361.3′2′07155—dc21   97-48592

Printed in Canada by University of Toronto Press Incorporated.

p 10 9 8 7 6 5 4 3 2 1

Contents

INTRODUCTION   ix

1. The Integration of Theory and Practice: The ITP Loop Model   3
The Integration of Theory and Social Work Practice   3
Understanding the ITP Loop Model of Field Instruction   11
The ITP Loop Model and Your Practice   25

2. The World of Field Instruction: The School, the Student, and
   the Agency   28
The School and the Agency   28
The School and the Field: Different Frames of Reference   28
Collaboration between Schools and Agencies   32
The Curriculum   37
The Educational Experience of the Field Instructor   41
Assessing the Student's Academic Preparation and Program   43
Practicum Objectives   44

3. The Beginning Phase   47
Pre-Practicum   48
Beginning   57

4. The Instructional Relationship   77
The ITP Loop and Your Own Experience as a Student   77
The Importance of the Student–Field Instructor Relationship   81
The Qualities of an Effective Student–Field Instructor Relationship   90

Processes to Enhance the Relationship   92
Challenges to Effective Relationships   96
Organizational Context   107

5. Guiding the Learning Process   110
Using the ITP Loop Model   110
Developing a Strategy for Teaching   113
Feedback   118
Methods of Guiding the Learning Process   120
On Writing Skills   138

6. Special Situations   140
Age and Experience   140
The Exceptionally Good Student   142
The Resistant Student   143
The Student with Disabilities   144

7. Legal Aspects of Field Instruction   149
Liability Issues   149
Informed Consent   152
Record-keeping   154
Privileged Communication and Confidentiality   154
The Duty to Report and to Warn   157
Disclosure of Student Status   157
Students in Potentially Dangerous Practicum Situations   160
Strategy for Collective Agreement Strikes   160
Sexual Harassment   161

8. Evaluation and Ending   163
Issues in Evaluation   164
The Final or Summative Evaluation   171
The Marginal or Failing Student   177
Appeal of a Failing Grade   183
Evaluation of the Field Instructor and the Setting   185
The Importance of Endings   186

APPENDIX: A Teaching Guide

1. The Integration of Theory and Practice: The ITP Loop Model   195
The ITP Loop Model   195

The Ecological Framework for Social Work Practice 201
The ITP Loop Model and Field Instruction 203
Using the ITP Loop Model with a Range of Retrieval Methods 204

2. The World of Field Instruction: The School, the Student, and
   the Agency 205
The School/Agency Interface 205
Assessing the Fit between the Academic Courses and the
   Practicum 207
Practicum Objectives 208

3. The Beginning Phase 210
The Phases of Field Instruction 210
Anticipation and Preparation of the Field Instructor and the
   Setting 211
Characteristics of a Learning Contract 213
How to Develop a Learning Contract 215
Selecting Assignments 218

4. The Instructional Relationship 219
The Importance of Relationship 219
Qualities of an Effective Student–Field Instructor Relationship 220
Learning and Teaching Styles 221
Challenges to Effective Relationships 222

5. Guiding the Learning Process 231
Developing a Strategy for Guiding and Monitoring Learning 231
Giving and Receiving Effective Feedback 234
Using the ITP Loop Model 235

6. Special Situations 239
Age as an Issue 239
The Student with Prior Social Work Experience 240
The Exceptionally Good Student 241
The Resistant Student 241
Students with Disabilities 242

7. Legal Aspects of Field Instruction 246
Liability Issues 246
Informed Consent 247

Privileged Communication and Confidentiality   247
Students in Potentially Dangerous Practicum Situations   247

8. Evaluation   250
Formative or Ongoing Evaluation   250
Evaluation of Competence   250
Maintaining Objectivity   253
The Final or Summative Evaluation   253
The Marginal or Failing Student   253
Evaluation of the Field Instructor and the Setting   255
Evaluation of the Seminar   257

REFERENCES   259

Introduction

We began our first edition of this book with the premise that accreditation granted to an institution providing social work education guarantees that the curriculum is providing a field education component, also referred to as field work or field practicum. Field instruction, though derived from the school curriculum and from an older model of apprenticeship, is a unique approach to professional education which demands thoughtful preparation by the school and the agency. Academic courses alone are not enough, nor is an apprenticeship requirement *per se* sufficient to qualify for a social work degree. The field instructor must learn to travel a new road between the university system and the service provider.

Field instructors are those persons who are selected or who volunteer to guide students through the practicum requirement of the social work curriculum. They may be attached either to a community agency or service or may come from within the school itself. Effective field instructors should have current practice experience as well as a commitment to social work education. Neither a faculty-based educator with no direct involvement in practice nor a practitioner disinterested in the educational process is properly equipped to provide the guidance that is required.

Nomenclature can be confusing because various titles are used to describe persons engaged in field instruction, such as practice teacher, field instructor, field educator, or agency supervisor. In order to be consistent, the title of field instructor will be used throughout this book. Regardless of title, it is the function of the field instructor that will be examined.

A revised edition of our book, first published in 1986, was undertaken because we believed it was time to revisit our original formulation of our model, the Integration of Theory and Practice (ITP) Loop, as an approach to field education. We had learned much from our own direct teaching experience with field instructors and from many field coordinators who use our book in training. Field instructors affiliated with our institutions and field coordinators from other universities gave us support and encouragement as well as excellent suggestions for clarification and presentation of concepts, letting us know what worked and what needed more work. In addition, there is continuing research and a growing body of literature on social work field education that we wished to consider in relation to emerging developments and emphases in professional preparation.

This edition includes what we believe is an important expansion of the basic components of the Integration of Theory and Practice Loop. The added elements are four specific situational elements: contextual or societal, organizational, psycho-social, and interactive factors which assume different weighting as the looping process recurs. We have included many examples that help to illuminate these concepts.

We have also incorporated into the appendix of this edition the teaching modules which were developed for the teaching manual published in 1993. They include teaching suggestions, examples, and exercises to be used by practicum coordinators in orientation and training groups for field instructors. Individual readers may find they can use some of these educational activities on their own.

We still believe our model and approach to be generic and applicable to social work practice in any setting, using any modality and serving diverse populations. In these times of shrinking financial support and diminished service resources, it is more important than ever to develop competent practitioners, able to respond to clients and communities with skill and imagination and to understand the uses of advocacy. We believe the approach presented in these pages will facilitate this high level of practice.

THE PRACTICE OF FIELD INSTRUCTION IN SOCIAL WORK: THEORY AND PROCESS

1

The Integration of Theory and Practice: The ITP Loop Model

The Integration of Theory and Social Work Practice

Practitioners and educators in social work have always characterized the business of the practicum as the place where theory is integrated with practice. All too frequently this statement stands without further definition. Integration of theory and practice (ITP), without examination, may be a kind of magical incantation through which educators, like alchemists, hope to transform a social work student into a professional social worker. Recognizing the limits of magic, even for social workers, this chapter will engage field instructors in the work of demystifying ITP and giving it operational meaning.

Practitioners, to become educators, must be able to examine their own practice and articulate the thoughts, attitudes, values, and feelings that affect the actions they take. Practitioners feel that many of these actions have become 'second nature,' so that plans and behaviours may appear, to the observer, to evolve naturally. In fact, professional behaviour is based on implicit ideas and beliefs that social workers have developed through their own educational and practice experiences. This 'integrated knowledge' has to be identified so that the field educator can communicate it to the student (Bogo and Vayda 1987, 1991). In order to illustrate how to unravel 'integrated knowledge,' we will follow two case examples, one a practice situation with an individual and one involving community practice and service planning.

The worker in both examples might imagine a looping process. Since social work activity is both cumulative and ongoing, looping is a useful image. Each practice encounter must incorporate past experience, new knowledge, and future speculation and planning. This is demonstrated in figure 1.

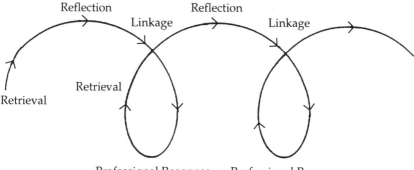

Figure 1

Retrieval

The starting point of the loop is information gathering, which we call retrieval. Retrieval is the recall of information about a specific practice situation and would include preparatory thinking as well as the contact itself. To put it another way, we mean the facts that distinguish and define any situation at the beginning of involvement.

Retrieved information from any social work situation can be divided into psycho-social, interactive, contextual, and organizational factors (Vayda and Bogo 1991). The worker and client focus on the most pressing factors, which may change with time. As new information is retrieved, the worker moves through the loop again and again until the situation is resolved.

Psycho-social factors are familiar concepts to social workers and refer to specific information about individuals, families, groups, and communities. Included are observations about behaviour, affect, and cognition, and information about formal and informal support systems. Psycho-social factors direct attention to the client system. Interactive factors refer to the creation of a new system composed of social worker and client exchanges. The quality of the interaction plays a key role in the disclosure of information and facilitates elaboration. In demonstrating the loop, we have been deliberately selective and reductive. We will focus on psycho-social and interactive factors first, and add contextual and organizational factors later.

RETRIEVAL: INDIVIDUAL PRACTICE: EXAMPLE 1

The social worker is employed in a shelter for battered women. The client, a woman, aged thirty-four years, has three children, ages six, eight, and ten years, and is physically abused repeatedly by her husband. Although the police have been involved, no charges have been laid. The woman has sought refuge in the shelter several times in the past, but has always made a decision to return home. Her family has counselled her to return to her husband. She has never held a paying job and has a grade 10 education.

RETRIEVAL: COMMUNITY PRACTICE: EXAMPLE 2

In a large metropolitan city, a South Asian feminist women's group approaches the local planning council for help in establishing a service for battered women in their community. Increasing awareness has developed that wife abuse is considered a criminal offence in the wider society but is tolerated by some in the community. Males and elders in the community are feeling threatened by the militancy of some of the younger women in the community who have publicized, in the mainstream media, the fact of wife abuse in their community.
This information is illustrative of retrieval. In actual practice, more information would have been retrieved and reflected upon at this point.

Reflection

Social workers are trained to subject the information they have gathered to a reflective process, which we have identified as the next step in the loop. Reflection contains elements of the rubric of 'self-awareness,' which has been a standard principle of social work practice. Reflection, as it is used in the loop, is an exploration of the social worker's personal associations with respect to the practice situation. Personal associations may arise from personality style, idiosyncratic reactions to similar life experiences, or internalized cultural values. The purpose of reflection is to gain self-knowledge of each of these processes.

Personal subjective reactions can be recalled through reflection and examined regarding their potential effect on the work to be done. It is equally important to examine assumptions and beliefs that may be perceived as truth but are cultural constructs belonging to a personal world-view shaped by one's ethnicity, race, culture, and gender. By acknowledging the validity of other assumptions and beliefs, an open dialogue can begin between worker and client. Personal experience must also be acknowledged when it is relevant to the situation of the client. While similar experiences can aid joining and understanding, it is important to acknowledge that each individual has a unique response to the same life event.

In addition, as the situation progresses and the loop repeats itself, the worker reflects on the effectiveness of interventions undertaken to bring about change. In this way, reflection begins to build an ongoing evaluation of the work accomplished.

REFLECTION: INDIVIDUAL PRACTICE: EXAMPLE 1

The worker is a strong feminist who herself had left an abusive relationship and subsequently earned a graduate degree while supporting herself through part-time employment. Through reflection she confronts her impatience with the client's pattern of returning to her abusive husband. She becomes aware that she must separate her experience from that of her client. She recalls her immediate labelling of the client as helpless and dependent, unable or unwilling to make decisions and act upon them. The worker knows that she can be judgmental and that this attitude could undermine her capacity for empathy and joining.

REFLECTION: COMMUNITY PRACTICE: EXAMPLE 2

The worker is a middle-aged Hispanic male with a strong sense of the importance of family preservation and the value of shared beliefs and cultural solidarity. Upon reflection, he becomes aware that he has a tendency to identify with the males and elders in the community. He becomes aware that he must find a way to join with the needs of the younger women, without losing his sense of the value the community places on family stability.

Linkage

Less familiar to social workers is the conscious application of theory to practice. This step is what we have labelled as linkage. Linkage is that part of the loop that uses cognitive associations to retrieved information and to the associations elicited through reflection, and links them with knowledge learned from reading, research studies, lectures, and general experience. The purpose is to identify and label knowledge that will help explain the practice data and the subjective reactions that have been evoked, and ultimately to use that knowledge in planning professional responses. Linkage requires that facts and attitudes about the situation be abstracted or generalized to identify common elements that relate to a knowledge base. A social worker's practice is likely to be based on a well-integrated knowledge and value base consisting of practice wisdom, concepts from various theories, and empirically validated findings. Additionally, approaches or therapies that may be characteristic of a specific setting provide the theoretical linkage. These 'pieces' of knowledge become part of the practitioner's art and are used in a seemingly intuitive fashion in interacting with a practice situation (Schon 1987, 1995). Specialized practice models such as task-centred, family systems, group, and community development approaches interpret human behaviour and interpersonal adaptation, and provide social workers with specific techniques to involve clients in intervention approaches to bring about desired change.

LINKAGE: INDIVIDUAL PRACTICE: EXAMPLE 1

Psycho-social knowledge may involve recognizing the impact of the client's cultural expectations about traditional female behaviour in a marriage on her self-identity, self-esteem, and her fears about permanently leaving the relationship. Knowledge of family dynamics are also relevant, such as the emotional impact on the children and the reactivation of the woman's experience of violence in her family of origin. Knowledge of specific practice models for intervention may focus attention on eliciting support and safety planning from informal support networks such as a local single mothers' group and her family of origin. Formal support networks might include financial maintenance, subsidized housing, vocational training and education, and provisions for day care.

LINKAGE: COMMUNITY PRACTICE: EXAMPLE 2

Linking to 'pieces of knowledge' about immigration and relocation, such as an understanding of cultural beliefs brought from the country of origin, and the effect of a different set of societal expectations in the new country on identity, may inform the worker's approach to this situation. The worker asks himself, 'What do I need to think about to better understand this situation, and what do I need to know to intervene effectively?' The worker uses the practice principle of involving participants in all aspects of the process to acknowledge the group's concerns and enlists them in developing a strategy to identify and engage key persons in the community who play formal and informal roles.

Professional Response

To practice social work means to take some action. This step is what we have labelled as professional response to a given set of facts at a particular point in time. Each situation requires the worker and client to select the issues of highest priority for immediate focus. Using this part of the loop, the social worker grounds the ideas, knowledge, and insights just uncovered to develop specific plans and behaviours for dealing with the situation. Professional response is the selection and implementation of a plan that will inform the next encounter. Consideration of all parts of the loop conveys the dynamic interrelationship between concepts and action.

PROFESSIONAL RESPONSE: INDIVIDUAL PRACTICE: EXAMPLE 1

The worker might choose to open a discussion with the client about what choices the client feels are immediately necessary and possible for her at the time, specifically encouraging her to plan for the safety of herself and her children, through contacts with appropriate informal and formal systems, such as neighbours, extended family, and police. Later, the worker might discuss with the client her family's attitudes, experiences, and expectations.

PROFESSIONAL RESPONSE: COMMUNITY PRACTICE: EXAMPLE 2

The social worker begins to work with the women's group to help them identify all the stakeholders in the community who need to be involved from the beginning in planning a response to this community issue. The next step is to work out a detailed plan of how to involve these various potential participants and to begin implementation of the plan.

We have thus far focused on retrieval of psycho-social and interactive factors in going through the loop. However, two other important factors, contextual and organizational, influence all social work situations and need to be acknowledged. Contextual factors refer to the economic and political structures embedded in society that affect individuals and disempower certain groups through discrimination based on gender, race, ethnicity, age, and disability. In addition, societal attitudes may erect boundaries that exclude specific groups; for example, a suburban community may seem a hostile environment to visible minority persons. A particular community group may have fixed beliefs about homosexuals or lesbians, homeless persons, persons who have committed criminal offences, or persons who are either mentally or physically disabled. Social workers are committed to connect these issues to their ongoing practice responses and work toward shifts in empowerment for their clients.

CONTEXTUAL FACTORS: INDIVIDUAL PRACTICE: EXAMPLE 1

In a period of budgetary constraints, the community is less sympathetic to providing adequate resources for battered women. The re-emergence of beliefs in the sanctity and primacy of the family have created a hostile climate for women who may need protection from their partners. The attitudes of the police and the justice system toward family violence often keep women at risk. In addition, there are negative economic consequences for single women living alone with children.

Integrating this perspective expands the worker's previous professional response to include advocacy. The worker might join with others to plan a strategy for presenting the needs of battered women to the media and to various levels of government.

CONTEXTUAL FACTORS: COMMUNITY PRACTICE: EXAMPLE 2

In a period of financial constraint, the government is unlikely to fund services aimed at a specific ethnic group. Many people in the community have experienced discrimination which they believe is based on racial difference.

Taking this into account, the worker's professional response might be to help the women identify funding sources in their own community as well as publicizing the information from the needs assessment in the wider community.

Organizational factors refer to bureaucratic systems and to how their ideology and assumptions, rules, and procedures affect program delivery and service provision. These factors include an organization's mandate, its climate, roles and procedures, including decision-making procedures, its structure and funding, board composition, and its relationships with a network of other community agencies. Social workers use knowledge of organizational dynamics to develop interventions to make organizations more effective.

ORGANIZATIONAL FACTORS: INDIVIDUAL PRACTICE: EXAMPLE 1

The shelter's board of directors has placed a three-week limit on the length of time any woman may remain in the shelter. The worker feels this is insufficient time for adequate planning to take place and may be a reason why some clients return home to a dangerous situation before an alternative plan is in place.

The worker may seek the support of other workers, clients, and the director in making a request to meet with the board to present her concerns.

ORGANIZATIONAL FACTORS: COMMUNITY PRACTICE: EXAMPLE 2

The planning council has just published a study which some local community leaders have branded as unfair because they feel it focuses on racial divisions and criminal activity in their community. The director of the council is very sensitive to this criticism and has asked the staff to avoid any activity which could jeopardize the council.
The worker knows that survival of the council is dependent on public funding. However, he recognizes an ethical dilemma between responsibility to protect the council and responsibility to respond to community needs. The worker may inform the director that he understands the director's concern, but that he cannot let it interfere with his responsibility to provide assistance to community groups. He may agree to keep the director informed about any action which would be potentially significant to the council.
These case examples and discussion provide an introduction to how the ITP Loop Model as a process can be applied to the content of social work practice. It is a model that is generic and comprehensive, and provides a unifying structure for both practice and field instruction. Figure 2 illustrates how this framework unifies content and process.

THE ITP LOOP MODEL APPLIED TO SOCIAL WORK PRACTICE: PROCESS AND CONTENT				
PROCESS	Retrieval	Reflection	Linkage	Professional Response
CONTENT	Psycho-social Factors			
	Interactive Factors			
	Contextual Factors			
	Organizational Factors			

Figure 2

Content

We have diagrammed the looping process, and we will return to a discussion of each step in this process. More complicated and complex are the factors we have labelled as content. These factors coincide with an ecological metaphor which has been widely adopted in social work practice theory to capture the profession's commitment to the transactional bonds between the person and his or her social and physical context (Hartman 1994). We have described all social work situations as involving psycho-social, interactive, societal or contextual, and organizational factors. In actual practice, however, instructors and students must consciously choose to consider only those factors which are meaningful to the specific practice situation at any point in time. This requires scanning the whole to focus attention on the most relevant factors, which, in turn, may change with time, thus requiring the selection of still other factors. Though this process sounds complex, scanning to facilitate focus is a common mental activity.

Understanding the ITP Loop Model of Field Instruction

Implicit in preparing students for service in the field is a process whereby the information, knowledge, and critical analytic base acquired by students in the academic part of professional education is translated into an ability to relate to persons seeking help and to arrive at professional decisions in a service context. Each social work school or program has developed a unique philosophy of education, specific curriculum objectives, and specific practicum regulations and procedures. However, field instruction is more than a structural arrangement between academy and agency in which actors follow a set of procedures; and field instruction requires more than providing an example for a student to observe and emulate, as a master teacher would do for an apprentice, or establishing a facilitative relationship between student and field instructor. The ITP Loop Model should assist field instructors in examining their own practice and that of their students, as well as the interaction between student and field instructor. The organizing principle is the belief that field instruction is a branch of social work practice that possesses a distinctive blend of knowledge, values, and skills that can be articulated and learned. The ITP Loop Model is applicable to all levels of practice, whether with individuals, families, groups, or communities, or in administration, policy development, or planning. It can be used in well-established or developing settings, urban or rural settings, and with undergraduate and graduate students.

To review, we use the image of a looping process to depict the cumulative and ongoing nature of both practice and field instruction. For purposes of presentation, we will discuss each phase of the ITP Loop Model sequentially. However, practice and field instruction are fluid, dynamic, and integrated, and cannot be so neatly organized. In using the loop at a given time, any part will be joined with other parts as the process of retrieval, reflection, linkage, and professional response occurs. Having described a model that integrates social work theory and practice, we are ready to focus on how the practitioner, now functioning as a field educator, can use the model with students in practicum settings.

Retrieval

Since the distinctive feature of the practicum is the primacy of practice, field instruction starts with and always returns to a practice event. The entry point in the loop for the process of field instruction is the retrieval or recall of information, namely, the facts describing the given practice experience. It involves use of the observing ego, a 'mind's eye' phenomenon wherein the field instructor or student recalls a professional situation as both an observer and a participant. We have already said that social work situations include psycho-social, interactive, organizational, and contextual factors. These are reviewed as the field instructor and the student move through the loop again and again until the situation is resolved. Retrieval may involve consideration of the known facts of a situation in order to prepare for the first contact, or it may involve reactions flowing from a professional response that evolved from the preceding practice activity. Practice activities in which students are involved include individual, family, or group interviews, team or committee meetings, presentations, and reading and writing reports. Field instructors may retrieve student practice data through such methods as verbal reports, process and summary recordings, audio or video tapes, live supervision, or co-working experiences.

Students new to social work are likely to retrieve and report practice observations that are personally meaningful to them but that may not be focused. The bridge between the familiar role of social persona and purposeful intervenor is difficult to negotiate. Workers know that it is the context of the encounter or the agency's service mandate that empowers the worker to investigate any situation. Students, wanting to be accepted and liked by the person they are seeing, find it difficult to ask for information which they feel might insult, embarrass, alienate, or anger the other person. For example, the student at a child protection agency sent to investigate a complaint of potential child abuse talks with the mother for nearly an hour. She reports to her field instructor that the mother was friendly, seemed very nice, and denied ever hitting or spanking her child. In response to a question from the field instructor, she said she did not ask how the mother might discipline the child or if the child ever made her angry. Rather, they mainly discussed the mother's concerns about the recent decrease in her welfare support.

The task of the field instructor is to present a structure which will frame students' random observations and affect their selection and definition of what constitutes relevant data. In the above case, the field instructor and student talked about the agency's charge to ensure that children are protected and what the student, as the instrument of that charge, needs to ask the mother, who may be ambivalent about her parenting role. The field instructor also acknowledged that governmental changes in the level of support available to single mothers were affecting many of the clients of the agency. In this example, the field instructor and the student have identified relevant psycho-social, interactive, organizational, and contextual content.

Reflection

Reflection is a familiar concept in social work education. It refers to the worker's thoughtful consideration of the practice activity and, as it is used in the loop, focuses on two elements: subjective meanings and objective effects. Reflection on subjective meanings entails an exploration of the personal associations that the student or the field instructor might have with respect to the practice situation. It involves the identification of the values, beliefs, assumptions, and attitudes which we attach to observed facts in order to make them understandable within a personal context and in accordance with our internalized notions of what is 'right.'

Social work practice has long recognized that the 'self' of the practitioner exerts a powerful influence on interpretations of and reactions to professional situations. Approaches to field instruction have given more or less attention to the student's personality dynamics, and to past or current issues in the student's life which affect his or her ability to offer effective service (George 1982). Models which used a therapeutic approach tended to interpret students' subjective reactions negatively, seeing them as interfering and hence in need of being controlled. Too often this resulted in a quasi-therapeutic supervisory model which blurred the boundaries between education and personal growth (Siporin 1981), with the result that this approach became problematic and fell into disfavour. We recognize that in their practice social workers are often confronted with extremely challenging situations, such as those of people who have been victimized in violent intimate relationships, refugees who have suffered trauma and torture, people who are dying of AIDS, and children who have been sexually abused. It is normal that these situations will elicit strong personal reactions from social workers and students. As Grossman, Levine-Jordano, and Shearer (1990) have observed, social work education has often abdicated its role of helping students learn to deal with their emotional reactions to practice. Through the phase of reflection in the loop model, the field instructor can include this focus and work with the student to identify subjective responses. These can be used to advance both self-understanding and understanding of the client, and to formulate professional responses that will be helpful.

In some instances, the student will have had personal experiences similar to those of the practice situation. While these experiences can aid joining and understanding, it is important to acknowledge different reactions and unique responses to the same life event. The intent of identification of similar experiences is not to intrude into the personal life of the student; rather, when students and educators feel that their own experiences are relevant to the practice situation, the aim is to acknowledge and consciously use them. It is the practice situation that stimulates and guides the search for personal experience that will promote or retard students' ability to empathize.

Reflection is a process that has taken on a new urgency as people from many different races and cultures are struggling to find an identity and to survive in North America. Trying to meet the needs of such a diverse population is straining established practice repertoires and traditional attitudes. In addition, gender roles are shifting, conventional attitudes toward sexual preferences are being challenged, and cherished concepts of family and social support are in great need of redefinition (Hartman 1990a). Through reflection, social workers can gain self-knowledge and become aware of the influence of assumptions and beliefs that may be perceived as truth but are actually cultural constructs belonging to a personal world-view.

In summary, reflection aims to help the student gain access to personal subjective reactions to practice phenomena with which the student is engaged. These reactions can reflect internalized cultural values, idiosyncratic reactions to similar life experiences, or personality styles. Through reflection, the student's feelings, beliefs, values, and assumptions are made explicit and subjected to critical thinking about their impact on interactions with the clients or participants in the practice situation, on assessments and judgments being made, and on the effectiveness of plans and interventions. Students are helped to recognize the challenges and changes that are occurring, or that need to occur, as long-held beliefs and reactions are confronted by new knowledge and experience.

In reflecting on personal associations to practice, four sets of factors must be considered: psycho-social, interactive, contextual, and organizational. Psycho-social factors might include subjective reactions to characteristics of people in the situation; to certain social problems (e.g., substance abuse or the homeless populations); and to systemic or structural factors (e.g., race, unemployment, or incarceration). Interactive factors might include reactions based on transference or counter-transference phenomena; and idiosyncratic reactions to specific areas of comfort and enthusiasm or discomfort and anxiety.

Contextual factors may also direct student and field instructor to recall life experiences relevant to the practice situation that have produced their belief systems, social class assumptions, and cultural, ethnic, and gender-based assumptions. For example, life transition experiences such as adolescence, marriage, parenthood, aging, separation and loss, crisis reactions, and the effects of isolation all form the basis for empathy. These universal experiences, however, are filtered by poverty, social class, culture, race, and gender. The commonalities and the differences need to be reviewed and applied to the practice situation.

Organizational factors might include reactions to specific agency policies and procedures, to a climate of openness or rigidity, or to an institutionalized approach to problems based on regulations. Large bureaucratic structures may be hierarchical and authoritarian, or they may permit democratic participation; and small services may be egalitarian, or they may be charged with factionalism and tension. These factors influence the interactions between social worker and client, and between student and teacher.

Table 1 outlines the factors that can be scanned by the field instructor and student in order to select those elements that may be personally relevant to the practice situation.

TABLE 1
Reflection: Personal associations to the encounter

Psycho-social factors:
Reaction to characteristics of people in the situation.
Reaction to social problems (e.g., homelessness).

Interactive factors:
Awareness of areas of comfort and enthusiasm, and of discomfort and anxiety, in contact situations.
Awareness of the effects of transferring subjective meanings, feelings, and reactions on the part of both workers and other persons.

Contextual factors:
Relevant life experiences.
Relevant belief systems; social class assumptions; culture, ethnicity, and race; and gender-based assumptions.
Awareness of the influence of specific systemic and structural factors.

Organizational factors:
Reaction to the agency's approach to clients and social problems.
Reaction to the agency's approach to suggestions for innovation.

The following example illustrates how the process and content of reflection inform the work of the field instructor. The student is placed at a community neighbourhood centre in a working-class area that provides various drop-in programs, a legal clinic, and advocacy assistance and planning for groups responding to changing community needs and concerns. The municipality has purchased a large old home and, after making extensive renovations, announced publicly its plans for an AIDS hospice and a counselling centre for gays and lesbians. The neighbourhood is already the site of various group homes and shelters and a large mental health hospital. Many residents feel stressed and angry that this facility is being foisted upon them. They have circulated petitions demanding that it be located somewhere else. The placement agency's board and the executive director believe that the proposed facility will meet a long-standing need, but they also anticipated a negative reaction in the community.

A public meeting is organized and publicized by the centre to discuss the issue, and the student and another worker are assigned to be facilitators. Following the first meeting, the student reports to the field instructor that he lost control when people began talking and shouting at once and he was unable to impose order. He said that he lost his temper and called them a bunch of bigots. He apologized quickly, but he feels he seriously damaged his chances to work with this group in a constructive way.

The field instructor said she could appreciate the student's pain and embarrassment at what happened, but all was probably not lost. The student then said that he might have handled the shouting, but what really upset him was the homophobia he felt as he faced the group. He said his brother was gay, and he knew the prejudice his brother faced even from their own family. He just felt overwhelmed by the belief that nothing would ever change, even though the city was now ready to offer services and support.

Using reflection, the field instructor and student talked about attitudinal change as a long and often difficult process. Reflective field instruction begins with a discussion of the student's own reaction based on his experience and then has to move from this interior space to connect to the professional situation by helping him to reflect on the experience and beliefs of those persons in the community who were so opposed to the hospice and centre. Together, the field instructor and the student speculated about what made these persons fearful and angry. Homophobia was a factor, but social class also played a role in their belief that more powerful people did not want social services for troubled and troublesome people located in their own communities but always seemed to choose this community. The field instructor pointed out that the centre had worked hard to be seen as one that was willing to hear out the thoughts of persons living in that community and to consider their needs and wishes. They planned how the student could use these insights to try to begin a real dialogue at the next planned meeting. This example suggests how all factors, psycho-social, interactive, contextual, and organizational, were useful and necessary to expand the student's reflective process.

Reflection must also provide for the opportunity to consider the effectiveness of an interaction or professional response that is retrieved as the situation reloops back to retrieval and reflection. For example, the student in the child protection agency, working with the potential abuse situation already described, had begun to work with the mother, seeing her twice a week. After six weeks, both the student and field instructor felt that the mother was ready to be referred to a group of other young single mothers who met weekly for companionship, relaxation, and general discussion of topics of their choice. Regular contacts with the student were discontinued. All went well for several months, and then the group facilitator reported that the mother had not attended for three weeks. The agency also received a phone call from a neighbour saying that she heard the child crying for hours at a time. The student called on the mother and reported that she had found her withdrawn and depressed.

On reflection, the student and field instructor agreed that the student's contact with the mother might have ended too abruptly and prematurely. Possibly the mother found the group support insufficient for her to gain the strength needed to cope more competently.

For the purpose of demonstrating how the ITP Loop Model looks when uncoiled, we can see that each of the content components is operant, although in teaching from this model, each component does not always have to be specifically labelled by field instructor and student. We can see, however, that psycho-social and interactive factors reviewed reflectively were linked with the knowledge that the relationship between client and worker cannot be too quickly or lightly dismissed even when the organizational demand on the agency for service creates pressure for very short-term service. Contextual factors influencing the current crisis in the mother's situation, such as the recent decrease in welfare support, need consideration by the student at this point as well. In addition there is a possibility that new events have occurred, such as the loss of a significant person or the threat of eviction, which might explain her current depression. The loop begins again as the student and field instructor retrieve the information necessary to understand this new development, reflect, link, and move to a new professional response.

Thus far we have focused our discussion of reflection on helping the student identify personal associations to a professional encounter. Obviously the field instructor will also have subjective reactions which reflect personality style, life experiences, or cultural values. Reflection poses a dilemma for the interactive process between field instructor and student. To what extent is it useful to share personal feelings, associations, and experiences with the student? The test is the relevance of the experience either to the practice situation or to the field instructor–student dyad.

When the field instructor feels that the student is unable to empathize with or understand a practice situation either because of lack of personal experience or unwillingness to relate to personal experience, it may be necessary for the field instructor to use her or his own experience to help the student make a connection. Whenever personal disclosure is sought or given in field instruction, it is the discloser who must always remain in control by selecting what and how much it feels comfortable to reveal. For example, disclosing personal feelings and behaviour in reaction to a loss or separation may stimulate the student to think empathetically and respond in a productive way. Students may have a range of reactions to hearing about their field instructors' subjective experiences related to a practice situation. In some instances, the student will find the experience very powerful, and this might facilitate understanding or increase empathy with the practice situation. The student might feel flattered or special that the field instructor has chosen to share personal experiences, and this might further solidify the field instructor–student dyad. On the other hand, some students may feel burdened by hearing the 'story' of the field instructor, uncertain about what reaction is expected, and uncomfortable with personal disclosure. Obviously students' reactions to field instructors' subjective experiences vary according to personality and level of development. The field instructor should be sensitive to how disclosure might be received.

Linkage

This step moves to a search for the professional knowledge base that makes it possible to choose a specific response to a situation from among a variety of competing responses. Linkage is that part of the loop that uses cognitive associations of both student and field instructor to the retrieved data and the associations elicited through reflection. The purpose is to identify and label knowledge that will help explain the practice data and the subjective reactions that have been evoked, and ultimately to use that knowledge in planning professional responses. Linkage addresses the way in which a knowledge base finds expression in practice, and is reconstructed as a result of practice. It encourages the student to select, from competing concepts, what is needed to construct a cognitive system of understanding that fits what has been retrieved and subjected to reflection. It is the degree to which a working hypothesis fits the situation that both student and field instructor must agree upon.

Linkage requires that facts and attitudes about the situation be abstracted or generalized to identify common elements that relate to a knowledge base. It is a process of moving back and forth between the general and the specific. In this phase, field educators conceptualize practice so that it can be clearly communicated in terms of applicable generalizations (Kadushin 1991), and they link these generalizations to the understanding of and response to a specific situation. This process is analytical. It is a search for concepts, learned by the student or practised by the field instructor, that derive from theoretical bases such as ecological systems, structural analysis, empowerment theory, feminist theory, psycho-dynamic theory, communication theory, or developmental theory. This list is not exhaustive.

The field instructor's task is not only to draw the student's attention to theoretical and empirical knowledge but also to help the student apply that knowledge in relation to a specific practice situation. What is stated in general practice principles must be made situation specific. For example, how can 'start where the client is' be related to the specific student assignment? We are not suggesting that the field instructor must teach theory which may already have been taught by the school. Students carry an overload of theoretical content from the classroom which they have difficulty transferring to practice. It is the concrete situation which makes it possible for the field instructor to help the student link knowledge in order to understand the phenomena of practice.

In working with field instructors, we have found that linkage seems the most difficult component to comprehend and the most controversial. The field instructor's practice is likely to be based on a well-integrated knowledge and value base consisting of practice wisdom, concepts from various theories, and empirically validated findings. These 'pieces' of knowledge become part of the practitioner's art and are used in a seemingly intuitive fashion in interacting with a practice situation (Schon 1987, 1995). In addition, the agency may structure service in accordance with a particular therapeutic or service model. As an educator, the practitioner must search for the underlying ideas that constitute his or her cognitive system of understanding, communicate that knowledge to the student, and assist the student in developing his or her own cognitive system.

In a book aptly titled *Social Work as Art*, England (1986) states that the integration of theory and practice is a unique and intuitive process, but the social worker must be articulate about the problems and about her or his own thinking, citing the specific and selecting from the general. He argues that the worker uses theoretical knowledge, not to apply formulae, but to construct coherence from immediate complexity.

For example, in identifying isolation as a concern for an individual who seems to have no supportive network, we are connecting to a knowledge and value base affirming that human isolation is an unhealthy state. In identifying an individual's sense of powerlessness to alter noxious conditions of living, we link to a theoretical base that teaches that one can effect change through understanding the institutionalization of oppression as an external force that otherwise may be perceived as personal deficiency. This understanding might suggest empowering collective action to exert pressure for change on those institutions. In identifying a struggle between adolescent and parent, we link to a theoretical base that examines appropriate developmental stages and behaviours for individuals and family members and the effect of recurring dysfunctional transactions within the family that could maintain a paralysing power struggle. Faced with a hospital team headed by an administrator who wants beds immediately, even if it means sending a patient to an inappropriate facility, we link to the knowledge that a client problem can be created by the very system charged with the resolution of problems. In working with family caregivers of the chronically ill, we link to the knowledge that counselling without some attention to the provision of concrete relief for the caregivers will be of little benefit. These are examples of practice wisdom, but they are at the same time examples of applied theory.

In field education, the student and field instructor review all knowledge relevant to a situation. This may mean exploring a variety of frames or theoretical stances to determine the best guide for understanding and acting in the current situation. This provides an opportunity for the student to use knowledge from the classroom in examining practice data. Both faculty and field educators may long for a simpler time when there was a greater uniformity of thought between faculty and agency. The issue of fit between class and field has a long and tortured history in North American social work education. Each school of social work has the responsibility to communicate to the field instructors its philosophical and theoretical approaches and the content of courses, and to decide the degree to which it hopes to achieve congruence between what is taught in the school and what philosophical and theoretical approaches inform the practice of social work in the field.

Controversy exists in social work regarding what theories and approaches contemporary practitioners need to know (Reamer 1994). There seems to be a belief that practice is either radical or traditional – an old social work battle-cry that refuses to be silenced. Currently some argue for teaching primarily empirically validated intervention approaches, while others champion postmodernism and the deconstruction of positivistic methodologies as a requisite for knowledge-building. We believe that linkage encourages students to bring to the practicum knowledge from the classroom, or a specific perspective for assessment

TABLE 2
Linkage: Cognitive associations of both student and field instructor
to retrieved data and reflective awareness

Psycho-social knowledge:
Explanatory knowledge, model, or theory for understanding affective, cognitive, and
behavioural observations of clients or groups.

Interactive knowledge:
Explanatory knowledge, model, or theory for understanding transactions.

Contextual knowledge:
Explanatory knowledge, model, or theory for understanding structural and environmental
factors.

Organizational knowledge:
Explanatory knowledge, model, or theory for understanding organizational behaviour and
how to influence change.

---

of a situation. In some instances there will be a good fit between the philo-sophical, theoretical, and empirical approaches taught and the practice experience. In others, the lack of congruence will help the student learn that no single approach or formulation applies to a specific situation without considerable custom tailoring. The student can be encouraged to apply new ideas to the current experiences in the practicum.

Assessment, and therefore intervention, must consider not only the client's psycho-social issues, but the helping system itself, as well as societal and organizational biases and blockages. Strategies flow from a full consideration of explanatory theories and remain tentative and uncertain. The ability to tolerate uncertainty resulting from the tentative quality of current theories is a quality required of all social workers. Retrieval, reflection, linkage, and a professional response which is then subjected to the relooping process help workers maintain a cautious scepticism. This can lead to rethinking and research that yields new knowledge.

Table 2 outlines the bodies of knowledge that can be scanned by the field instructor and student in order to select those concepts which may be relevant to the practice situation.

Professional Response

Professional response is the selection of a plan that will inform the next encounter with the specific situation. This plan must derive from the preceding process. It is an exercise in 'if this ... then that.' Each situation requires the worker and client to select the issues of highest priority for immediate focus. As the process of relooping occurs, there will be opportunity to respond to other aspects of the information retrieved initially, as well as to re-evaluated and emerging information.

The field instructor, using this part of the loop, grounds the ideas, knowledge, and insights just uncovered through reflection and linkage to develop specific plans and behaviours for dealing with the situation. The field instructor should not move too quickly to case management and response without moving through the previous phases. It may be that several possible theoretical frames have been identified through linkage, each having its unique appropriate intervention. Specialized practice models, such as task-centred, family systems, group, and community development approaches, interpret human behaviour and interpersonal adaptation, and provide social workers with specific techniques to use in professional response.

Through discussion of a variety of perspectives, the student has an opportunity to make comparisons and to anticipate the possible effects of a specific intervention. A response or action is selected, and its effect then becomes the focus of the same process. The use of the ITP Loop Model should facilitate the student's conceptual understanding of the situation, and hence make possible a more informed response to the practice situation as the contact continues. If field instructors use the loop after each encounter, the student should feel a growing sense of control over the uncertain elements of practice.

Consideration of all factors inherent in any social work situation conveys to the student the dynamic interrelationship between concepts and action. Integration demands that professional actions be informed by selection of preferred outcomes based on understanding probable consequences on the systems and actors involved. This implies that the student is encouraged to examine possible responses at psycho-social, interactive, contextual, and organizational levels, and to consider the relative effects of actions directed at one, several, or all systems. No single theory or construct is likely to provide a sufficient frame of reference. Selection of knowledge is eclectic and based on developing a preferred outcome, which is then negotiated with the systems involved. Because the process is applied to complex human events, it remains tentative and is subject to revision, modification, or even abandonment on the basis of subsequent work. The looping process then returns to retrieval of the effect of the plan or action on the situation, new data are gathered, and the process begins again.

TABLE 3
Professional response: Selection of a plan that will inform the next encounter the student has with this specific situation

Psycho-social response:
A plan or action that will respond to the concerns or behaviours identified.

Interactive response:
A plan or action that will respond to interactive factors identified.

Contextual response:
A plan or action that will respond to the environmental or structural aspects of the situation. This plan may be for immediate action or part of a long-range strategy.

Organizational response:
A plan or action that will respond to the identified organizational issues. This plan may be for immediate action or part of a long-range strategy.

Table 3 outlines the factors that can be scanned by the field instructor and student in order to select a plan which may be relevant to the practice situation.

It is probably practice wisdom that leads social workers to use the ITP loop intuitively, but in many cases with omissions. The steps of retrieval and professional action, for example, are undoubtedly always operative, but we believe that either reflection or linkage may be omitted as practice competence becomes more routine. Since students need to think through their practice responses, they must be encouraged to go through the entire cycle. Both field instructor and student need to take the time to engage in reflection and linkage.

Field instruction can teach an analytic process that begins with a practice act and moves through the loop. The ITP Loop Model provides a structure for the integration of cognitive and affective processes that we believe form the core of social work practice. It permits these two processes to be unhooked and hooked again through a conscious, analytic process. In addition, it will succeed whether one chooses to focus widely on a global problem or concern, or narrowly on a specific episode of student-client communication. For example, it can be used to focus on a single interchange in a family therapy interview; or the focus can be widened to examine a case management problem, or to consider a neighbourhood analysis of significant actors in order to develop an effective strategy for community development.

The loop can be used to teach social work practice at any level of intervention with a variety of populations, purposes, and settings. It can be microscopic or macroscopic, depending on what facts are retrieved. The choice of ends and the degree of magnification depend on the practice activity and the specific intent of the field instructor.

The ITP Loop Model and Your Practice

As we stated earlier, when social workers assume the role of field instructor, they make a transition from practitioner to educator. Social workers ask themselves, 'What do I do? Why do I practice this way? What do I know? What do I believe is important to teach?' The beginning field instructor is a competent practitioner, so that understanding the basis of your own competency is essential to achieving the skill to guide the student through the necessary steps of analytical thinking and practice interventions. Practitioners in all professions recognize that ongoing education is a lifelong process. In fact, many social workers choose to become field instructors as a way to reconnect with the university and learn new social work knowledge. As a field instructor, you may find it helpful to begin by reflecting on your own comfort as a competent practitioner, recognizing areas where you feel uncomfortable and where you feel you have more to learn. The ITP Loop Model can provide a tool to help you identify the assumptions, values, thoughts, and beliefs that underpin the actions you take in professional situations.

Using the ITP loop, retrieve a recent practice experience of yours such as working with a client, supervising staff, or conducting a community activity or a policy and planning activity. Recall your thoughts, feelings, and responses, and subject these elements to critical self-analysis using the loop. Reflect on your subjective beliefs and attitudes that were operating in your actions. What aspects of your personality, life experiences, cultural values, and personal world-view were evident in the judgments you made and in your responses? You may find it helpful to scan table 1 and select those elements that are personally relevant to you in thinking about this particular situation. These elements may be universally present in your practice, or they may be stimulated by unique features in your retrieved example. This exercise may confirm what you already know about yourself and the link between your personal self and your professional self, or the exercise may provide new insights. Reflection also focuses on the effectiveness of an interaction and provides the opportunity for you to critically analyse the impact of your professional response.

The next step is linkage, in which you will identify and label the knowledge you use. Articulate for yourself what was done and why it was done. What informed your choice of approach, direction, or response? Did you think about using a specific approach and then reject it for another? What ideas were operating in this decision? In this way, you will begin to articulate the cognitive system of understanding which underpins your practice. Again, scanning table 2 may help you to elucidate the concepts you use in your thinking.

The aim of linkage is not necessarily to discover global or large-scale theory. Rather, the purpose is to uncover the ideas that inform your interventions with the specific situation at hand. The use of knowledge is complex since, as practice situations unfold, social workers find themselves using multiple concepts for understanding and intervening. For example, a wife has requested help with a difficult marriage but says that her husband refuses to accompany her for counselling. You have agreed to see her to focus on how she might engage with her husband about attending joint sessions. This is an initial limited goal based on research findings that individual counselling for marital distress is more likely to result in separation or divorce than is couple counselling from the outset. While this is a valid use of general empirically based knowledge, as the work progresses, you and your client realize that her husband will not participate. This is the point at which human complexity demands flexibility and openness in helping the wife set goals and work through the ambivalence that must accompany them. Theoretical knowledge about the dynamics of bonding and separation supports this later shift in intervention.

At this point, you might want to recall a specific intervention from your own work and try to relate it to knowledge that would support that intervention, using the example just presented as a guide. You may recall how your cognitive system has changed over time and remember the influences on the development of your current views of social work. You may recollect the practice assignments, supervisors, workshops, lectures, and readings that you drew upon in the construction of your knowledge base for your practice.

Finally, think about your professional response and examine how systematic you were in integrating the insights uncovered in reflection and linkage. In retrospect, would you describe your actions as 'intuitive'? Through using the looping process, you may have arrived at new insights and ideas that you can use in planning your next encounter with this practice situation.

Reviewing your own practice experience using the loop gives you familiarity with its applicability and flexibility. As a field instructor, you will be better able to teach the loop to the student by engaging in the process of retrieval, reflection, linkage, and professional response with respect to the student's practice. Your new role of educator will involve you in helping the student build and reinforce a level of practice capability that will meet professional standards.

2

The World of Field Instruction: The School, the Student, and the Agency

The School and the Agency

The field practicum takes place within the context of two organizations, the university-based school and the community-based agency or department. As a field instructor, you are part of the school and thus belong to two different organizations simultaneously. Similarly, students in the field practicum and faculty members with field responsibilities participate in an activity which takes place in 'two worlds' and is affected by both these contexts. This is demonstrated in figure 3.

As a social worker in a service organization, you are knowledgeable about its practices. As a field instructor, you will need to learn enough about the particular school to represent its field program in your work with the student. A general understanding of the school as part of the university, including its values and methods of operating, is a useful beginning point for a new field instructor. In effect, anticipating your role as a field instructor starts with an organizational analysis of these two worlds. Such an understanding will help all parties to identify the common goals and to minimize conflict over divergent goals.

The School and the Field: Different Frames of Reference

The school and the field setting are two organizations with different purposes, values, and processes. As well, each differs in defining social work practice, social problems, and appropriate interventions. These differences create a dynamic tension between schools of social work and social work service providers (Cohen 1977; Frumkin 1980; Gibbs and Locke 1989; Tropman 1980). Table 4 highlights differences between the two institutions.

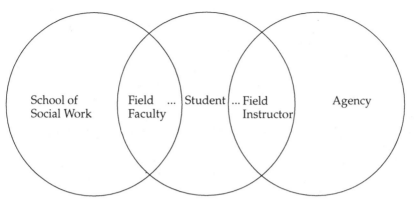

Figure 3

TABLE 4
School/field: Frames of reference

	School	Field
Purpose and mission	Education Knowledge-building	Service
Valued activities	Teaching Research Scholarship	Effectiveness and efficiency in service delivery
Time perspective	Future-oriented goals	Present-oriented goals

Primary focus	Analysis and critique of
	    current practice
	Experimentation
		Maintenance and
		    enhancement of
		    current programs
		Evaluation of
		    effectiveness

Rewarded behaviours	Critical analysis
	Developing, testing,
	    reporting new ideas
	Independent activity
		Competent job
		    performance
		System maintenance
		Interdependent
		    activity/teamwork

Approach to social work	General Abstract	Specific Concrete
Method of governance	Collegial Consensus	Centralized Hierarchical

Note: For purposes of illustration, dominant trends are characterized as polarities. Characteristics attributed here to educational institutions are often a valued part of social service settings, and vice versa.

Purpose and Mission

The purpose and mission of the university-based school is to educate for practice and to contribute to knowledge-building. Valued activities are teaching, research, and scholarship. The university's time perspective is primarily future-oriented. The school's primary focus is analysis and critique of current forms of practice, and experimentation leading to new intervention approaches. While practice methods are taught, it is the theoretical which takes precedence over practical application.

The purpose of the agency is to provide services within its specific mandate to people in need. The valued activity is the delivery of effective and efficient service. The agency's time perspective is primarily present-oriented, and its primary concerns are maintaining and enhancing current programs, and dealing with the insistent demand for service and crisis resolution.

Expectations and Rewards

Organizational expectations are reinforced through rewarding and sanctioning employee performance. In general, the university expects its members to employ critical analysis, to conduct research and experimentation, to disseminate new knowledge, and to function independently. Therefore, development, testing, and reporting of new ideas are rewarded, as are individuality and autonomy. These values are imparted to students in direct and indirect ways, and it is probable that they create two student responses to practice which irritate and perplex field instructors: beginning students are often characterized as inept in actual client contact and/or as arrogantly critical of agency practice.

The agency expects it members to perform their job function, as it is defined by the organization, in a competent manner. In general, the agency rewards members who work interdependently within the norms of the agency and contribute to system maintenance. Many students feel immediately more comfortable with this approach and have asserted for many years that the practicum was the best part of their education.

Approach to Social Work

The university addresses itself to social work in its general and broad sense. Its concerns are with the totality of the discipline of social work. As such its scope tends to be broad and abstract. Students learn knowledge and skills which are generic in nature and transferable to practice in a range of settings and with a range of client problems or social situations. The curriculum includes courses which focus on specific groups, such as the elderly, the mentally ill, children, and adolescents, but the focus is on these groups as a general population.

The agency addresses itself to a specific part of social work, embodied in a legislative mandate or a mission statement, and its scope, therefore, tends to be particular and concrete. Its focus may be on a particular population, such as children in need of protection, or a particular issue, such as housing. Students learn knowledge and skills reflective of the specific practice functions and client needs of that agency. Agencies, confronted with severe financial restraints, have increasingly adopted specialized time-limited intervention models or service approaches.

Governance

Universities pride themselves on functioning as communities and are highly committed to collegial decision-making processes. Issues are discussed and debated in a multitude of bodies which represent many constituencies, such as university governors, administrators, teaching faculty, students, alumni, and staff. Critics of universities have challenged these methods as inefficient and unlikely to bring about the rapid changes currently needed for restructuring. Schools of social work adopt the university model of governance and are likely to have a plethora of policy-making committees with representation of many groups. While the school's dean, director, or chair has responsibility for administrative decisions, significant input will come from others, especially faculty members. For example, when a school embarks on a curriculum change, typically there is extensive consultation with students and faculty, as well as perhaps with field instructors, prospective employers, and alumni. Proposals are presented to committees and are discussed, debated, and changed before a final curriculum is ultimately adopted.

Agencies have a variety of governance structures, depending on whether their source of funding is governmental or private. While most agencies have a board of directors, representation from service recipients and staff members may be very limited. Generally, responsibility for decision-making and administration is centralized and rests with senior management. For example, hospital administrators who have reorganized from discipline-specific departments to a program management model have initiated little or no consultation with social workers or service recipients.

As social workers and faculty members work in their respective institutions, their values, perceptions, and behaviours are influenced by the organizational context. Increasingly, there is a tendency to adapt and conform to organizational expectations. To do otherwise risks isolation within or termination from the organization. For example, continuing financial cutbacks have led agencies to focus on costs, efficiencies, and productivity. The worker who wishes to expand her or his role to include research and teaching must still carry the expected service load. Similar situations also exist in the university. During the past decade, the university has increased the expectations for productivity in scholarship and research for faculty members (Feld 1988; Gibbs and Locke 1989). New faculty members must pursue focused programs of research and contribute, through publication, to the dissemination of new knowledge. Otherwise they risk being denied tenure and loosing their university position (Hartman 1990b). Those wishing to pursue an interest in practice must integrate it with the university's expectations of scholarship.

Faculty members and field instructors, as a result of their respective employment affiliations, have different expertise, interests, and perspectives about social work practice and education. These differences will manifest themselves especially as they work together in the field practicum. In addition to the tension that can arise from such differences, there are also benefits. Through understanding the characteristics of each organization and their differences, one can broaden and change perceptions. Through understanding the impact of organizational demands and pressures on the two kinds of participants – the social work field instructor in the agency and the faculty member in the university – more realistic expectations of each can be formed. Through collaboration between faculty and field, both the university and the agency can contribute to the development of social work education, knowledge-building, and practice. In other words, real community demands on practice must inform university social work education, while a critical challenge to the political agendas that influence agency policy and practice must be acknowledged by the field in order to advance the profession.

Collaboration between Schools and Agencies

In an attempt to address the inter-organizational dynamics between university and field settings, Bogo and Globerman (1995) identified four key components. These are: organizational commitment to education, organizational supports and resources, effective communication and collaborative relationships, and reciprocity. The field instruction you offer occurs within the context of the inter-organizational relationships between your agency and the educational institution. Therefore you may find it useful to review these components to clarify where there are strong bonds and where there is a need for further development.

Commitment and Resources

Field organizations' commitment to education varies greatly, depending on a number of factors such as the agency's mandate and funding base. For example, there are settings which are affiliated with universities and have, as part of their mandate, the education of students from many professions. University teaching hospitals are an example of such a setting, and typically these hospitals expect all professional disciplines to offer an educational program for students. In many of these hospitals, a senior social worker is appointed as an educational coordinator, with responsibility for a field education program involving multiple learning opportunities (Showers 1990). Students participate in many interdisciplinary educational activities in these hospitals, while special learning opportunities for social work students are offered in small group seminars or case conferences. Even though students are matched with individual field instructors, they also have assignments with two or more staff social workers. In these large settings, field instructors have available opportunities for formal and informal peer consultation about student learning and progress.

Most social service agencies do not have such formal continuing affiliation agreements with universities. Schools of social work usually develop annual contracts with these field settings for one or more student practica. Despite the lack of formal affiliation, many settings have established long-term relationships with schools in their communities and provide quality practicum experiences. A cadre of experienced and effective field instructors work individually or together to create a field experience for students. In addition, students learn, formally or informally, from others, from participating on a team, and from the continuing education activities for staff offered in the setting. These agencies, by their agreement to have social workers use part of their time to provide field instruction to students, commit resources to social work education.

Many schools of social work expand their practicum offerings beyond

established social service and health organizations to include more settings engaged in community organization practice, agencies serving
specific ethno-racial communities, or fledgling front-line community
organizations serving special needs groups. Many of these settings lack
a firm funding base, have very limited resources, and may not employ
personnel with professional social work degrees. Students in these settings require resources for teaching, but they also serve as a resource for
offering extra programs and services. An exchange occurs which is evident in the balance that is struck between the volume of the student's
workload and the staff time allotted to educational activities. In these
settings, it is critical that the educational purpose of the practicum is primary and must be built into the contract between the agency and the
school. Students can then learn from the unique opportunities available
in these settings, where schools have been willing and able to develop
creative and innovative methods for field instruction (Allen and
Shragge 1995; Ruffolo and Miller 1994).

Your organization's commitment to education will affect your experience as a field instructor. To the extent that your organization has a student educational program, your setting may provide resources that you
will find helpful as a field instructor. In a study of new field instructors,
Bogo and Power (1992) found that instructors valued the following
agency supports: reduced practice load; release time to attend seminars
for new field instructors and other educational events at the university;
organized educational activities to augment the student's learning with
the primary field instructor, such as seminars and opportunities to
observe other social workers' practice; the provision of relevant social
work literature not readily available in the agency; and administrative
assistance to locate office space and telephones for students. In some settings, these resources are centrally provided; in others, the individual field
instructor must make all the arrangements for the student. If your agency
does not have a student program, you may wish to initiate a process with
other field instructors and the agency administration to plan centralized
educational opportunities for students. These experiences broaden students' learning by exposing them to the rich diversity in any setting and
decrease students' sole reliance on their primary field instructors.

Relationships and Reciprocity

Another important aspect of university-agency collaboration is the
working relationships established between agency and school person-

nel. These relationships occur at many levels: between the agency's and school's directors, between the agency's senior personnel and the school's practicum coordinator, and between the school's faculty-field liaison and the agency's field instructor. Clear definitions of the role and responsibilities of each, along with adequate processes for communication, cooperation, and coordination are associated with effectiveness (Fellin 1982, Rosenblum and Raphael 1983). The role of the faculty-field liaison, as described in the literature, consists of facilitating the linkage between the practicum and the classroom, monitoring the practicum experience, evaluating field instruction and student learning, and actively managing problems in the field (Raphael and Rosenblum 1987, Rosenblum and Raphael 1983). In a study of field instructors' perception of the role of the faculty-field liaison, Smith, Faria, and Brownstein (1986) identified ten categories of liaison activities: linkage, mediating, monitoring, evaluating, consulting, teaching, advising, advocacy, practicum placement, and administration. Rosenfeld (1989) found that increased frequency of contact with the school, via direct or telephone contacts with the liaison, group meetings, and written communication, were highly rated by field instructors.

There is, however, criticism of this traditional definition of the role. Field experts are concerned that the role of faculty-field liaison is not implemented by teaching faculty in the way it is ideally conceptualized (Raskin 1994). In actuality, field instructors and students are reluctant to turn to the liaison for help with problems, and they do not agree on the overall value of the role to the field instructor (Fortune et al. 1995). This may be partly a result of a triangle effect. Since the primary teaching relationship is between the student and the field instructor, the faculty-field liaison role is more formal and more distant. Furthermore, the traditional role of monitoring and supervision on the part of the faculty-field liaison is inappropriate if the preferred model is a collegial partnership between two educators, one in the university, the faculty-field liaison, and one in the practice setting, the field instructor (Globerman and Bogo 1996). In a recent study of field instructors in two faculty-field liaison models, one an intensive model and one a troubleshooting model, Fortune and her colleagues (1995) found that both groups of respondents ranked teaching-related activities as most important. Liaisons who are readily accessible when problems arise were ranked as the most important resource the school can provide.

Clearly there is variation in current views of the faculty-field liaison role within schools of social work. It is important for you as a field instructor to receive the resources and educational support that you feel you need to perform your role effectively. Try to identify what faculty-field liaison model has been defined by the school with which you are associated. Does it involve regular visits with the liaison, or is it a trouble-shooting model in which you are encouraged to call as needed? If there are regular visits, what is the purpose of these meetings, who sets the agenda, do the meetings meet your needs? If there is a trouble-shooting model, do you know your liaison well enough to telephone should you have a concern? Do you feel there are barriers which would stop you from calling? If so, can a colleague at the agency or the school's practicum coordinator help you address these barriers?

In some schools of social work, the university requires that grades be given by the faculty-field liaison. The grade is based on the final evaluation which is developed by the student and the field instructor and written by the field instructor according to the school's evaluation outline. It would be important that both the student and the field instructor be aware of this procedure.

Concerns you identify about the faculty-field liaison model may reflect the need for changes in the working relationship between your agency and the school, or they may reflect the need for changes in the school's field program. If these issues are specific to your agency, you can discuss them with agency colleagues who are field instructors and with the agency's educational coordinator, if you have one. Together you can clarify the concerns and approach the school to engage in joint problem-solving. For those issues that are likely to affect most field instructors, we urge you to find a vehicle for direct discussion with the faculty or practicum coordinator. Most schools of social work have a structure in which field instructors, as a group, have the opportunity to give ongoing feedback to the practicum office or to the social work program and to work together to refine the program. This structure may be a field education committee, an advisory board, an association of field instructors, or a curriculum committee. In a recent exploratory study, Rosenblum (1997) found that 40 per cent (119 respondents) of schools of social work in the study sample reported that they have a field advisory group which consists of the field director or field coordinator, field instructors, community practitioners, and agency directors. Some schools also included faculty-field liaisons and students. Other members of the group ranged from alumni and retired professors to representatives of the professional association. These advisory groups addressed a wide range of issues relevant to the development, evaluation, and revision of the field education program, including curriculum, evaluation of students, training of field instructors, and quality of practicum sites. Respondents generally reported that these groups were useful and supportive, leading Rosenblum (1997) to conclude that they provide important information to schools about the complexity of practice and emerging issues in the field and help keep social work programs grounded. Clearly, field instructors can contribute valued and informed ideas to the development of quality field education programs, and it is important that you feel empowered to work with the school's faculty in this endeavour.

Finally, reciprocity in inter-organizational exchanges has been identified as another factor in promoting effective working relationships between the two organizations. Reciprocal activities go beyond the joint focus on practicum education. They address the needs and interests of both organizations with respect to knowledge-building and practice in social work and social welfare. Joint research studies, continuing education programs, joint sponsorship of conferences and visiting lecturers on relevant topics, sharing audio-visual library collections, participation in colloquia at the university and conferences in the setting, and employing experts from the agencies to offer specialized courses at the university are some examples of successful reciprocal activities (Bogo and Globerman, 1995).

The Curriculum

Field instructors are often mystified by the school's curriculum as it relates to the practicum. They wonder why the curriculum includes certain areas and omits others. Some field instructors critique the educational programs as too theoretical. They are concerned that students are not prepared with the practice skills needed to engage in service delivery to clients of the agency. They query why student learning is so general and why it does not provide the specific knowledge base useful for the particular agency's service mandate, population, or approach. Others wonder why curriculum change is not faster, anticipating societal, service, and practice needs. Social work educators and practitioners feel the scorn of the critics because we are positioned at the very interface of the client and the institutions. Field instructors often ask about 'the faculty's perspective of social work,' as if there were a unified and agreed-upon view of the profession and its knowledge base that is held by all members of the teaching faculty. It has been observed that although students read the literature critical of social work practice, they still wish to learn skills that will make them marketable employees. Compartmentalization comes to the rescue: skills for the practicum; critical analysis in the classroom (Vayda 1980).

The curriculum of a school of social work is an expression of the views of its creators about the knowledge base of the profession, its principal ideas, values, methodological approaches, and skills at a particular point in time. It constitutes a belief about what every social worker needs to know. There has always been debate about the central components of the knowledge base, a topic that has been the subject of numerous conferences, reports, and books. Reamer (1994) has recently edited an important contribution to this literature, in which leading social work educators contribute their perspective on current substantive areas. These include social work practice, social welfare policy and services, human behaviour and the social environment, research and evaluation, field education, values and ethics, oppression and social injustice, and diversity and populations at risk (ethnic minorities and people of colour, women, lesbians and gays, and people with disabilities). This debate about the knowledge base and what students should be taught, about 'the merits and demerits of particular schools of thought and practice, ranging from theories of human behavior and intervention techniques to the political aims and agenda of the profession' (Reamer 1994, ix), is essential to the growth of any vibrant and socially relevant profession. Therefore one would expect, as part of this tradition of debate, that there will be critique, as well as support and agreement, by field instructors of a school's curriculum content and focus.

Shaping the curriculum, building and changing it, involves a complex set of processes and players. Numerous stakeholders, with different goals and objectives, participate in the evolution and change of a school's curriculum. Active involvement comes from teaching faculty, students, alumni, field instructors, agency employers, the professional association, and consumers. The final curriculum represents the end point of a process of accommodation and negotiation between these groups. Kolevzon (1992, 10) states that 'despite the rhetoric which undergirds our accreditation standards, curriculum building represents an accumulated series of political compromises in an effort to accommodate divergent and, at times, opposing interest groups. Each of these groups advocates in behalf of its own values and beliefs regarding what constitutes the "minimum base" that every graduate level social worker should know, believe, value, and be able to do.' A school's program, therefore, reflects many elements, including the characteristics or needs of its community or region, the mission of the university, the scholarly interests of the teaching faculty, the professional interests of the students, the job market, and project-funding opportunities.

Schools of social work, as they develop and change the curriculum, are also operating in accordance with the policies and guidelines established by their national accrediting bodies. In the United States, the Council on Social Work Education (CSWE) establishes educational policy and standards which are used for accreditation and re-accreditation of undergraduate and graduate programs. In Canada, the Canadian Association of Schools of Social Work (CASSW) is the body which sets educational policy and carries out the accreditation function. In Great Britain, the Central Council for Education and Training in Social Work (CCETSW) is charged with the responsibility, by law, to regulate the quality of social work education.

As a field instructor, it is important for you to know that a curriculum is the result of this complex and political interaction of forces. The perspectives and participation of stakeholders, the standards of accreditation bodies, and the expectations of the university are all present in the construction and negotiation of the final end product. The curriculum of a school is rarely static. Most schools have a standing curriculum committee, which is concerned with evaluation. Periodic self-study for university reviews or for re-accreditation lead to an examination of the curriculum. If you are interested in participating in curriculum change, your faculty-field liaison or the practicum coordinator can direct you to committees where you can become involved.

As a field instructor, your primary interest in the curriculum is likely to be in relation to understanding your students' educational experience. Each school generally provides their field instructors with some orientation to the educational program and the courses offered. Course outlines and bibliographies can be requested for those courses you are especially interested in, or you can ask your students to share their materials with you. Some social work programs adopt a specific model or approach to practice which they feel should be understood and applied by the student in the practicum. When the school expects field instructors to use this model in the practicum, this expectation is made clear in contracting between the school and the setting. Orientation and training for field instructors in the model may also be necessary.

*Ensuring Multicultural and Multiracial Equity in Schools
and Service Settings*

Social work educators and practitioners have become increasingly committed to educating students to practise with the diverse multicultural and multiracial communities that currently characterize North America. It is expected that content on diversity will be included not only in specialized courses, but throughout the curriculum and in the practicum. Field instructors will need to find field opportunities for all students to develop competence. This includes learning how racism and oppression operate at structural, organizational, and interpersonal levels as well as learning how to bring about change. Moreover, students need to learn how to work with clients, community participants, and other service providers with cultural and ethnic identities different from their own.

Some schools of social work have actively promoted the admission of students from many ethnic groups representative of the general population in their communities. In addition, in the last decade, students who have recently come from African and East Asian countries as immigrants and refugees have entered social work programs. The curriculum in many of these schools places a special emphasis on ethnic issues taught by faculty with interest and expertise in culture, ethnicity, and race.

The practicum may be seen as an opportunity to extend this interest into the community. Practicum settings are sought in ethno-specific agencies, but, in addition, students may also arrive at other more traditional agencies primed to seek out opportunities to use their heightened awareness of ethnic issues. They have an interest in what it is like to have to learn to integrate cultures, to be visibly different from the mainstream culture, and to experience discrimination from mainstream structures such as police, justice systems, schools, or health care systems. These students may also have an interest in the effect of race and culture on the organizational hierarchy of the agency, the composition of the board, as well as the sensitivity of administrators about whether there are appropriate and accessible community services. Field instructors, aware of the school's curriculum emphasis, are better prepared to be open to discussion of these issues and of how they affect practice in their agency and in the local community.

Faculty-field liaisons need to be aware that persons from cultures different from those of North America may bring with them ingrained but subtle cues about the meaning of status, region of origin, education, dialect, dress, and gender-appropriate behaviour that are unfamiliar to

Canadians or Americans. This is similar to interpretation of cues observed in North American regional populations that inform North American attitudes. A practicum assignment in an ethno-specific agency might cause discomfort to a student who seems to share a generic ethnic background but for whom these subtle, regional factors provoke unexpected attitudes and responses. It may be useful for the faculty-field liaison to explore this issue with a student interested in an ethno-specific agency practicum.

The Educational Experience of the Field Instructor

A curriculum is organized to operationalize the school's mission and objectives in an educational design. Academic courses and a practicum are structured to achieve educational goals. Extensive involvement with a curriculum is required to fully understand it, so that a general understanding is all that can be expected of a new field instructor. However, this is sufficient for the instructor to become familiar with the student's academic experience.

As we said earlier, curricula are always changing. Re-accreditation reviews engage social work programs in a form of self-study that encourages responsiveness to changing practice, community, and educational concerns. Teaching faculty who are active scholars and researchers are eager to integrate new knowledge in the curriculum, and students are vocal about what they view as missing from their educational experience. With the constant restructuring and reorganization of social and health services, the requirements of the job market are rapidly changing.

The curriculum that you experienced as a student may be different from the current focus of the school with which you are now associated. Using your experience as a starting point, it may be useful to compare the similarities and differences with respect to the following factors: undergraduate or graduate program level; educational objectives, including ideology and mission; curriculum design; core courses and elective courses; and how the practicum fits into the curriculum.

Undergraduate and Graduate Students: Is There a Difference?

Since social work education is offered at both undergraduate and graduate levels, it is reasonable to expect differences in programs, outcome expectations, and the field education component. Social work education at the first university level leads to a bachelor of social work (BSW) degree and takes the form of professional studies within the context of general university education. BSW curricula are designed primarily to prepare generalist social workers. These programs provide the professional foundation of basic values, knowledge, and skills.

Social work education at the second university level leads to a master of social work (MSW) degree and reflects graduate level university education and professional purpose. Generally, the first-year or foundation-year curriculum in two-year MSW programs is designed to provide the professional foundation. The second-year curriculum in the majority of MSW programs is intended to prepare students for advanced and specialized practice (Raymond, Teare, and Atherton 1996, Vinton and White 1995). Students select specializations or concentrations in levels of practice, such as micro- or macro-level practice, and fields of practice, such as geriatrics, mental health, physical health, child and family service, corrections, schools, or some combination of both. Some MSW programs prepare students for advanced generalist practice with no specialization. Students who possess a BSW degree may be admitted to the second year of the MSW program at most schools of social work.

Levels of social work education suggest there is a continuum moving from foundation to advanced stages. While many educators support this view, some disagree that a steady progression reflects reality. Raymond and his colleagues (1996) reviewed studies of the job activities of BSW and MSW practitioners and observed that the data did not provide strong evidence of there being differences in job tasks between these two groups, nor of differences in the needed skills among various specialized fields of practice. Some exceptions were that MSWs were more likely to work in mental health, provide specialized therapeutic interventions, and hold middle-management positions than were BSWs. Their findings support the conclusion that much of what social workers do seems to be common to social work practice in all practice areas and settings. Reviewing the same studies, Fortune (1994) concluded that there is little evidence to support the notion that BSW and MSW practitioners are at different stages of a single career path or educational progression. Fortune (1994) identified a core of common knowledge and skills that all practitioners must learn, both BSW and MSW graduates. These core competencies can be considered the 'foundation' field curriculum. The core knowledge and skill competencies she recommends include: practice with individuals and families; professional commitment and development; practice in an organizational context; and practice that uses service delivery organizations and community resources. In fact, these categories and the specific knowledge and skill competencies are similar to the practicum goals and objectives, or competency models, used by schools of social work. The objectives are the same for all students. The differences arise as a result of the agency. In order to practise and to learn in any setting there are a set of both unique and specialized knowledge and skill competencies which the student, BSW or MSW, must master in order to deliver a service. For example, in a mental health clinic situated in a neighbourhood with many refugees from South Asia, all students must learn about reactions to trauma and interventions which are effective in helping individuals who have experienced loss and crises as a result of war, torture, dislocation, and disruption of extended family ties. In addition, all students in this clinic need to learn about the specific societies from which this population comes and how cultural forms affect the refugee experience, mental health issues, and the interventions offered.

Together, the school and the agency, through the contracting process, will make some determination about the appropriateness of offering a practicum to a beginning student or one further along in their studies. Both BSW and MSW students include not only 'typical' students in their late teenage years or early twenties, but also students returning to professional studies after obtaining other degrees, or with professional work experience and greater maturity. Therefore assumptions based on the youth, inexperience, or appropriateness of the 'typical student' in BSW or MSW programs are difficult to make and are unreliable. Decisions about offering a practicum cannot be made simply on the basis of whether the student is a candidate for a BSW or MSW degree; these decisions should be based on the learning opportunities in the setting, the school's general practicum objectives, and the characteristics of the individual student.

Assessing the Student's Academic Preparation and Program

Field instructors frequently query whether the student 'knows enough' to practise in their setting, whether the student has the appropriate knowledge base, and whether field instructors are expected to teach theory. In contracting the practicum, the field instructor should discuss with the faculty-field liaison the practice and learning experiences available in the setting. Together they can identify the knowledge base that will support field learning and determine whether that content is available in the school's current offerings. For example, social work on a medical service might include the opportunity to learn to work in an interdisciplinary model; to learn short-term, task-focused intervention with adults; and to learn about community resources for disabled people. Knowledge about multi-disciplinary teams, the psycho-social impact of illness on individuals and families, crisis intervention, and health policy and programs for the disabled would support field learning. Such a discussion might make it possible for the faculty liaison to ensure that the student take appropriate supporting courses. If such courses are not available, a reading list can be developed to address gaps in the student's knowledge base. The faculty-field liaison may be able to assist field instructors and students with this task.

It is helpful to engage students in a discussion to identify their experiences that will help them learn in the field setting. Students can reflect on volunteer and work activities, life experiences, and academic courses. In focusing this discussion on the learning opportunities that the practicum can provide, the student can identify useful and transferable knowledge and skills as well as existing gaps and determine whether these gaps can be addressed through academic courses. As discussed earlier, the focus of academic courses tends to be at a general and abstract level of conceptualization. For this material to be useful in the field, a more specialized focus may be needed. For example, the student may have taken a course in social welfare policy but not have studied the specifics of health policy and programs affecting the disabled, the client group served in the field setting. Again, the field instructor can help the student fill this gap through suggested readings or by speaking with experts in the setting. Given the diversity of practice settings and approaches, and the knowledge explosion in social work, the student's courses and the knowledge used in the practice setting are not likely to fit perfectly. The student can engage with the field instructor to assess academic overlap, fit, and gaps. Together the student and field instructor can develop an educational plan and identify resources to access for knowledge that will support practicum learning.

Practicum Objectives

Fortune (1994) points out that field education has two purposes in the overall curriculum. Firstly, it provides the opportunity for students to apply and integrate content they have been exposed to elsewhere in the curriculum. For example, students may have used a feminist analysis to examine the persistence of the care-giving role of women in Western society, despite changes in their participation in the labour force. A practicum in a long-term care institution for the elderly provides the student with the opportunity to speak to family members and observe that daughters and daughters-in-law are more frequent visitors to the senior residents than sons or sons-in-law, to learn about who does what household chores, and to observe that many women are carrying a double burden in caring for both their senior relatives and their own nuclear families. Concrete experiences such as these bring theoretical concepts to life. This type of learning cannot be structured. Rather it is a result of the unique experiences a student encounters in a practice setting.

The second purpose of field education is the application of theory in practice. This component of field learning is structured with its own objectives and curriculum content. There is considerable debate about what constitutes the content for field practicum learning, what students should learn, and what they should be able to do when they have completed their field experience. Social work has not answered these questions definitively. Several expert panels have agreed that identifying objectives for field education and determining criteria that distinguish graduate from undergraduate learning are important, but as yet unmet, concerns (Raskin 1983, 1994; Skolnick 1989). Instead, each educational program sets broad educational objectives which field instructors and students use to construct individualized learning plans.

All schools develop educational goals for the practicum which are expressed as competency models, performance criteria, or learning objectives. These models generally include a core of knowledge and skills for working with people in systems, for understanding and changing community and organizational contexts, and for social reform (Fortune 1994). The expression of core competencies in general and abstract terms again reflects a difference between the university and the agency. The university, concerned with the totality of the discipline of social work, defines practice broadly. Practicum learning objectives are expressed in global terms. Since social work is practised in settings that are problem or population specific, field instructors can, most usefully, view these objectives as a framework and guide. The next step is to translate these general goals into setting-specific knowledge and skill components. These specific learning objectives will reflect the agency practice in relation to its mandate, practice approaches, needs of the clients or projects, and value positions. For example, all schools include in their educational objectives the expectation that the student learn assessment skills. The student engaged in community development in an outreach project on a native reserve will learn to assess, even though the specific assessment skills may be quite different from those required by the student studying a particular family therapy approach in a children's mental health centre. Both will have learned the general concept of assessment; specificity is based on the expertise, purpose, ideology, and model of the field setting.

Using the school's practicum objectives demonstrates an essential feature of field teaching: linking the general with the specific. The articulation by the instructor of the important components for effective practice in that setting serves as the curriculum for the practicum. These components are used in contracting with students to identify the most important educational goals, are a guide in selecting appropriate learning assignments, focus the learning and teaching, and finally are used in evaluating educational outcomes.

3

The Beginning Phase

The practicum is composed of phases or stages, each of which requires the completion of a range of activities and tasks. As in social work practice, the process of field learning is cumulative, with the work of each phase resting on the experiences of earlier ones and, in turn, influencing the effectiveness of the subsequent phases.

The first phase is the pre-practicum stage, which includes negotiation, anticipation, and preparation. Negotiation is the process of arriving at a working agreement with the agency, the school, and the student. Anticipation precedes participation in any activity and is the psychological preparation for any new role, usually involving a mental rehearsal of the possible positive and negative aspects of the endeavour. Preparation refers to the actual tasks that must be done before the student begins the practicum in the agency. They include the field instructor's meeting with the school's representative to gain an understanding of the educational program: the practicum objectives, the school's expectations of the agency and the field instructor, and the educational supports provided by the school. This information is useful to the potential field instructor, who is well advised to consult with others in the agency, such as the director, supervisor, or team, to consider the feasibility of incorporating a student. In many schools, field instructors have preliminary meetings with one or more students to determine whether a suitable match is possible between the setting, the student, and the field instructor.

The beginning phase of the practicum sets the stage for what is to come. Orientation is crucial and places in motion the structure and expectations of the practicum. The relationships among the student, the field instructor, the team, and the setting begin to take shape, and the first learning assignments are introduced. In this stage, the pre-practicum discussions are revisited, and a more thorough contracting process is undertaken. Objectives, learning assignments, methods of teaching, and evaluation criteria are specified.

The middle phase focuses on teaching that flows from the assigned learning activities. The ITP Loop Model can be used as a framework and guide for the educational process. For example, to operationalize the ecological and multi-factorial perspective, assignments will need to ensure that there will be learning experiences in which these concepts come to life. Decisions will be made about which of the various methods for retrieving practice – such as reports, audio- and videotapes, and observation – will be used, as well as concerning the timing of their introduction and use. The student and field instructor will select the most effective methods to promote student learning that are possible in the setting. During the middle phase, new learning objectives are often identified and form the basis for re-contracting. Schools structure a mid-semester evaluation, which provides a formal time for mutual evaluation of the practicum.

The final stage of the practicum is allocated to evaluation and termination. The original contract, additional objectives which emerged through the course of the practicum, and the school's practicum objectives form the basis for the evaluation of student learning. Assessing the student's progress in achieving these educational goals is the primary task of this phase, and the evaluation will highlight areas for further development and provide a direction for continuing professional education. This phase also includes formal evaluation of the contributions of the agency, the field instructor, other personnel, and various activities to the student's learning. Hopes, disappointments, and accomplishments are worked through in a manner similar to that in the termination phase of any other social work activity.

Pre-Practicum

Negotiating the Practicum

Chapter 2 presented the context of field education, a world where the university-based school, the community-based agency, and the social work student meet. With this framework in mind, the negotiation phase sets a number of processes in motion which will ultimately result in the assignment of a specific student to a specific field instructor. In this phase, meetings take place among a variety of individuals: the school's and agency's representatives and potential field instructors; the field instructor and one or more students; and the field instructor and other staff in the setting. The aim is to decide whether a practicum will be offered and who the participants will be.

The first step, considering whether to offer a practicum, may be initiated by a staff social worker, an agency's educational coordinator, supervisor, or director, or by the school. A meeting is held between a representative of the school and the potential field instructor to explore educational opportunities and, if possible, to negotiate a student practicum. The focus of this discussion is whether there is a fit between the practicum learning objectives of the school and the learning opportunities in the setting. It is important that the prospective field instructor involves the significant members in the workplace in making this decision, such as other social workers, staff from other disciplines, and administrative and support staff. The goal is to ensure agreement to incorporate a social work student practicum into the work of the unit or setting so that there will be commitment, on some level, to providing learning and teaching opportunities for the student. In this way, students are not solely the responsibility of the field instructor and can therefore expect to have their learning enriched and supported by others. Similarly, the field instructor need not feel he or she owns the student and must bear the total responsibility. In settings where education is part of the mandate of the organization and expected of all staff, agency commitment may be a routine matter. In new settings the social worker may wish to have a representative of the school meet with the staff to orient them to the program and the expectations and benefits of a practicum.

In many schools, a pre-practicum meeting between the student and the field instructor is an essential part of the negotiation process prior to the decision to embark on the practicum. The purpose of this interview is twofold: to determine whether there is a fit between the student's learning interests and the agency's practicum, and whether there is a subjective feeling of comfort between the student and the field instructor. This is an important meeting and merits thoughtful anticipation by both field instructor and student. Either the student or the school should provide the field instructor with a résumé which contains basic information that can then be expanded in the interview. As with all preliminary information, the field instructor can make some tentative speculations drawn from the student's age, education, work and volunteer experience, and level of the requested practicum. The field instructor should have decided whether it is important that the student already have some skills in place or whether basic skill development can be one of the goals of the practicum. Some field instructors enjoy the challenge of working with an inexperienced student when the work of the agency makes it possible to accommodate these learning needs.

The content of the interview will generally be focused on why the student wishes to learn in that particular setting, what relevant work or volunteer experience the student brings, academic courses already taken, and the nature of the student's long-range social work goals. The field instructor will be expected to answer questions about the nature of the agency and the type of experiences that can be provided to the student. Beginning students may find it more difficult to respond to questions about what they want to learn and may make very general statements that seem vague and uninformed. Students are accustomed to academic courses in which a curriculum is presented to them and therefore may not make the adjustment quickly to the practice focus. The ITP Loop Model is helpful here, because students may not have learned the relationship between theory and practice and how to connect the two. Some students, however, seem put off by questions about theory and seem to fumble, as if they have had no conceptual exposure. Again, it may be that the integration aspect has never been emphasized, so that theory and practice remain relatively unrelated. Students who are further along in the education program are likely to be far more specific about learning objectives.

It is always a good idea to check on whether the expectations students have about what can be accomplished match with the reality of what can be offered as student experiences. The field instructor should be specific in describing practice activities and learning resources. Examples of practice activities are work with individuals, families, specific types of client groups, and community groups such as committees, as well as a range of activities in administrative projects. In addition, it is important for field instructors to inform students of their expectations of the student. For example, if the agency or field instructor uses a specific model of practice, it should be made clear to students that they will be expected to learn that model. Field instructors in direct practice might prepare students for the use of audio-visual facilities and live supervision via one-way mirrors. Field instructors offering a practicum in community practice or administration might advise students to be prepared for weekend work, travel, and public presentations. Because of the importance of learning and teaching styles, field instructors might ask students how they would describe themselves as learners. For example, do they prefer considerable direction or, in general, prefer to find their own way? Students might also be asked what facilitates their learning, that is, do they like to learn from reading, from discussion, or directly from experience? These are, of course, general tendencies and are not mutually exclusive. The field instructor will use this initial discussion to help the student develop the learning contract once the practicum begins.

For the field instructor, the first impression made by the student is a decisive factor in determining whether or not to proceed with the practicum. First impressions condense a multitude of factors and can produce strong feelings that are either positive or negative. The ITP Loop Model may be useful in examining these reactions. For example, suppose you retrieve your observation of a student who made poor eye contact and demonstrated a markedly passive manner. Reflection leads you to recognize that the student's background may be one in which deference to authority is expressed by a relatively silent comportment and avoidance of a direct gaze, characteristics which may make you uncomfortable. Theory linkage tells you that the capacity for interpersonal relationships is critical for all levels of practice. You consider whether the student might learn that relationship behaviours are modified by social context, and you make a decision based on weighing all considerations. We all respond positively or negatively to specific characteristics as irrational and unrelated to the task of social work practice as physical appearance, patterns of laughter and speech, awkwardness, age, and manifestations of sexuality. If you feel strong antipathy toward a student, you will probably decide not to accept that student. In those schools in which a preliminary meeting is not expected or is not possible, these guidelines should shape your first meeting with a student who has been assigned to you.

If your decision is to accept the student and there is a mutual decision to proceed with the practicum, you and the student have already begun the relationship which is so critical to the success of the practicum. However, if your decision is negative, you may feel uneasy about conveying it to the student. Some field instructors feel comfortable with telling the student why they feel it would not be a good experience for the student in that particular setting. Others may be able to ask the field coordinator to inform the student about why he or she will not be offered a practicum in the setting. The student may also have reservations about the field instructor, the setting, or both, and may feel relieved about the decision. Whether a negative decision is discussed directly by the field instructor or indirectly through the field coordinator, insofar as possible, it should be a learning experience for the student. It is always important to inform the field coordinator about the nature and outcome of the pre-practicum interview, whether positive or negative.

Anticipating the Practicum

Field instructors contemplate the practicum with both positive feelings of anticipation and some anxieties and reservations. For field instructors, students bring many advantages and serve multiple needs. Field instructors report that they enjoy teaching students and influencing another's professional development. Teaching provides intellectual stimulation and a fresh view of practice as well as reinforcing a sense of practice competence. Field instructors feel they are contributing to the profession at the same time as they are sharpening their own practice knowledge and skills. Also, students provide a break in the routine of practice and a connection to the university.

Field instructors, when they retrieve and reflect on their own experiences in the practicum, often report that their field instructors were so important and helpful to them that they wish in turn to provide a learning experience for a student. Despite many competing demands on their time, a strong identification with a positive role model motivates social workers to contribute to the profession through 'giving back.' This personal commitment to professional education is a commendable characteristic of social workers. In essence, they volunteer part of their time to provide field instruction in the absence of financial remuneration from universities or adjustments in their workloads from the agency. Schools of social work are cognizant of this contribution and have a range of recognition activities, such as the provision of a university library card, conducting workshops on new practice models, awarding a certificate for being an instructor, conducting a recognition ceremony, or conferring adjunct professor status (Lacerte, Ray, and Irwin 1989). While field instructors appreciate these incentives, their primary motivations for continuing as field instructors come from their personal enjoyment of teaching students and the value they place on contributing to the profession (Bogo and Power 1992).

Some social workers recall negative experiences in their own practicum and consider the effect this will have on their motivation to take a student. For some, offering a practicum represents an attempt to 'do it better,' to provide for a student those ingredients which were missing in their own education. In such cases, a negative model serves as a guide for what not to do as a field instructor. In general, however, effective field instruction involves the application of universal principles to the unique situation presented by each student. Therefore, one of the important tasks for field instructors in the pre-practicum stage is to identify the positive and negative aspects of their own experiences and to examine how these might influence the planning of the current practicum. This preparation helps to separate one's unique reactions as a student from current experience as a field instructor.

Field instructors may wish to go one step further and clarify their own thoughts about field education. The following questions can assist in the development of a personal model of field instruction. What do you consider to be the ingredients of a successful practicum? Conversely, what would a difficult practicum look like? What are or what might be your strengths as a field instructor? What are or what might be your limitations? What areas will you need to improve? (AASWWE 1991).

Students enter social work education with concerns about their ability to learn the practice of social work and to become competent enough to find fulfilling employment, and they rely on their field instructors for help with these issues. Students enter the practicum with a range of anxieties and hopes, but so do field instructors. Field instructors have developed a sense of competence and self-esteem about their professional practice. They recognize, however, that education is different from practice and wonder if they will be able to teach what they do. In addition, subjecting one's own work to the scrutiny of a student involves a degree of risk which may not feel entirely comfortable. Some may wonder if they have a well enough thought-out approach to practice that can be articulated and communicated to students. Field instructors also worry about how much time they will have to commit to the student and whether they will be equal to the task. Field instructors feel the basic anxiety of any new interpersonal experience, namely, whether each of the participants will understand the other and whether they will get along. Both students and field instructors are going through a similar process of assuming a new role and experiencing a range of anxieties and expectations. This concept of analogous or parallel process is a useful way to empathize with the student and prepare for relationship-building in the early stage.

Field instructors may wish to take the time to become aware of their anxieties and expectations about the beginning of the practicum and identify steps to take to respond to the various issues. For example, one social worker was concerned that she did not use a specific model of practice in her work in child protective services. Comparing herself to other field instructors at the school's orientation session, who spoke with confidence and authority about the brief solution-focused model or a narrative approach to practice, she felt anxious about her ability to help the student link theory and practice. She discussed this with an agency colleague, who stated that she had felt the same way when she first took a student. She said that most of her practice was eclectic, and reassured her that somehow students made the links. This response was not sufficient for the social worker, and she decided to spend some time looking at the recent child welfare journals in the agency's library. While she found interesting papers on specific aspects of child welfare and recognized some of the principles that she used in her work, a clear model did not emerge. The worker decided to begin to articulate the main features of her own approach to conducting child abuse investigations. She started by writing what she believed were the most important things she did in each stage of her work. She used the stages in the ITP Loop Model to guide her. She retrieved recent practice examples and reflected on her practice. She asked herself questions such as Why did I ask that question in the interview? and Why did I make that suggestion? to identify some of the beliefs underlying the actions she had taken. She became more aware of her own thought processes while in interviews with clients over the next few weeks. On the basis of these reflections, she continued to expand her list and formulate it as her practice principles. She then reread some of the literature and found that in some instances there was a link between her practice behaviours and generic concepts in child welfare. It became apparent that she was practising from a 'model,' not necessarily one that is presented with a specific designation, such as task-centred social work or brief solution–focused therapy; rather, her practice represented an integrated set of beliefs, assumptions, and guidelines, which she had developed through many years of work in the setting and which were authentic and effective.

   In another example, as a field instructor began to plan for the student's arrival, she became concerned about the amount of time that she perceived would be needed to provide a quality field experience. As a result of recent changes to her workload, she felt stressed by her earlier commitment to take a student and raised her concerns with her team. Other team members were also experiencing similar time pressures;

however, since they had originally supported the decision to take a student, they worked together to develop strategies to share the teaching. Two workers who co-led a group offered to include the student in that activity and provide the associated instruction. The team leader offered to debrief with the student following team meetings. Anticipating issues and actively problem-solving them is an important task of the pre-practicum stage and contributes to the field instructor's feeling more confident.

Preparation

An important aspect of preparation is related to the organizational context of field instruction, that is, the school and the agency and their respective policies, procedures, and expectations. Thoughtful planning of the student's orientation to all aspects of field education will result in a structured and focused beginning.

Orientation to the university program with which the student is associated is an important part of preparation. Two aspects merit attention: the school's educational objectives and requirements for the student's practicum; and the educational supports for the field instructor. Each school of social work has a practicum manual which provides the framework for the practicum and includes policies, objectives, and expectations. The school may also provide additional information about the academic component of the program. It is likely that this material will be introduced in the field instructor's meeting with the school to negotiate a practicum. In some instances, a formal orientation session is offered for new field instructors. Manuals are dense but should come to life as they are used in the appropriate phases of the practicum. What is helpful in this early stage is that the field instructor have a general sense of the academic program, the specific practicum expectations, and some ideas about how the practicum objectives can be met in the setting.

The second component is the educational supports for new and continuing field instructors. Field education is a branch of social work with a theory and practice. Recognizing this, many schools have instituted training for new field instructors; while, in other situations, new field instructors themselves have requested training. Accrediting bodies have more recently instituted a requirement for training. Schools offer a range of educational activities, including courses on field instruction, which are taken concurrently with the student's practicum. Other formats are intensive workshops or periodic seminars. Some schools provide continuing education events for all field instructors, such as workshops or lectures on specific topics. As discussed in chapter 2, a variety of faculty-field liaison models exist for the purpose of linking the academic and field components in social work education. It is important for field instructors to know about the model used in the program with which they are associated and to have a clear understanding of the respective roles of, and expectations for, the student, the field instructor, and the faculty-field liaison.

Once the decision to accept a particular student has been finalized with the school, field instructors can prepare the agency for the arrival of the student. Where the decision to offer a practicum was made with the participation of other staff or team members, they may be ready to take part in the learning plan. In other settings, the decision may have been made only by the field instructor, and some advance planning is necessary. Other social workers and members of other disciplines should be informed as well as support staff. There are distinct advantages for both the student and the field instructor in this preparatory activity. The field instructor has signalled to the agency that the student is to be a part of the agency's total function and is not only the responsibility of the field instructor. The field instructor can discuss what aspects of the student's learning could best be undertaken by various staff members. Accountability for learning, authority, and responsibility for evaluation will need to be clarified, bearing in mind that students report that they prefer field settings that provide a wide range of diverse learning experiences.

It is helpful to have space already selected and prepared and necessary supplies gathered. If there are requirements regarding audio and video taping, arrangements for scheduling and equipment should be in place. If it is a large agency, there may be bureaucratic forms and rituals to set in motion, such as scheduling an introduction to the director, attendance at an agency-sponsored orientation, and taking a driver's test. Some field instructors find it useful to collect written material for students to supplement the agency's orientation process. Manuals for new staff members provide important information about the setting and its mandate, its policies and procedures, and the documents and forms that will be required. Field instructors are encouraged to prepare a bibliography or package of readings relevant to their practice. For example, a hospital social worker on a renal unit may suggest literature on basic kidney function and disease, the psycho-social effects of this illness, and effective social work interventions. Time spent in preparation will produce for the student a sense of having been anticipated, expected, and welcomed by the agency.

In a secondary setting, preparation by the field instructor assumes even more importance. Hospitals, schools, or correctional facilities are complex, and special care has to be taken to inform key persons, such as nurses, principals, department heads, and support staff, about the student's arrival, learning needs, and timetable. Such planning paves the way for the student to follow up and establish important connections.

Some settings have established policies requiring students to wear identification plates signifying their status as student social workers. This usually occurs in hospitals, where it is customary for personnel to wear some identification. Other settings require students to be introduced to clients as student social workers. Obviously, if the agency has established a policy, this must be presented to the student, who then is expected to conform to that regulation. If no specific policy exists, field instructors should think through the implications for clients of specific designation as a student social worker and make a decision that gives the student clear direction. Clients should be informed about who will be involved in discussing their situation and who will have access to information concerning them.

Finally, thought should be given to how orientation will be structured during the first day and week of the practicum. The goal is to establish the right balance between the needs of the inexperienced student, who requires a structure, and those of the student who can take some initiative in getting information from the field instructor and others. If possible, the field instructor should plan to spend time during the first day with the student, preferably when the student arrives, outlining the activities and plans for that day and week. Recognizing that anxiety is high, the field instructor who has some case or project assignments ready for the student has taken a step toward anchoring this anxiety. Beginnings, as we know, are significant, and there is nothing so undermining of the heightened sense that accompanies a beginning as hours of neglect, confusing directions, or offhand, unthoughtful suggestions for activity.

Beginning

The beginning phase of the practicum aims to accomplish three major tasks: orientation, developing a learning plan, and assigning clients or projects to the student. These activities take place within the context of the developing relationship between the student and the field instructor. The way in which these early tasks are structured and carried out, and the reactions of both student and field instructor to each other in this process, will have an important effect on this critical dimension of the practicum.

Orientation

Orientation can be both formal and informal, and is both substantive and interpersonal. Formal orientation should contain information on relevant legislation mandating and regulating the practice in the setting or agency. It should provide instruction on required procedures in regard to both clients and personnel policies. It should focus on the process of decision-making in the agency by providing some understanding of the agency's organizational structure, from board to executive director, supervisory personnel, and staff. Some field instructors encourage or require students to make opportunities to interview key personnel to get some concept of the range of services provided by the agency. Some settings, such as child welfare or large mental health facilities, have established orientation sessions for new staff and students to familiarize them with terminology and procedures specific to these settings. Students in such settings need to be encouraged by field instructors to take the time to learn unfamiliar terms and procedures which they could not be expected to understand at the outset of a practicum. Field instructors should be certain to discuss the agency's manual or the orientation with the student to clarify and augment what can be a confusing mass of information not easily digested until seen in context.

Since social workers increasingly find themselves in situations where violence may occur, most agencies have developed safety-related policies and training. Safety issues are also discussed in practice courses and by faculty-field liaisons (Tully, Kropf, and Price 1993). Field instructors should ensure that students receive orientation about violence and personal safety so that they can identify the kind of behaviours that may pose a threat to their personal safety. Warning signs need to be interpreted within the particular setting, and responses will differ depending on whether the student is in an institutional setting, a community organization, or on a community or home visit. For example, violence in an inpatient psychiatric unit which is a result of a patient refusing regular medication will pose a somewhat different threat than violence in a home visit which is a result of a discussion about taking a child into care. Instructors need to take the time to help students learn to assess and minimize potential risks to themselves and to know how to defuse a situation which is potentially dangerous. Understandably, most students are likely to find this topic uncomfortable; however, it is the responsibility of both the school and the agency to prepare students for the realities of practice.

The informal and interpersonal aspects of orientation are a continuation of the preliminary preparation already begun by the field instructor. Introductions to other key personnel and staff should be made. Students might be encouraged to note key names. Some attention should be paid to physical orientation if the agency is large, especially key locations such as washrooms and lunch rooms. It is particularly important that with respect to lunch routines, students feel included and welcome. It makes a difference if there are several students or only one. Expected attendance at staff meetings or team meetings should be clarified with students, along with some discussion of how they are expected to participate. The thrust of the orientation is to encourage students to perceive themselves as members of the social work staff with as many of the privileges and responsibilities as the circumstances of a specific setting will permit.

A thorough orientation to the structure and processes of the student's and field instructor's educational work together begins to provide the student with the knowledge and information she or he needs to become an active participant in the teaching and learning process. Such an orientation includes defining the expectations of the agency, clarifying the roles and responsibilities of the student and the field instructor, and introducing the methods of field instruction. While the following is not exhaustive, it can provide a checklist of important elements. Knowing the expectations of the agency will include knowing the required hours of attendance at the setting, whom to notify when illness or emergency prevents attendance, the agency's recording requirements, any procedures relevant to the student's service role, and whether attendance is optional or mandatory at educational seminars, staff meetings, and any other meetings, such as team meetings.

Clarifying the respective roles of student and field instructor as mutual participants in field education will be introduced in this early phase. The working relationship will be a product of how well both the student and field instructor can negotiate and manage the fit between their respective expectations of field instruction and their preferred learning and teaching styles. However, it is crucial from the beginning to frame the relationship as a partnership with joint responsibility for, and commitment to, its success. Establishing the structure and methods for field instruction serves to ground these nebulous concepts about relationships and mutuality. It is crucial to the establishment of a working relationship to set up as soon as possible a regular field instruction conference time. Guidelines about the field instructor's availability outside of the conference time and whom to call in the field instructor's absence provide a sense that the student is not being left alone in unfamiliar situations. It is also useful to discuss how both the student and the field instructor will contribute to the conference agenda, and to clarify what materials will be used in the sessions (e.g., written reports or tapes), how they will be prepared, and when they are to be submitted.

Instructors who use the ITP Loop Model presented in chapter 1 will introduce the student to both the phases in the model's loop and its ecological and multi-factorial focus. Providing examples from the agency's practice illustrates these concepts and immediately links theory and practice. Students can be encouraged to begin to apply the ITP Loop Model by being asked to read relevant information on a situation or case carried by the field instructor prior to observing the field instructor's practice. The student and the field instructor can then reflect on and analyse this shared experience. The student can then submit a written analysis of the practice situation to the field instructor prior to their next meeting so that the conference can be used for discussion. Following the structure of the ITP Loop Model, the written analysis would include retrieval of the relevant facts of the situation; reflection about the student's subjective reactions to the situation and the student's impressions of the effect of the field instructor's professional responses; linkage of ideas the student uses to understand the practice situation as well as concepts or theories the student is currently learning in academic courses which might be used to explain the practice situation; and professional responses which the student thinks would be useful in the next contact.

A written learning contract or plan will eventually be developed that summarizes the roles and responsibilities of student and field instructor. What is important initially is that both student and field instructor have the opportunity to discuss the various components of the practicum, and to reach agreement about how they will proceed. Much of the anxiety associated with beginnings can be contained with clarity about what is expected of the student and what the student can expect of the field instructor.

Field learning is about practice, and the sooner the field instructor can assign a client, task, or project to the student the better. Students should also observe the field instructor's work as soon as possible to get a feeling for approach and process. Delay in assignment of concrete practice tasks seems to heighten anxiety and dissatisfaction in students. In the beginning phase, especially with inexperienced students, field instructors need to be more available as a guide and resource. In the pre-practicum meeting, the student and field instructor will have discussed the nature of the learning assignments available in the setting, and these agreements will guide the initial selection. Principles useful in selecting appropriate learning assignments will be elaborated on later in this chapter.

Since the first week of the practicum can be stressful for a student, the field instructor may wish to give the student a brief written plan for his or her first week in the agency. In developing this plan, the field instructor will give thought to what he or she wants to accomplish as the practicum gets under way. The ideas presented here about orientation can be used as a guide.

Developing a Learning Contract or Agreement

WHAT IS A LEARNING CONTRACT OR AGREEMENT?

Social work literature reflects the acceptance of a concept of contract development both in practice with clients and in field instruction. We feel that 'agreement' or 'plan' might be better terms because 'contract' has a legal connotation for many people. As used in social work, a contract implies a flexible, dynamic document subject to renegotiation, rather than one that is static and binding (Seabury 1976). Field instructors should feel comfortable in selecting a term that suits them.

A learning contract is a document developed by the student and field instructor which is based on what the field instructor and the agency can teach, what the school expects the student to learn, and what the student wishes to learn. The contract establishes clear goals and specifies the means to achieve those goals, the indicators of successful achievement or the evaluation criteria, and a time frame. Though based on the field objectives of the school, the contract individualizes a student's learning program in a particular agency. The contract explicates the roles and norms for participation of the partners in field instruction.

Formulating a learning contract involves a process, the end product of which can be written down and shared with the school if required. But it is important to remember that the contract is developed to serve the student–field instructor learning and teaching function; it should therefore be a working document and not an onerous barrier to the learning and teaching function. Contracting engages both student and instructor in observation and retrieval of practice behaviour, reflection about that behaviour, linkage to a professional knowledge base, and in professional responses expressed as the outcome objectives expected by the school. Through this process, the field instructor and student can assess the student's base level of competence and plan a learning experience that will facilitate growth. Formulating the contract serves to shift the role of the field instructor away from that of 'all-knowing expert' toward that of a partner in planning student learning. The strength of the contracting process lies in its emphasis on mutual development and mutual commitment to a plan. As well, significant learning takes place as a product of this process. The contract provides a vehicle for the student to learn how to become a more self-directed learner, an essential component of adult learning, and, once written, it can serve as a stimulus to further assessment and planning as it is used to measure accomplishment at various points in the practicum. Its regular use to determine progress leads naturally into the evaluation process.

WHY USE LEARNING CONTRACTS OR AGREEMENTS?

The past two decades have witnessed a growing attempt on the part of the profession and educational programs to define competent social work practice (Arkava and Brennan 1976; Dore, Epstein, and Herrerias 1992; Gross 1981). Schools of social work have defined competency expectations for students' learning in the practicum, which are defined in more or less specific behavioural terms. Students need ongoing assistance to assess their level of skill in relation to these competencies. Contracting serves the purpose of assessment and indicates the student's performance level in relation to the outcome objectives. The contract formalizes in explicit terms what the student needs to work toward. It does so not only at the general level expressed in the school's field objectives but in a specific way that reflects the professional behaviours and activities in the particular field setting. This provides students with the opportunity to link the abstract to the concrete. The specificity inherent in the contract enables students to participate more actively in the evaluation of their own learning.

While contracting has received acceptance in the social work and field instruction literature, there is no research to support its effectiveness. Adult education theory promotes the process of contracting on the premise that what adults learn on their own initiative they learn more deeply and permanently than what they learn by being taught. Unlike traditional education, in which the learning activities tend to be structured by the teacher, adult educators use a mutual process of contracting which should ideally result in students feeling more involved in the learning activity. Knowles (1980) notes that learning from a field experience contains elements of personal development as well as acquisition of specific skills and attitudes demanded for entry into a profession. Learning contracts provide a means for negotiating a reconciliation between these external needs and expectations and the learner's internal needs and interests.

Students who have experienced the modern educational system in a university are accustomed to courses structured by the teacher. A set curriculum, a course outline, a bibliography, and assignments are introduced at the beginning of the course. The lecturer tells the student what and how they are to learn, and how evaluation will be conducted. This encourages dependency, passivity, and acceptance. When students are faced with a different educational process, that of mutual involvement in designing a learning program, some students may become anxious, confused, and worried. Others may feel liberated and experience the process as truly empowering. Students entering social work education with limited familiarity of the field will need to learn how to participate actively in designing the contract. They will need to learn how to define what is to be learned. With some students, field instructors will have to be more directive in developing the contract until the student is more knowledgeable about what needs to be learned. Therefore, field instructors need to pay attention to both the content of contract construction and students' comfort with this process.

While there is general acceptance of the concepts of contract and contracting, there has been critique as well. Some social workers have been concerned with an apparent contradiction between humanist values and stating measurable behavioural objectives for students. Humanists are concerned with the complexity of behaviour, its variety, and the nature of the unexpected in human dynamics. Learning, to be a human endeavour, must accommodate the uniqueness of experience and should not be made to fit into an instructional unit stated in behavioural terms, a process which may become mechanistic and focused solely on the demonstration of discrete performance skills.

Some students and field instructors may experience the contract as an assignment requested by the school and of no use in field instruction. Some students want field instructors to write the contract because they believe that the instructor should decide what they will learn; while some field instructors want the student to write the contract because they believe it should reflect only what the student wants to learn. However, as stated above, the contract, when collaboratively designed, can provide an opportunity for the student to experience a process which is mutual, collaborative, and empowering. Similar to its use in social work practice, contracting is a complex process and requires learning how to cooperate, negotiate, and give and take feedback. Since the process is analogous to contracting with clients, it serves as a model for teaching students these skills.

HOW TO DEVELOP A LEARNING CONTRACT OR AGREEMENT

It may be helpful to consider two very different kinds of contracts, one which may be easily drawn up at the beginning of the practicum if it is deemed desirable, and a second learning contract, which involves more time and process, and cannot be drawn up until the practicum is under way.

The first type of contract can be termed a working contract. Some schools provide a field instruction manual which contains guidelines pertaining to the expectations and responsibilities of both field instructor and student. If such a manual is not available or if the setting is new or non-traditional, a working contract can provide specific agreements about practicum time expectations, agency policies and procedures to be followed, roles and responsibilities in field instruction, and initial practice assignments. Even if a manual is provided, it may still be important to draw up a specific working agreement that reflects the actual circumstances of the practicum setting so that expectations can be mutually expressed. This learning contract focuses on the instrumental aspects of the practicum.

The second type of learning contract is used to develop a specific plan for the practicum, identifying the objectives, the learning experiences available to meet those objectives, and the evaluation methods to be used to determine when those objectives have been achieved. It provides a clear and explicit focus for the practicum, though it should be used flexibly to allow for change as objectives are achieved and new ones developed. This contract consists of three parts: learning objectives, learning activities and resources, and evaluation methods.

Hamilton and Else (1983) have offered some useful suggestions for writing learning contracts. In developing a framework for constructing learning contracts, they use specific verbs which provide clarity in differentiating among goals, objectives, and specific learning activities. For example, goals are concepts with broad, long-term purposes whose attainment cannot be specifically measured:

1. To be an effective group worker.
2. To be an effective program planner.
3. To be an effective school social worker.

Objectives are framed as specific observable behaviours. Such verbs as 'defines,' 'identifies,' 'distinguishes between,' 'interprets,' 'prepares,' 'demonstrates,' 'uses,' and 'formulates' are examples of verbs which can specify objectives:

1. Demonstrates knowledge of group roles and identifies those roles.
2. Identifies the advantages and disadvantages of a proposed staff training program.
3. Interprets to a parent the relevant sections of legislation about education for children with special needs.

Learning activities are those tasks and situations which are undertaken in order to achieve the learning objectives. Useful verbs for structuring learning activities include: 'interview,' 'write,' 'observe,' 'simulate,' 'role play,' 'participate,' 'accompany,' 'contract,' 'tape,' 'teach,' 'attend,' 'summarize,' and 'co-lead':

1. Co-lead a group of recently separated women.
2. Accompany a pupil to a hearing for special placement.
3. Summarize a meeting of agency directors interested in developing community day programs for seniors.

SETTING LEARNING OBJECTIVES

The school will outline overall learning objectives for students in the field practicum. These objectives are likely to define practice in general terms applicable to a variety of practice approaches with a range of clients or projects. The student and field instructor will use these objectives as a framework and relate them to the specific practice of that field setting. The instructor will need to identify what the student needs to learn in this work situation in order to carry a service role. Discussions with the faculty member contracting the practicum and with the student will help determine to what extent the academic curriculum provides the necessary components to support that learning and to what extent specific required knowledge will have to be mastered by the student through readings or seminars at the field setting. Students can be helped to explore the preparation they have gained from volunteer and work activities, life experiences, and academic courses in order to identify knowledge and skills already developed. Through focusing this discussion on the practicum setting, it may be possible to identify transferable competencies as well as existing gaps.

LEARNING OBJECTIVES AND AN ECOLOGICAL FRAMEWORK

The ITP Loop Model presents an ecological and multi-factorial perspective. To ensure that the commitment to societal and organizational issues does not remain at only a conceptual or ideological level, learning objectives need to be developed to reflect this emphasis. Attention to the ecological framework is a hallmark of social work practice, differentiating it from other helping professions such as clinical nursing, psychology, or counselling, which focus more exclusively on interpersonal helping. Advocacy is a useful concept to use to ground learning objectives and practice assignments that aim to develop student competence in using an ecological perspective. Advocacy can be defined narrowly as activities undertaken to plead a client's cause or more broadly as creating bridges to facilitate understanding and responsive organizational and societal change. Both definitions are important and are dependent on the specific situation. Students in the practicum need to be encouraged to see that in some situations their help to individuals, families, and groups will prove ineffective without considerable focus on organizational and societal change. Social work practice should be understood by students as a bridging profession that moves from a holistic perspective in assessment to focus attention on those parts of the system that may be contributing to the dysfunction of any specific part. It is important that field instructors include this aspect of practice in the learning objectives that they and students construct. In every practicum, three areas can be identified which all students must understand: (1) the organization or agency itself, its philosophy, structure, policies, and procedures; (2) the community, its demography, resources, uniqueness, and special problems; and (3) the nature of the population served and its position in the mainstream power structure.

Advocacy can easily be omitted from the practicum contract as both student and field instructor focus on learning skills of interviewing, facilitating interpersonal intervention, and mastering specific practice models. Students are more concerned with learning these skills and may designate the practicum as their skills laboratory. The danger residing in this narrow definition of the focus and purpose of the practicum lies in the separation of theory and practice. Unity of social work theory and practice should be a practicum goal. The ITP Loop Model can be helpful in ensuring a holistic, ecological, and multi-factorial approach because it insists that through linkage to professional knowledge, relevant knowledge be canvassed for guidance in selecting a professional response.

BASELINE ASSESSMENT OF STUDENT'S COMPETENCE

For a contract to be relevant to the student's actual ability, it is necessary for the instructor and student to obtain a baseline assessment of the student's competence. It is our conviction that this assessment is meaningful only insofar as it arises out of the student's actual performance. We suggest the following methods to achieve that assessment: observation of the field instructor's practice and observation of the student's practice.

Observation of the field instructor's work should be followed by a discussion focused on the student's observations about the client or project and the field instructor's interventions, as well as suggestions for continued intervention. In this way, the field instructor can begin to develop some idea about the student's ability to conceptualize and link theory and practice. In addition, the field instructor models openness and demonstrates the ability to receive feedback by exposing her or his own practice to observation, analysis, and critique.

The field instructor may observe the student's work by participating in a session or a meeting, observing through a one-way mirror, listening to an audio tape, or watching a video tape with an accompanying analysis prepared by the student. Through discussion of the client or project and the student's practice behaviours, the field instructor will have an opportunity to assess the student's level of skill and ability to conceptualize. From a few such observation and discussion sequences, the field instructor and student will be able to develop specific learning objectives, which can then be summarized in a written contract.

The activities of observation, discussion, and setting learning objectives involve the student immediately in the process of integrating theory and practice. The ITP Loop Model provides a framework for this process. Practice behaviours are retrieved and reflected upon in relation to meanings, assumptions, and values. As the discussion moves to linking an understanding of practice phenomena and interventions to professional knowledge, the field instructor can identify with the student useful concepts to be mastered. Similarly, as student practice behaviours are examined, an assessment of the student's skill level is made. This assessment, based on observable data, is made in relation to an end goal, which can then be expressed as a learning objective, a new professional behaviour. Through using the ecological, multi-factorial framework in the ITP Loop Model, the field instructor can assess to which levels the student attends and which levels are omitted. Again, gaps are formulated as learning objectives. We suggest the phase of assessment and goal setting, as in most social work practice models, takes place early, and the written contract be completed within four to six weeks. It is likely that new learning objectives will be established as the student continues to practise. These objectives should be added to the contract.

SPECIFYING LEARNING ACTIVITIES AND RESOURCES

The next task is to determine how the learning objectives will be realized. For example, what clients or projects will the student be assigned? What educational resources will be available and how will they be structured? What methods will be used by the field instructor to give the student ongoing feedback about his or her practice? Activities such as visits to relevant resources, attendance at seminars, observation of other workers, and relevant readings may be suggested and arranged. Assignments and activities derive from the learning objectives, and it should be obvious to students how they will facilitate their achieving their educational goals.

In chapter 4 we will introduce the concept of learning styles. It may be helpful for the field instructor to become familiar with this material and, with the student, make a preliminary assessment of some of the many dimensions associated with this concept. This information is useful in selecting educational experiences and teaching approaches which are initially complementary and support the student's preferred learning style. The learning contract can include plans to help the student expand his or her learning-style preferences, so that the student can have access to a wider range of educational activities.

Since the field instruction relationship is perceived by students as central to their field learning, it must be considered as the most important learning resource. In chapter 4 we will present the various aspects of this relationship, the importance of mutuality and communication, and the impact of the fit between expectations, learning and teaching approaches, and personal characteristics. We recommend instructors introduce and discuss these concepts early in the practicum, so that a mutually clear understanding of expectations and preferences can be achieved.

Contracting is a continuing process that provides an opportunity to use the relationship it involves to encourage growth. As discussed earlier, though field instructors should frame the work as a partnership, in the beginning they will need to take the lead in exploring useful activities and processes for learning, as well as perceptions of the student's and their own roles. At this stage, field instructors will encourage feedback from students. However, since students often have concerns about the power differential in the student–instructor relationship, they may be reluctant to be direct. Instructors, therefore, need to be sensitive to issues that are hinted at or avoided. Those who use the communication and relationship-building skills of social work practice, such as active listening and exploration, in a supportive and non-judgmental manner will help students feel more ready to participate in shaping the field instruction relationship. Two sensitive areas should be introduced as soon as possible. The first concerns expectations regarding the mutual responsibility for giving and receiving positive and critical feedback about the working relationship. The second stresses the freedom to make mistakes, to take risks, and to disagree with the field instructor in an open and honest manner.

The process of contracting goes on over time as the implications of these agreements are tested in the activities of daily learning and practice. Agreements will be discussed, clarified, and perhaps changed in response to such dialogue. The learning contract serves as a road map for the practicum. To pursue this metaphor, it is to be expected that over time detours will occur and new roads will open and re-contracting will occur. This process also provides a model wherein students will learn about contracting and re-contracting with clients or consumers.

SPECIFYING EVALUATION METHODS

Finally, the question is addressed of who will evaluate what in order to determine whether the learning objectives have been achieved. Though the field instructor has primary responsibility for evaluation, the student participates fully as well, and other professionals in the setting, the faculty-field liaison, or other field instructors may be involved. When staff other than the field instructor are involved in student activity, the contract should specify their role in evaluation.

The field instructor and student will decide what data will be used to evaluate progress. Data may include direct practice data, such as observation (or audio or video tapes) of interviews, meetings, and interactions with colleagues and significant others in the setting, case, or project; indirect practice data, such as process or summary records and reflection logs; documentation prepared in practice, such as letters, minutes, summaries, assessments, briefs, proposals, and reports; agency information-system statistics about the number of activities performed and attended; and practice outcomes based on systematic protocols or user satisfaction indicators.

The following are two examples of setting a learning objective and specifying learning activities and evaluation methods.

Example One: Learning Objective

The student will demonstrate understanding of the multiple consequences for people who suffer lay-offs as a consequence of downsizing of industries or businesses.

Learning Activities
1. Read relevant literature and interview two unemployed people and their families to gain knowledge about the effect on workers of downsizing.
2. Gain knowledge about current services available to laid-off workers and visit two programs.
3. Participate in the agency's outreach initiatives to laid-off workers to involve them in community counselling and upgrading programs.
4. Work with a group of laid-off workers to help them gain knowledge about the personal and political dimensions of their situation.
5. Participate in any social change initiatives in the community with respect to this issue, such as a rally planned by a labour union.

Evaluation Methods
The student's and field instructor's observations, focusing on the student's evolving knowledge and understanding as evidenced during joint outreach activities, group meetings, and field instruction sessions.

Example Two: Learning Objective

The student will demonstrate competence in the use of the interviewing skills of clarification, exploration, and confrontation in practice with adolescents.

Learning Activities
1. Observe two interviews conducted by different social workers from behind a one-way mirror and make notes of their different styles in using these interviewing skills.
2. Role play the use of these skills with the other students and with the field instructor.
3. Serve as primary social worker for three adolescent clients with different presenting problems.
4. Tape all interviews with these clients and provide an analysis of interviewing skills used in a twenty-minute segment. This segment will be discussed in the weekly field instruction conference.

Evaluation Methods
Using the school's standardized rating scale for assessing competence in interviewing, the student and field instructor will independently rate the student's use of the interviewing skills in two interviews, one at mid-semester and one prior to the end of the semester.

Selecting Learning Assignments

The development and selection of learning assignments requires consideration of a number of factors: the objectives of the practicum; the teaching resources of the setting; and the unique abilities, needs, and goals of the student. The learning contract or agreement aims to integrate these elements and provide some direction for assigning learning tasks.

COMPLEXITY

The question of selection of appropriate learning assignments for students is always problematic for instructors. To protect or expose are the horns of the dilemma. Conventional wisdom has directed field instructors to choose assignments carefully so that students would confront relatively uncomplicated situations and would experience initial success. Indeed, in some agencies, cases were labelled as 'student' cases and passed on from student to student. These cases usually involved clients with chronic concerns. It is to be hoped that this practice, which discouraged both clients and students by perpetuating feelings of powerlessness, has fallen into disrepute. Even this practice, however, would sometimes be infused with energy by a student who was capable of taking a fresh look at the situation.

Many feel that students need an incremental induction into practice situations of increasing complexity. In reality, the best-protected assignment can convert quickly to a complicated situation because of unpredictable events. Lemberger and Marshack (1991) note that agency practice is increasingly complex and there are no uncomplicated or protected learning assignments. Matorin (1979) queries whether students need such protection and guidance through sequential learning. She wonders whether they might be better equipped to enter the profession by exposure to all kinds of situations. It seems reasonable to accept the fact that such precise sequential assignments are not possible and, more importantly, not useful. Front-line positions are held frequently by beginning workers, who need the knowledge and skills to function in complex and/or crisis situations. Demanding practicum experiences that develop this capacity are to be valued. The protection required by students as they learn can be provided through the careful monitoring of their work, so that students feel that immediate guidance and support will keep them afloat no matter what the presenting situation. Supportive instructors have been defined as persons who can tolerate complexity and share with students their own feelings of how difficult it is to work with such complexity, both interpersonal and societal. These field instructors can acknowledge their own errors and encourage students to take risks by sharing mistakes they have made and how they learned from them. The best measure of the range of assignments may be found in the student's expressed interest in the acquisition of new skills.

In the beginning phase, field instructors might consider having students work more closely with them as co-leaders in family interviews or groups. Initially the student's role may be one of participant observer. Often co-leadership or observation leaves students feeling dazzled by their instructors' abilities or confused about why they intervened in specific ways, and quite immobilized regarding what actions they should take. The ITP Loop Model can demystify practice and provide an educational, rather than an apprenticeship, focus to these learning activities. The student and field instructor can easily retrieve the practice data they both experienced, and share and compare their observations and assumptions. These in turn can be linked to professional concepts. Together they can plan professional responses for the next session and develop specific interventions which the student will carry out. This method gives the student the structure and guidance needed in the beginning, rather than leaving him or her to 'figure out' what was observed, passively absorb it, or flounder in the sessions.

In every practice situation there is the opportunity for a variety of learning experiences, some more complex than others, some with a greater focus on psycho-social factors, and others with a greater focus on organizational or contextual issues. In the beginning, learning assignments may focus more on concrete tasks which are achievable. For example, a student assigned to a single mother who is reestablishing herself after leaving an abusing husband may work with the client to find job retraining resources, link her to services, and support her as she prepares to take a training program. At a later phase in the student's practice, the student may be expected to research the possibility for inter-agency action on job retraining or may work with the client on individual personality issues related to her hopes for establishing new relationships. A student in community practice may begin by gathering important background data for a committee or a project team. Later in the student's practicum, the assignment might be to prepare and make a presentation of this information to the committee, a community meeting, and the agency's management team. Concrete manageable practice tasks give the student a beginning sense of accomplishment and prepare him or her for the more complex learning tasks of the middle phase.

WORKLOAD

The number and variety of assignments are more amenable to control than is the factor of complexity. Students differ in their capacity to learn and the speed with which they can assimilate skills. It is almost an aphorism universal to practicum manuals that the school places a premium on education above service as an appropriate guide to student load. The field instructor needs to assess the pace which keeps the student busy and progressing, but not frenzied and overwhelmed or bored and restless. Some students, anxious to learn as much as possible, want to take on more than can be assimilated. Others may be reluctant to undertake assignments because they feel inadequate. Communication which is sensitive and frequent can help field instructors respond to this anxiety. Evaluation begins with the setting of the learning contract, and field instructors need to keep in mind that a range of experiences is important for evaluation of professional competence.

LEARNING ASSIGNMENTS AND AN ECOLOGICAL FRAMEWORK

The ITP Loop Model and its ecological and multi-factorial perspective can be operationalized in the learning contract. Practice assignments can provide concrete examples of how contextual issues can exert pressures on people and how social work interventions might ameliorate those pressures. The extent and scope of contextual interventions will vary from setting to setting, but some advocacy activity should always be included in a social work practicum.

Field instructors, starting again from the base of their own experience, should examine their practice and that of other workers to identify examples of advocacy activities directed toward organizational change either within their own agency or within other institutions. For example, a worker in a family service setting may be trying to change the agency's policy which favours a short-term intervention model and define indicators for exceptions. A worker in a child protective setting may be part of a coalition of workers advocating for investigation of racist practices in the local welfare office. Similarly a school social worker may be involved with the welfare system on behalf of an adolescent student who has left an abusive family and has no means of support or shelter. Examples give specificity to concepts and help students understand their role in this aspect of social work practice. Social work values which emphasize enhancing human dignity and self-worth may then be transformed from vague, global, and passive words to concepts capable of serving as guides to planned actions in the service of client well-being and empowerment.

In order to create meaningful learning assignments at the organizational level, students first need to learn how decisions, both formal and informal, are made within the agency or institution. Instructors should discuss with students ways in which they can influence these decisions effectively and sensitively, how they can marshal the necessary facts to influence decisions through a planned strategy, and how they can recognize and deal with resistance to change at any level. This is particularly important when the setting is not a primary social work agency but rather a secondary setting.

The ITP Loop Model directs attention outside the agency's organizational structure as well as within. Field instructors can develop a learning assignment to help students become familiar with the community in which the agency is located. Prepared by this investigation, field instructor and student can discuss the social, economic, cultural, and ethnic characteristics of the community, and a variety of social indicators such as whether it has a cohesive or transient population or whether the housing is adequate or substandard. Another meaningful assignment is the task of learning about the network of community resources available to meet the needs of the populations served by the agency. Especially in communities with diverse racial and ethnic populations, services, including the agency, can be analysed with respect to their information and outreach efforts to diverse communities, the appropriateness and relevance of the approaches used, and the perceptions of community members of the helpfulness of these services. Students can examine the extent to which community organizations include the multiple populations in the community in their board composition, staff complement, and clients served.

Learning assignments such as these may uncover needs for resources that the community does not provide or barriers to service delivery for all members of the community. When a student identifies a need or barrier, the field instructor can guide the student to think through strategies that may generate resource-building to meet the need or organizational action to change the practice. Other interested workers or key figures in the community can be mobilized to join with the student in formulating a strategy. Such activities may lead to the formulation of proposals for new services, such as transportation for the disabled and frail elderly, or extended school programs for children of working parents. Removal of barriers to underserved populations and the creation of more effective outreach and inclusionary practices may result from efforts at promoting equitable service accessibility.

Finally, students in some settings need to learn about societal factors as expressed in socio-legal procedures, such as appeals for welfare, health insurance reimbursements, workers' compensation, immigration and refugee claims, or how patients are protected or placed at risk by mental health legislation. Many administrative decisions are discretionary ones which can be challenged and brought up for review. Where the law is unclear, these appeals are often decided in favour of the claimant (Vayda 1980). Students become interested in these matters when their application is immediate and when they are encouraged to work with others, such as community legal personnel. Learning assignments can be designed so that students become knowledgeable in a way that allows them to respond appropriately to practice situations involving legal and administrative matters.

In conclusion, beginnings represent the opportunity to launch a successful practicum if field instructors recognize the high anxiety associated with embarking on any new activity. In this stage, an effective start will most likely be achieved by anticipating issues for the student, the field instructor, and the agency, and by providing thoughtful planning, structure, and focus. Reflecting on our experiences as field coordinators who were consulted by field instructors about difficulty with students, we concluded that most situations could have been avoided had there been a good start in the beginning phase. The critical ingredients appear to be providing structure, clarifying expectations, assigning clients and projects early, providing the socio-emotional ingredients for relationship-building, and a welcoming atmosphere in the organization.

4

The Instructional Relationship

The ITP Loop and Your Own Experience as a Student

As practitioners become educators, it is likely that their assumptions and beliefs about what constitutes effective field instruction are largely influenced by their own experiences as students. Traces of field instructors' practicum experiences, positive or negative, will shape their concept of what they wish to convey to students and what climate is felt to be desirable. Take the time to reflect upon your own practicum experience and try to put it into words. The purpose of this exercise is to identify issues you felt were relevant when you were a student and to examine how they affected your learning. It is important to ask how these issues were handled by the field instruction participants – you as a student, your field instructor, and others in the agency – and to realize their influence on your ideas about field education. Thus, the process of preparation for field instruction begins at 'the point where the field instructor is'; that is, you begin by retrieval of elements of your own student experience. If your student experience was a positive one, in which you learned and developed your professional practice, try to identify the elements that promoted development and growth. Conversely, if your student field experience was unpleasant or not conducive to growth, try to identify those elements that inhibited learning.

You will recall that retrieval is the entry into the ITP loop; in this case, retrieval of your student practicum experience. Reflection on these retrieved memories provides the opportunity to review your practicum from a distance and from a perspective of more experience and understanding.

As you move to linkage, you may be able to relate positive and negative aspects of your student experience to theories, such as those of adult education, learning styles, and supervisory relationships, that may reveal why some memories produce positive feelings that learning was enhanced and encouraged while other memories bring back negative feelings that learning was impeded.

Professional response, the next step in the loop, may be demonstrated by a resolve that the learning experience for your student is partly informed by re-experiencing and examining your own practicum. In other words, you make a conscious decision about how you will behave toward your student. The looping process now begins anew as the present encounter with your student tests the usefulness and the limitations of this decision. For example, if you adopt an approach to your student totally based on your own retrieved practicum experience and fail to separate your reactions as a student from those of your present student, you may have made an assumption that your retrieved memories of your unmet needs are universally valid. One social worker recalled how her field instructor was very task focused and did not provide sufficient time for her to express her feelings about the work she was doing with her clients. She felt she needed more emotional support from her field instructor. Therefore she deliberately encouraged her current student to talk about his reactions and probed for unexplored and unexpressed affect. Finally, in a field instruction session, the student was able to say that talking so much about his feelings seemed like a waste of their limited time together, and he would prefer more focus on strategies to move the client situation forward. She realized that she had assumed that her student wanted the support she had not received and so had overlooked his need to understand through objective planning.

Contextual Factors

The ITP Loop Model also takes into account layers of experiential complexity in that it requires a consideration of context and the influence of macro issues, as well as organizational factors, interpersonal interaction, and psycho-social factors; therefore, it is ecological and multi-factorial. It bridges macro and micro levels and incorporates structural, organizational, interpersonal, and personal elements. This model highlights the importance of contextual factors and how these factors may affect the organization and the nature of the student–field instructor relationship. For example, recently many agencies, facing financial cutbacks, have responded by downsizing, which has resulted in increased caseloads for social workers. If those same agencies remain committed to field education, they may expect their social workers to offer field instruction while maintaining high levels of client service. The individual social worker must then strike a balance between time given to student education and time given to service. Hence, the student may experience the field instructor as inconsistent, sometimes interested and easily accessible, and at other times harried and preoccupied. This behaviour may be more a result of the agency's current service pressures than of the field instructor's style. It is an example of how political decisions and the agency's organization affect the educational relationship between student and field instructor.

The agency's mandate and organization also influence the type of learning assignments and practice models available for student learning. Field instructors, interested in providing students with a range of learning experiences, may, in flexible settings, include activities other than those preferred or mandated by the agency's official approach. For example, students may be able to do long-term work, even though the agency's service model is short-term and time-limited. Agencies that are committed to education will include students in a rich range of learning activities, such as staff development, journal clubs, case conferences, and the opportunity to observe or practise with experienced staff in the setting. An organizational climate that values education will provide a supportive and helpful context for the work of the student and field instructor. Conversely, in settings where the student's education is seen as exclusively the responsibility of the field instructor, the instructor may feel less supported. The student may feel that she or he is a burden to the field instructor and become overly protective of the instructor's time at the expense of his or her own learning needs. These examples are provided to illustrate the subtle effect of organizational factors on the interpersonal and educational relationship between the student and field instructor.

Inter-organizational relationships between the agency and the school also have an effect on the student's practicum. In chapter 2 we discussed the world of field instruction and noted that the context of the practicum is within and between two organizations. The faculty-field liaison and the field instructor are employed by two different organizations, while the student must navigate both worlds, the university and the community agency. Variations in both faculty-field liaison models and approaches to social work were discussed. These differences will also have an impact on the student's practicum. Meetings with the student, the faculty-field liaison, and the field instructor can be synergistic and promote greater learning. They can also highlight differences, and students can become caught in the middle or ally with either the field instructor or the liaison. Using retrieval, social workers have recalled a variety of interactions they experienced in the school-agency interface. Some retrieve benign experiences, some helpful ones, and others destructive encounters. Some will recall the liaison as a person who helped integrate classroom and field, and contributed to lively discussions about different professional viewpoints. Others recall involvement fraught with differences of opinion between school and agency. Acrimonious discussions about what constitutes competent social work practice often leave the student feeling powerless and frightened.

The instructional relationship between the student and field instructor is embedded in these organizational contexts and is affected by them. You may wish to consider the following questions as you reflect on your practicum experience. What were the contextual issues that were operating in both the agency and the school? How did these issues affect your practicum and how were they dealt with? In retrospect, how might they have been dealt with differently? Have you developed any beliefs, values, or assumptions about field education from that experience that shape planning for your student? Are these beliefs helpful or are they your history and not necessarily applicable to the current experience with your student?

Relationship

Social workers who have used this exercise, in which they revisit their student practicum experience, almost universally comment on the significant impact of the student–field instructor relationship on their learning. Social workers have shared experiences which highlight how their learning needs were met by field instructors who were excellent teachers, mentors, and role models. Others have shared experiences in which their personal characteristics, learning styles, or practice approaches did not fit well with those of their instructors. Strong feelings of disappointment or anger may still be connected to those experiences, even though they occurred many years ago.

Take the time to reflect on the relationship between you and your field instructors. What were the qualities of your field instructor that you most and least admired? What were important issues in the relationship? Did they relate to issues of vulnerability and trust, authority and power, control and autonomy? You may recall past misunderstandings and acknowledge the subjectivity of meanings, feelings, and reactions. Identify how these issues were handled productively and when they were not successfully dealt with. Have you developed some ideas about how you intend to proceed as a field instructor as a result of your own experience?

The process of retrieving your own experience as a student and reflecting on the feelings, assumptions, and beliefs that emanate from it provides you with important self-knowledge. The retrieved material can be focused and linked to a body of field instruction knowledge via the ITP Loop Model. The exercise also puts you in touch with the normal anxieties and expectations students bring to the practicum, so that you can connect with empathy.

The Importance of the Student–Field Instructor Relationship

Study after study concludes that the field instructor is key to a positive field experience for the student. Tolson and Kopp (1988) conducted a study to investigate the transfer of knowledge learned in the classroom to the field. They found that the practicum instructor's orientation appears to relate more significantly to the student's practice orientation and behaviour than any other variables thought to influence practice, such as client characteristics, type of agency, or orientation of the classroom instructor. They conclude that the most important influence on the development of students' practice is the practicum.

Raskin (1989) found that students' satisfaction with the practicum is likely to influence student learning and may even be a necessary condition for learning. A number of studies found that the relationship between the field instructor and student has the power to affect the student's learning positively or negatively and predicts satisfaction (Amacher 1976; Fortune et al. 1985; Fortune and Abramson 1993; Kahn 1981; Marshall 1982). Fortune and Abramson (1993), investigating potential predictors of satisfaction, found higher scores significantly associated with three factors: the quality of field instruction, agency desirability and inclusion, and a field instructor who provided explanations. In summary, these studies provide empirical support for a social work practice principle: the importance of relationship in facilitating change, learning, and growth. Research findings demonstrate that what happens in the working relationship with the field instructor is the best predictor of satisfaction.

Why is this relationship so important and so pivotal to effective practicum learning? In the classroom, student learning is divorced from the actual world of practice. The student is surrounded by peers and is largely protected from self-exposure. Students know what is expected in a university course. Learning is intellectual and provided in the familiar formats of lectures, presentations, or discussions. While the personal may be engaged affectively, students can maintain as much privacy as they wish with regard to their feelings about the material being presented. Evaluation is conducted through 'objective' methods such as examinations or papers. Behavioural or performance competence is rarely part of evaluation in an academic course. The relationship with the classroom instructor is generally impersonal and distant. In contrast, the field practicum takes place in the real world of practice, where learning occurs through providing a service to a client, group, or community. While there may be other students in the agency, the student is usually the only one assigned to a particular field instructor. Hence, this educational dyad takes on the qualities of a primary relationship; that is, two people meet regularly and frequently in face-to-face contact. The material they work on is often anxiety-provoking, elicits more or less intense affect, and requires not only intellectual understanding but also the ability to act in a helpful and professional way. Unlike the classroom, field learning requires self-exposure and a constant challenge to the student's sense of competence and self-confidence. In the process of learning to become a competent professional social worker, many personal and professional issues are activated within the dyadic relationship of student and field instructor, but the impact of the relationship itself is seldom acknowledged with the student.

The following section deals with some of the issues which confront students during the course of their professional preparation and which should be recognized as fairly universal themes. As in social work practice, specific responses are based on the uniqueness of the situation, and timing and specific words cannot be prescribed. However, the following issues are fairly common, and can be introduced by the field instructor for discussion and problem-solving with the student.

Career Choice, Preparation, and Job Competition

In the recent past, social service and health delivery systems have been undergoing massive changes. Economic and organizational restructuring, changes to government policy and programs, the growing influence of managed care, and the decline of private voluntary agencies are some of the factors which have created an uncertain and highly competitive employment market for social workers. Whereas only a decade ago graduates of social work programs could be relatively confident that they would find employment in fields of their choice, today social work students and practising social workers are faced with uncertain job prospects, the lack of permanent positions, and the possibility of not finding employment in the field or location of their choice.

In addition, schools of social work are admitting more students who have already completed a first university degree. These students are seeking specialized education to increase their employability, or they are changing careers. Typically, these students have a bachelor's degree in arts; however, there are increasing numbers with professional degrees (e.g., in education, nursing, and law) and with graduate degrees in social sciences and humanities.

Aware of the tight job market, students feel pressured to develop visible competence, to master knowledge and skills that will enable them to deliver a service. Students often seek a niche, a set of marketable capabilities that will make them stand out from colleagues with whom they are competing for the scarce and desirable positions. Students know that where they do their practicum and what set of practice competencies they develop will be crucial in finding future jobs.

There are also personal issues connected to career choice and beginning professional education. Students in any field inevitably question whether they have made the right choice. Is this the right profession for me? Should I have chosen something else? In social work, students have always been concerned with the enormity of the social and personal issues confronted by the client groups they work with. They are anxious about their ability to learn the knowledge and competencies that will make a difference in promoting a more just society, and about their ability to cope with the challenges and disappointments of a career in social work. Many students become overwhelmed by their inability to make any impact against the structural, political, and economic forces that are so destructive to the lives of many of their clients.

Self-esteem

Social work is a profession in which the practitioner as a person is the instrument of intervention. This fact creates heightened anxiety for both field instructor and student. Our knowledge base is diffuse and demands an integration of concepts from several different disciplines. Though other professions, such as medicine, nursing, or law, demand interpersonal skills, they have, in addition, precise and visible technical skills which must be learned and applied, but which have no counterpart in social work practice. Kadushin (1968) has pointed out that students become anxious because they begin to perceive that change may be required that can affect not only their ideas but also their behaviour and quite possibly their personalities. The diffuseness of the knowledge base, combined with what is perceived as demands on the personality itself, can quickly undermine the student's sense of adequacy and self-esteem.

Furthermore, the position of learner leads to an awareness of 'what I don't know' – a position that can engender a feeling of being 'not-competent' and, at times, 'in-competent.' Learning social work in the classroom makes use of familiar intellectual and cognitive abilities that have been developed through university education. The study, analysis, and critique of a multitude of social issues, practice problems, theories, and approaches can be stimulating, interesting, and broadening. Learning in the field is a completely different matter. Since learning in the field is a by-product of carrying a service role, the student must make sense of the multitude of theories, concepts, competing empirical findings, and alternative frameworks and paradigms, so that a direction for practice emerges. Practice confronts students with 'real problems' presented by real people, and students feel the need to learn quickly so that they can provide something useful to the client or consumer. This circumstance inevitably stirs up feelings about one's competence and self-esteem. Kaplan (1991a) observes that 'social work learning in the practicum is a complex process that implies considerable personal and professional risk for students. It requires that students deal with unfamiliar situations, utilize creativity in selecting interventions and determine optimal direction for clients. Indeed, they are asked to begin doing something before they have learned to do so' (106).

Graduating students and alumni, reflecting on the course of their learning in professional school, have described a stage of demoralization when they realized that learning to practise 'is tough' and takes a long time. They recall searching for safe places where they could express their uncertainties, risk 'not knowing,' ask, and not feel totally inadequate in the process. Field education is often the place where these struggles are most evident; and the relationship with the field instructor, the most facilitative and supportive place to work out these normal and ubiquitous issues in personal and professional development.

Many beginning social work students, especially students who have little social work or life experience, have up to this point been socialized to relate to others with politeness, to desire to be seen by others as helpful and likable, to respect the personal and private space of others, in short, to be a 'nice' person. This is the internalized self-image which many students bring to the practicum. As the practicum develops, the student becomes aware that this is not a 'good enough' self to bring to work with clients. Probing into another's personal space, hearing and responding to fears, pain, anger, sadness, and ambivalences, are essential to developing into a competent social worker, and these demands create a dissonance which threatens comfortable behaviour patterns and personality integrity. It is important that field instructors empathize with students' confusion and anxiety from the beginning of the practicum in regard to the newness of the social worker role contrasted with their image of themselves as helping and kind persons. This supportive attitude will form the cornerstone of the learning and teaching relationship. Towle (1954) spoke of relationship as a means to learning which should develop the identity of the learner rather than obliterate it. Younghusband (1967) pointed out that learning in social work involves students' emotions and facing personal value judgments and subjecting them to professional discipline. This process of self-awareness sets in motion continuing behavioural change in the direction of increasing receptivity and perception. Hamilton (1954) observed that self-awareness in professional education is a by-product which is a form of attendant learning rather than primary learning. She felt that it occurs by increasing the student's capacity for self-acceptance, a conclusion that is still valid. The field instructor should approach the problem of stimulating self-awareness on the level of conscious motivation. In other words, promoting self-awareness is related to the needs of client situations and is not to be presented as a therapeutic intervention aimed at changing the student's personality. Self-awareness is essential for the student, but it is a by-product of the analysis of the experience of intervention.

Since many students in social work programs have considerable social work experience, life experience, or both, adult learning theory is useful to understand the issues they face. Drawing on experience can provide a rich resource for learning. However, since adults have a well-organized self-concept and sense of self-esteem, new learning activities and the expectation for change may be perceived as a threat to the self (Brundage and MacKeracher 1980). Fear of failure may impede active involvement in learning. Experienced students may be preoccupied with what they know and what they think they should know. On the one hand, there may be parts of their practicum which are very familiar to them and with which they can engage easily, feeling knowledgeable and competent; on the other hand, there will be new areas of learning in which they will feel like beginners again. Individual styles will affect how this will be handled. Some experienced students are quite distraught about not knowing, and are fearful of exposure and the possibility of failure. Feeling de-skilled and retreating to the position that they feel they know nothing, they might become highly dependent on the field instructor for guidance and direction. Others may react to not knowing by becoming critical of the agency, the practice model, or the field instructor. They may assume a position of knowing it all.

It is important for the field instructor to recognize multiple variations in students' reactions to new learning situations, and to understand the unique experience and reactions of a particular student. It is the field instructor's responsibility to introduce pertinent issues for discussion and to reach out to engage the student in a mutual process of reflection and exploration. By identifying what is at issue, the field instructor and student can then work together to arrive at the best possible educational responses.

Power and Control

Moving from the position of a beginning learner in a profession to an autonomous practitioner involves a process of moving from initial dependence on a teacher to an independent position. Students are realistically dependent upon field instructors' professional expertise, knowledge of and access to the setting, and power of evaluation. The student has less power in the institution, less practice competence, and less specialized knowledge than the instructor. Horner (1988) notes that the power differential renders the student vulnerable to the instructor's attitudes toward power. Field instructors can sensitively respond to this circumstance by recognizing and respecting students as adult learners who will soon be professional colleagues and avoiding the arbitrary use of their power. Horner (1988) cautions: 'Is it something to be used benevolently and reliably in the interest of the student's growth towards competence and autonomy, or is it to be used in the service of the supervisor's need to control, to maintain a posture of superiority, or to destroy the power of the other?' (9).

A variety of interpretations of the extent of the field instructor's power have been noted. Some students perceive the instructor as having so much power and themselves so little that they feel vulnerable at the hands of the instructor. They report feeling concerned about the instructor's potential to harm them. They expend considerable energy 'figuring out' what will please the instructor and trying to behave in accordance with those perceptions. Instructors can unwittingly collude with this stance and reinforce a one-down relationship with the student. This position mitigates against an atmosphere that is open, free, and facilitative of learning. Other students challenge the instructor continuously in an attempt to establish themselves and their expertise. Instructors who enable and accept students' questioning and create a reciprocal relationship of feedback and challenge can work well with such students. Others who experience challenge as a threat may find themselves in a struggle with the student.

In some instances, the power dynamics may include thoughts, feelings, and behaviours which are derived from other significant supervisory, learning, or personal relationships and which are activated by the intensity of the present relationship. They may seem irrational and not related to the reality of the current situation; in fact, they may be the result of previous experiences with authority characterized by fear, vulnerability, and the power to harm. Feelings transferred from such experiences and related directly to the present situation can lead the student or the instructor to behave in a manner not appropriate to a climate of participation and mutuality. Power and control also accrue to perceptions about race, gender, and age. These issues are discussed later in this section.

Even though field instructors may not subjectively experience themselves as having power, the respective roles of student and teacher confer power on them. In fact, many writers note that field instructors have initial difficulty with the authority inherent in their role (Hawthorne 1975; Kadushin 1968; Shulman 1982), and feel uncomfortable with the evaluative power granted to them. Some may avoid using their authority, act as if it is non-existent, and create a 'buddy' relationship with the student. Others may respond in an authoritarian, constrictive, and rigid manner. There is a power discrepancy between student and field instructor which needs to be acknowledged, clarified in operational terms, and re-clarified through the ongoing process as misperceptions, confusions, and misunderstandings arise.

The following case example demonstrates many of the issues presented thus far and some of the professional responses field instructors can use to solidify the working relationship in field instruction.

Prior to entering a social work degree program, Jim had worked for four years in the welfare department as a caseworker. In his final year, he had contracted for a practicum in a family-oriented agency. He had contracted with Sally, his field instructor, for a form of direct supervision wherein the instructor would participate in the interview sessions with him and intervene in his work with the client system as she thought appropriate. They would discuss the case process and their interventions after the session. As they were entering the interview room for the third family session, Jim turned to Sally and said, 'Would you please just observe today. Let me carry the session myself.' Sally was very surprised and said to Jim in an irritated tone, 'Well, in that case, you don't need me in the room. Just tape the interview and I'll see you at our next meeting.' She noticed he looked uncomfortable, as if he wanted to respond. She turned her back and went to her office.

Sally sat in her office and reflected on what had just happened. She identified that she was feeling angry and rejected by Jim's sudden breaking of their agreement that she would participate in the interviews. She asked herself what was it that she was so angry about. She had tried to be a good field instructor, to be sensitive to the student's need for control as an experienced worker. She had developed an approach to field instruction that emphasized mutuality and participation. In his rejection of this approach, she felt unappreciated and devalued. She acknowledged that feeling appreciated is important to her in interpersonal relationships. She began to speculate about Jim's possible reasons for not wanting her in that session. She drew on her knowledge that all behaviour has meaning and is the product of reciprocal interactions. She concluded that if their relationship was to continue in a productive fashion, they must both be involved in resolving this impasse. She decided to explore with Jim at their next meeting his reasons for abruptly changing the terms of their agreement. In this way, she did not continue to react with anger to the incident; rather, she chose a professional response.

When Sally introduced the topic at the next session, she began by sharing her reactions to his request. Jim was then able to describe how her critique of his handling of a previous interview had left him feeling unsure that he had any ability as a social worker. Sally was astonished to learn that what she thought was clear, direct feedback could have such a devastating effect. She decided to explore his past experience with positive and negative feedback. Jim told her that as an untrained worker he had been very sensitive to feedback from supervisors, fearing that he would lose his job if he was not good enough. In fact, he had received almost no negative feedback from his busy and preoccupied supervisor in the welfare department. It appeared that he had transferred into the current relationship thoughts, assumptions, and fears about job performance that were inappropriate to the educational task. These perceptions had affected the way he received feedback about his competence. His fear about dealing with authority manifested itself in attempts to control his instructor's input and perceived potential to harm him.

On the basis of this information, Sally suggested they review their contract in order to clarify the expectations each had of the other. Through this discussion, they articulated the differences in performance expectations between a learning situation and an employment situation. They also examined the difference between a field instruction and job supervision relationship. They clarified that Jim needed to feel validated in what he did know in addition to receiving feedback about what he did not know. As Jim left the office, Sally felt pleased that she had responded to her concern that 'something was going on' that had provoked such strong reactions on both their parts.

Modelling

Field instructors are role models for students. Much learning occurs through imitation, identification, and incorporating behaviours and attitudes experienced in the relationship between student and field instructor and transferring them to practice. Kadushin (1985) believes that especially in the development of professional attitudes, the most effective learning comes through identification with a supervisor who models the attitudes of a good social worker, rather than through didactic teaching.

While social work practice and practicum education are different activities, they share some similarities with respect to the qualities of helpful relationships, the stages of a change process, and the perceived implicit hierarchy between the participants. In both instances, the goal is empowerment. There are analogous processes in the student–field instructor relationship and in the worker-client relationship which can facilitate achieving the goal of empowerment. As the student experiences those processes in her or his educational work with the field instructor, the student learns through modelling and can generalize that learning in practice.

In conclusion, the field instructor–student relationship appears central to the practicum. It has the potential to affect significantly the development of the student into a self-confident, competent, and autonomous social worker. In the relationship, students learn both purposefully and through modelling social work attitudes, values, and approaches. Through participating with the field instructor, they can learn to deal with important issues impinging on their practice.

The Qualities of an Effective Student–Field Instructor Relationship

Numerous studies have found that the student's perception and experience of the relationship with the field instructor are the best predictors of satisfaction in the practicum. The following components appear to be of major importance: availability, support, structure, promoting student autonomy, feedback, and linking theory and practice.

Availability

Students value field instructors who are available and easily accessible (Baker and Smith 1987; Gray, Alperin, and Wik 1989; Hagen 1989; Knight 1996). Fortune and Abramson (1993) found that regular supervisory conferences were critical to establish a stable contact upon which a working relationship could be built. Together the student and field instructor will set a specific time for their field instruction sessions, which may vary with the needs of the practicum. In this way, students know they will see their field instructors at least once a week initially. What needs to be clarified is the instructor's availability outside of regularly scheduled sessions. Some field instructors react with panic to students who constantly look to them as being omnipotent and possessing all the answers. A common reaction is to try to pull away, to retreat from such devouring need. The student, however, sensing this withdrawal, may become even more anxious, and the cycle continues. With self-awareness, the field instructor may offer realistic reassurance and support, and by countering the sense that the student is alone, help to allay such anxiety. Particularly at the beginning of the practicum there needs to be easy accessibility and clarity about the field instructor's availability or backup for crises.

Support

Kadushin (1985), in his classic work on supervision, identified the importance of support in the work of the supervisor with both students and supervisees. Supportive aspects of field instruction attend to emotional issues and create a socio-emotional climate which is responsive to students' feelings (Fortune and Abramson 1993; Urbanowski and Dwyer 1988). These emotional reactions may be in response to practice situations and the effectiveness of student interventions. As well, feelings may be about issues associated with being a learner, such as self-esteem, dependency, and power. The following qualities and behaviours are associated with support: warmth and understanding, as contrasted with cold, aloof, and hostile interpersonal styles (Rosenblatt and Mayer 1975); openness, respectfulness, and trustworthiness (Fortune and Abramson 1993; Marshall 1982; Urbanowski and Dwyer 1988); accepting the student as a budding professional (Fortune and Abramson 1993); putting the student at ease and sensitivity to student needs (Baker and Smith 1987). Instructors who enjoy teaching (Fortune et al. 1985) and who recognize that students' mistakes are part of learning display additional supportive attributes (Hagen 1989). In a study investigating expected topics for the supervisory conference, Gray and colleagues (1989) found that students expected a greater amount of time to be allotted to supportive topics, such as students' personal strengths and weaknesses, and successes and failures, than did either the field instructors or the faculty members in their sample. Baker and Smith (1987) found that students' satisfaction with the field supervisor was more influenced by these socio-emotional factors than by task-related factors, such as the supervisor's practice knowledge and ability to train students.

Structure

Field instructors provide structure for the practicum through the timely selection of appropriate learning assignments and a range of relevant teaching methods (Baker and Smith 1987; Gitterman 1989). They clarify the roles and expectations of both the student and the field instructor with respect to the agency and the school (Hagen 1989; Knight 1996); and they provide information to structure and clarify the work situation (Rotholz and Werk 1984).

Promoting Student Autonomy

Autonomy-giving behaviour is designed to encourage independence and the student's active participation in learning (Rosenblatt and Mayer 1975; Urbanowski and Dwyer 1988). This includes encouraging the expression of the student's ideas (Fortune et al. 1985) and involving the student in planning and designing the learning experiences (Fortune and Abramson 1993).

Feedback and Evaluation

Evaluation that is ongoing and given as both formal and informal feedback about the student's learning and performance is associated with satisfaction. Many studies identify the importance of communicating clear expectations and goals, and giving feedback which is specific and constructive. Students value instructors who observe their practice, and give them systematic and critical comments about the skills they are acquiring (Baker and Smith 1987; Barth and Gambrill 1984; Fortune and Abramson 1993; Freeman 1985; Urbanowski and Dwyer 1988).

Feedback has been well developed for direct practice learning. It is equally important for all levels of practice, and instructors need to creatively find appropriate methods to access students' practice data and give feedback. Richan (1989) describes a field practicum in a low-income community designed to teach students empowerment practice. He found that the students' sense of empowerment and their ability to use this approach in practice depended on the kind of feedback received from the field instructor. Students in this project identified the importance of feedback given in a context which is positive, supportive, and accepting.

Linking Theory and Practice

Satisfactory field instruction promotes linkage between theory and practice. The instructor provides explanations that help clarify practice issues and interventions, makes connections between current learning and what should be done next in practice, and provides relevant readings (Fortune and Abramson 1993). Field instructors also teach students specific skills and techniques, and conceptualize these interventions using a variety of theories and classroom work (Gitterman 1989; Hagen 1989).

Processes to Enhance the Relationship

The six qualities and behaviours of field instructors identified with an ideal student–field instructor relationship can only serve as a preferred model. Each student and field instructor dyad is ultimately a reflection of the attributes and behaviours of each of the two participants and of their respective capacities to form a productive alliance. It is useful to view the relationship as a collaborative partnership in which both participants are committed to work together to achieve the educational goals of the student in the context of the school and the agency. It is the field instructor's responsibility to take the lead in developing and maintaining a positive working relationship. Social work practitioners have developed competence in building and maintaining relationships with clients, committee members, administrators, and consumers. This practice knowledge and skill can be adapted and used in field instruction. Relationship-building begins with the instructor's being available, giving attention to the socio-emotional aspects of the student's learning, and providing structure.

The student and field instructor, because of differences in their roles, knowledge, and skill, may have different perceptions about useful activities and processes for learning. Ongoing discussion and feedback are necessary so that adjustments can be made in the way they are working together. This includes being able to openly express differences. Raphael and Rosenblum (1989) conducted an exploratory study to determine the extent and effect of open expression of differences in field instruction. They note that the literature recognizes the value of instructors encouraging differences while acknowledging the impact of the power differential between student and field instructor. They found that when instructors responded to the concerns of the students empathetically and educationally, the students experienced these responses as supportive. They also perceived that it strengthened their practice and the relationship with the instructor. Conversely, when instructors' responses were not empathetic, they had negative effects on students' practice and learning. While it is self-evident that empathy is more effective, perceptions of empathy may differ widely. For example, a field instructor may feel that she or he is being supportive and encouraging, while the student complains of distance and coldness.

Most students have been socialized into a hierarchical model of education. An explicit statement from the instructor that feedback is necessary may not be sufficient to deal with apprehension about the power differential and the safety of open expression of differences or concerns. Students may not feel confident enough to raise concerns about misunderstandings, disagreements, and disappointments as they occur. Differences may be labelled as personality clashes that cannot be solved and so remain unspoken. It is useful for the instructor to be attuned to discrepancies between the student's verbal expressions – for example, 'everything is going just fine' – and behaviours which indicate the opposite. Indirect verbal and behavioural cues, and the instructor's own emotional reactions to these cues, can signal that something needs to be addressed.

For example, during the contracting phase, a field instructor informed the student that one of the expectations for evaluation is audiotaped recordings of client interviews, to be accompanied by process recordings of these interviews. The student provided the process recordings but told the instructor that she erased all the tapes because she was not aware that tapes were required. Using reflection in the ITP Loop Model, the instructor explored the possible meanings of this situation for both himself and the student. The instructor wondered whether he had communicated the expectation clearly, whether the student was indicating anxiety and fear of exposing her practice, and whether there had been other signs of anxiety which he may have missed. The phase of linkage connected him to knowledge that unstated issues that remain unresolved may affect behaviour in the educational relationship. He also drew on knowledge about the importance of raising issues, especially in the beginning phase, in an open and positive manner. In planning a professional response, the instructor decided to deal with the issue directly and try to elicit feedback that would indicate the student's perceptions. He appreciated that a low-key and non-judgmental stance on his part would more likely facilitate the kind of open discussion in which the student could express her views. Since practice involves complex and challenging situations, it is paradoxical to relate to students as if they are fragile and unable to deal directly with interpersonal tensions. In fact, the field instruction relationship provides a safe and important 'lab' where intersubjective perceptions and experiences can be examined, and common and different interpretations sorted out. This process provides experiential learning through modelling of attitudes and behaviours that contribute to effective relationship-building.

Returning to our example, in the next instruction conference, the field instructor began by telling the student that he was confused. He thought he had conveyed that taping was expected and yet it appeared that they did not have the same understanding. The student responded that she had thought that audiotapes were only necessary for the evaluation conference. They reviewed their earlier discussion, and each had different understandings of the expectation. The instructor felt that pursuing the details of how this misunderstanding arose would not be productive.

Instead he asked the student whether she had any experience in using tapes. The student told him of a course in interviewing skills she had taken. Students were expected to present tapes to the class for input and analysis. The instructor noticed her tense facial expression as she recalled that this had not been helpful for her learning. He gently asked what aspects were difficult. The student shared that the class had 'picked everything apart' and she had left feeling that she knew nothing. The instructor empathized with that experience and commented, 'Only receiving negative feedback can be pretty devastating. It's also useful to know what you're doing that's positive or what alternatives to try.' He asked the student if she thought the experience in her course was having an impact on her interest in using tapes in the field. She readily acknowledged that this was so. He clarified that the use of tapes was an expectation in the setting and asked her how they could use tapes together in a way that would be helpful for her. After thinking about this, the student suggested that she might identify parts in the tapes that were positive and parts that were negative. She would also like to highlight where she was lost and have the instructor help her form alternative responses.

In this example, the field instructor recognized the issues of self-esteem and demoralization which the student had experienced in her previous use of tapes. It was likely that she anticipated a similar experience with the instructor. It was not necessary to enter into an in-depth exploration of this topic. Rather, the instructor identified the issue in a way that encouraged partnership. The student easily joined him to find effective educational methods to alleviate her anxiety about being helpless and vulnerable to attack.

Depending on the student's educational stage of development, the instructor may need to take more or less leadership in this type of discussion. Students at the beginning of their first practicum may be uncomfortable with giving direct feedback to an authority figure. By contrast, a graduate student who can draw on undergraduate practicum and supervision experience is more likely to be accustomed to give and take with the instructor.

When students actually take the risk and respond to comments or raise concerns of their own, instructors' reactions will affect the next stage of the relationship work. Responses should reinforce the messages about openness. Subtle cues and defensive responses that convey that students' criticisms are not welcomed, or punitive, cold, or distancing reactions are likely to discourage any further attempts toward mutuality. Reframing the issues as the student's personality problem is counter-productive. For example, a student was concerned that the field instruction sessions, which focused on the client's dynamics, were not providing her with the direction she needed. The student took the risk of saying to the field instructor, 'I think I understand the client's problem, but I want to know what to do, and our field instruction sessions are not giving me enough help with that.' The field instructor had already labelled this student as passive-aggressive and responded, 'You seem angry at me for not telling you what to do. I wonder, do you tend to want other people to solve your problems for you?' One can speculate on how this comment was received by the student. It provides a good example of poor supervisory technique.

Challenges to Effective Relationships

Approval

Both student and field instructor share the human need for approval, a sense that one is accepted and liked. The task of field instruction is to learn practice. The role of the field instructor includes the responsibility to give both positive and negative feedback, to help the student critically evaluate his or her own practice behaviours. Some students may experience a negative comment as a withdrawal of approval, feeling a loss of self-esteem and adequacy. The instructor may be perplexed when the same student who has requested direct and clear feedback reacts in an upset manner when it is given. Similarly, the field instructor, who wants to help the student but also wants approval as a good instructor, may give support and encouragement by avoiding challenge, constructive criticism, and confrontation. While this pattern may feel comfortable, it risks maintaining the student in a status quo at the expense of growth and development.

Ruptures in Relationship

As the research has demonstrated, many students are able to accept negative feedback and challenges to their perceptions when given in a relational context which they experience as supportive and empathetic. However, some students experience negative feedback as hurtful and a signal that they must protect themselves from the instructor. In such a situation, the dynamics in the educational relationship become a barrier to learning (Bogo, 1993). Field instructors confronted with such a situation need to engage the student in reflecting together on the rupture in their working relationship. This will be a challenge since in these instances the very problem of the student's feeling vulnerable is heightened by such an exploration. Instructors can focus on clarifying unspoken feelings and assumptions, and work toward making them explicit. Increased understanding of difficulties should then lead to the discovery of more useful methods for learning and teaching to achieve educational goals.

The difficulty in such discussions seems to occur when instructors search for underlying explanations of students' behaviours by labelling personality issues and focusing on developmental and familial life events which may have contributed to current functioning. Some students will enter willingly into such a quasi-therapeutic exploration, but inevitably boundary issues develop when teaching is confused with therapy. Most students find a quasi-therapeutic approach invasive and feel even more vulnerable, becoming more anxious and guarded in field instruction.

An effective approach will focus discussion of the partnership in a way that invites mutual exploration that is receptive to the student's input and that is committed to working toward joint problem-solving to produce change in the way student and instructor are working together. Students struggle with whether they can trust the instructor's invitation to them and risk expressing their concerns. They can only develop this trust as they are helped to express concerns and discover that the field instructor's response will be helpful, not punitive as they may have feared. While trust is developed through the relational qualities of warmth, acceptance, genuineness, and interest, it is only tested as participants grapple with difference and recognize that they can risk disagreement and achieve resolution of some sort. This process takes time, understanding, and patience. Instructors are challenged to be open about their own reactions with respect to difficulties as well as attending to students' reactions. Since two individuals create the educational climate, instructors can assume that their attitudes and behaviours, as well as those of the students, may have a negative impact on learning. It can be difficult for field instructors to deal with their feelings of inadequacy or anger when students give them negative feedback. The faculty-field liaison can be helpful in this regard and also in working to resolve impasses in student–field instructor relationships. However, not all situations can be ideally resolved.

The following example illustrates some of these relationship issues. In this situation, the student had returned to university in middle age with life experience. She was a competent and intelligent woman who had done very well in her first practicum. She was matched with an experienced field instructor in a hospital setting. Within the first two months, the faculty-field liaison, on a regular visit, became aware that both the student and the field instructor were finding it difficult to work together. The student felt that the field instructor did not attend to her plans to deal directly with her client's concerns, but rather insisted that she focus her attention on reflection and analysis of personality factors. The student was becoming frustrated and angry, a reaction which the field instructor interpreted as resistance to acknowledging the power of emotions in social work interaction. Neither was wrong in that the fundamental problem was their respective inabilities to communicate their positions; namely, that the student put a prior value on action while the field instructor's first approach was to focus on affective understanding. The field instructor's approach, to his frustration, was to insist they look at what was happening in their supervisory relationship. This approach only heightened the student's sense that her own adequacy was being questioned. Once they had taken their oppositional stance, each supervisory encounter only served to entrench their positions, so that neither could leave the field or attempt to reach for a new perspective. The field instructor consulted with colleagues and realized that they respected the student and felt that she made sound contributions in staff meetings. They also told him that it might be that he and the student were not well matched in styles of working. The field instructor decided to back away from exploring the supervisory relationship with the student, realizing that this was probably counter-productive. The field instructor became more accepting of the student's approach, and the practicum succeeded. The student never felt altogether comfortable with the field instructor, who, in turn, was not satisfied that he had taught all he had wanted to teach about practice on his service.

Matching or Fit

Field instructors and students may be well matched, and a good fit results between the two. While many factors contribute to a good match, the following appear of particular importance: expectations of field instruction, learning and teaching approaches, ethnicity, race, and diversity.

Research studies have compared various components of field education from the perspective of students, field instructors, and faculty.
Hagen (1989) compared perceptions of forty-two role behaviours for
field instructors. Considerable agreement was found between students
and field instructors on a number of items. For example, there was
high agreement on the most important behaviours: that the field
instructor regularly confer with the student regarding process; point
out the student's strengths and weaknesses in skills; help the student
develop self-awareness; serve as a professional role model; provide
weekly supervisory time; help identify and clarify feelings about the
client; and help the student incorporate professional values. However,
significant disagreement was also found on the rating of 'very important' for some behaviours, with field instructors assigning higher
importance to the following: awareness of other employees' feelings
toward the student; improving the listening skills of the student; helping the student develop a work schedule; reviewing student assignments; and challenging student attitudes. Gray and colleagues (1989)
found similarity and differences between field instructors and students about expectations for supervisory conference topics. There was
agreement on the most important topics of discussing practice skills
and individual cases, and reviewing the student's ongoing performance. Disagreement was found on discussion of organization and
community issues, and supportive topics. Students expected more
time to be given to discussing personal strengths and weaknesses, and
successes and failures.

While these studies did not investigate similarities and differences in
pairs of students and their field instructors, they do highlight that, as
two groups, students and field instructors have some areas in which
there are different expectations of what the field instructor should do.
Therefore we recommend that early in the practicum each participant's
ideas about the field instructor's role, the student's role, and the topics
for the field instruction conference be clarified. We have proposed
throughout this chapter that relationships are the product of the negotiations and adaptations of the two parties. The recognition of different
expectations is not a problem. What is important is that assumptions of
similarity not be made, and differences become explicit and amenable to
change.

LEARNING AND TEACHING STYLES

Educational theorists and researchers have demonstrated that individuals learn differently and have preferred learning styles. Learning style refers to 'a student's consistent way of responding and using stimuli in the context of learning' (Claxton and Ralston 1978, 7). It describes the predominant and preferred approach which characterizes an individual's attitude and behaviour in a learning context. Hunt (1987) states that learning style describes a student in terms of those educational conditions under which he or she is most likely to learn and is a useful way to characterize interpersonal communication in education.

Many characteristics make up a person's learning style, such as a preference for structure or non-structure, method or intuition, the concrete or the abstract, the active or the reflective, individual or group learning, visual, auditory, or tactile modes, and self-directed or teacher-directed approaches. Kolb's (1984) experiential learning model is frequently referred to in social work and other professions to describe and assess learning style. He presented a four-stage cycle: (1) concrete experience is followed by (2) observation and reflection, which lead to (3) the formation of abstract concepts and generalizations, which leads to (4) hypotheses to be tested in future action, which in turn lead to new experience. A 'learning style inventory' is used to yield scores representing the individual's relative emphasis on each stage of the learning cycle. Two combination scores indicate an individual's emphasis on two axes: active and passive, concrete and abstract.

A number of studies have used Kolb's model to identify field instructors' and social work students' learning styles. Three studies found a preference for the accommodator learning style (Middleman and Rhodes 1985; Miller and Kennedy 1979; van Soest and Kruzich 1994), while one study found that undergraduate social work students favoured the accommodator learning style and graduate students and field instructors preferred the diverger learning style (Kruzich, Friesen, and Soest 1986). The accommodator style consists of a preference for concrete experience and active experimentation. The diverger learning style is a combination of concrete experience and reflective observation. The remaining styles are converger, a combination of abstract conceptualization and active experimentation; and assimilator, a combination of abstract conceptualization and reflective observation.

It is not assumed that a match of learning styles is most effective. Indeed, the educational theorist Thelen (1960) stated that 'the learner does not learn unless he does not know how to respond' (36). Educators have attempted to identify the optimal level of discomfort or comfort to produce an effective learning environment. While support is advocated so that learners will take risks, Rogers (1951) points out that our natural tendency as learners is to confine ourselves to those domains where we feel safe. Teachers have to help students engage in new and fearful domains, acknowledge discomfort, and set learning tasks to overcome the barriers of fear. Hunt (1970) stresses the importance of the relationship between the environment and development. He observes that if the environment is perfectly matched to the developmental level of the learners, they are likely to be arrested at that level. Optimal mismatch challenges a student's tendency to maintain familiar patterns, encourages movement to a new level, but does not overwhelm and immobilize the student. For example, when social work students are learning new skills, they are expected to demonstrate new behaviours through the use of tapes and one-way mirrors, or in co-working with the instructor. Students often report anxiety, discomfort, and stress connected with these new learning approaches in which the learning style is one of active experimentation. Instructors can support students to acknowledge and manage these threats to their comfort, while still expecting and encouraging them to use the new learning approaches. Furthermore, students may prefer to start with the learning activities with which they are most comfortable and avoid those they see as difficult. The academic process has reinforced intellectualization and teacher-initiated activities. For students who have not tested other styles such as active experimentation, new educational activities, such as role plays and direct observation of their practice, may result in increased anxiety about the exposure and risk in these approaches.

It is important that you, in your role as field instructor, identify your learning style as well as that of the student and that similarities and differences are acknowledged. Preferred learning styles can be identified through reflecting on past experiences and recalling what was effective and what was not effective. Discussion with an agency supervisor or peers may provide useful insights. Standard assessment inventories such as Kolb's *Learning Style Inventory* (1985) can help to assess your preferred characteristics within a particular educational model. Since teaching approaches are based on what we think we need in order to learn, your approach to your student may be based on your learning style. Therefore it is important to work with students to identify what they know about their own learning styles. Instructors and students can retrieve and reflect on past learning, observe and discuss what is and is not working in the present, and use assessment inventories.

A knowledge of learning styles can help you and your student construct the best possible educational environment. Instructors can examine the extent to which the learning environment provides educational opportunities that are responsive to the student's preferred learning style. This includes the methods and approaches used in field instruction, as well as opportunities in the setting for activities such as observation, discussion and conferencing, active participation, and preparation through the use of role plays. For example, students assigned to community-based organizations often comment that most of their learning is connected to concrete experience, and they miss the opportunity to engage in activities that focus on abstract conceptualization and reflective observation. Knowing the learning-style preferences of these students, instructors in such settings can create ways for students to connect to the concepts driving the community-action initiatives in which students participate.

Knowing what is favoured and what is not favoured in learning directs attention to approaches that may need to be developed to make optimal use of the available learning opportunities. Students can be encouraged to diversify their learning-style preferences and to participate in educational activities that require development of new learning approaches. For example, students who prefer reflective observation will find one-way-mirror viewing and discussing the work of experienced practitioners beneficial. However, they may become overwhelmed when expected to interview a family with the team behind the mirror. Students who prefer active experimentation may find watching others to be too slow and too passive, but they enjoy the opportunity to work directly with the family and receive the team's feedback. In settings that use these techniques in practice and teaching, students will be expected to make use of all these educational approaches. Another example of diversifying one's learning style is the student who learns best from a thorough reading and understanding of the literature before taking any action. This student can be asked to role play first and then identify learnings from the experience.

Similarities and differences in learning-style preferences appear to influence the perceptions that students and their field instructors have of each other. Using Kolb's model, van Soest and Kruzich (1994) found that the greater the difference between the student and the instructor on the concrete experience scale, the more negatively they rated the quality of their relationship and the skills of the other. They speculate that the negative perception might be the result of the mismatch and the use of learning activities associated with the concrete experience style. In their study, difference in style did not always result in negative perceptions. They found that the greater the difference on abstract conceptualization, the higher the student rated the field instructor's practice skills.

STRUCTURE AND DIRECTION

Since the 1970s, social work educators have been influenced by andragogical approaches that promote self-directed, experiential, problem-solving approaches for the education of adult learners. Knowles (1972; 1980) emphasizes a learning climate that is informal, mutually respectful, and collaborative. Through a mutual process, the student and the instructor diagnose learning needs, formulate learning objectives, and plan, conduct, and evaluate the learning. The educational process is determined by the learner's readiness and results from active involvement in experiential activities. The role of the teacher is that of facilitator of learning. Students are expected to be self-directing, to take initiative and responsibility for their own learning. Pedagogy, by contrast, is an authority-oriented, formal, and teacher-directed approach. Davenport and Davenport (1988) review the empirical base for andragogy and conclude that a preference for andragogical over pedagogical approaches is not necessarily related to age. Given the early phase of research about this concept, they caution against generalizations to all adult learners. They do note that female respondents in a number of studies tended to score higher on the andragogical end of a pedagogical-andragogical continuum. They recommend, as does the literature on learning styles, that field instructors understand these concepts and the learning activities associated with each, identify their preferred orientation and that of the student, and use that knowledge to inform the approaches used in field education. As with learning styles, they propose the flexible use of techniques not associated with the preferred orientation as these can broaden the available learning opportunities and encourage growth for the student. They note that this also prepares students for the 'real world' of agency practice, where ideal matching may be limited.

Some students approach the practicum with the hope that the field instructor will dispel all their confusion about social work practice and will teach them how to be a social worker. Such students, though adult, may want to assume a passive role in relation to an active teacher who will tell them directly how the job is to be done. Conversely, some students will approach the practicum feeling apprehensive about losing a sense of adult autonomy and will want a field instructor who will encourage independence.

Field instructors may place themselves on a continuum with respect to the degree of structure and the amount of direction they give to students. At one end of the continuum are those instructors who feel comfortable with a directive stance and tell the student what to do step-by-step. They check frequently on the student's execution of these directions. This style may be necessary in settings where there is a legal mandate; for example, in child protection or probation. At the next point on the continuum are field instructors who suggest mutual goal setting through ongoing negotiation with the student until they arrive at a consensus. The field instructor plays an active role but expects equal involvement and responsibility from the student. Finally, at the other end of the continuum are those instructors who may expect the student to articulate goals and initiate and plan the learning experience, using the field instructor as a consultant when needed.

Both match and mismatches of directive or non-directive field instructors with dependent or independent students will occur. It is important, therefore, that these approaches be introduced and discussed early in the practicum so that a clear understanding of expectations and preferences can be attained. Even a mismatched pair, once identified, can attempt to reach a workable resolution. Self-awareness can begin at this point. For example, a field instructor who wants more feedback than an independent student may provide, can remind the student: 'I feel more comfortable when I am in touch with all of our cases.' Or, in response to the student who wants to check out with the instructor planned interventions before taking any action: 'I know you can make that decision on your own once you are clear about options.'

Normally, as the practicum progresses and the student's learning is progressing at a satisfactory pace, the structure will relax so that the student is functioning with more autonomy than at the beginning of the practicum. This increasing autonomy can become an articulated goal which is set at the beginning of the practicum. The student might measure one aspect of growing competence through the increase in autonomous practice over a period of time.

Issues of Ethnicity, Race, and Diversity

Cultural diversity may be the most distinguishing feature of the last two decades of this century. Political and social upheaval in many parts of the world have brought to North American shores people from many cultures with expectations, beliefs, and values that are worlds apart. This continent was built on an ingathering of people from around the world, but at a slower pace in the earlier decades. During these early years, social workers believed in a myth of steady acculturation toward the values of a predominantly white and Christian culture for both themselves and their clients. We can no longer take refuge in this myth; a heightened awareness of differences in race, ethnicity, and values and beliefs has ruptured complacency. Awareness of decades of prejudice and discrimination toward native peoples, Afro-Americans, and Afro-Canadians has challenged old patterns of denial and indifference. Stereotypes and silence about race, gender roles, and ethnicity are no longer tolerated. Prefix Americans and Canadians abound in our agencies, among our clients and our colleagues, and, of course, among our students.

We need to search for an honest approach to diversity in the field instructor–student dyad, because to avoid the issues will diminish the mutuality and the quality of learning that can take place. Denial of difference impedes discovery of barriers to an effective learning and teaching relationship and will not enrich students' approaches to client diversity in ways that might make a personal and political difference.

In a study reported in 1994, new field instructors from a broad range of practice fields were asked to consider the impact on the educational experience of 'cultural, ethnic, gender, class, and age characteristics, and the implications of these similarities and/or differences for the teacher/ learner relationship' (Marshack, Hendricks, and Gladstein 1994, 78). The findings in this study reaffirmed the findings of an earlier study, which found that few field instructors identified issues of diversity in educational assessments of students (Gladstein and Mailick 1986). The recent study found that field instructors may be cognitively aware of diversity factors but rarely integrated this awareness into field teaching. In other words, valuable teaching opportunities are not developed, possibly because of the desire to avoid what can be perceived as sensitive and divisive areas.

Though diversity has many dimensions – for example, it can refer to culture, ethnicity, gender, sexual orientation, social class, age, physical disability, or religion – overriding all of these dimensions is the factor of power and the assumptions about power implicit in the thinking of both majority and minority groups. We start with the field instructor–student hierarchy and the obvious power vested in the field instructor by the school. We have already discussed this matter earlier. This is a given and a familiar imbalance, which most field instructors and students can more readily acknowledge and negotiate during the course of the practicum. Other perceptions of power imbalance are more subtle and often go unacknowledged in language, but not in attitudes and behaviour. It may be that a misperception of the social work value that stresses the inherent worth of each individual, expressed as global acceptance, obscures the need to recognize issues of diversity and their effect on perceptions of power. For some persons, the belief still persists that to acknowledge difference is akin to racism or an indication of inherent bigotry. To ignore difference is equated with neutrality and blind acceptance of all. Such an attitude is in reality a barrier to establishing a working relationship because it prevents disclosure and important information-sharing about relevant life experiences of both field instructor and student. How and when these differences are acknowledged, expressed, or acted out will comprise the unique content of the relationship. It is the field instructor who must take the primary responsibility for encouraging open discussion because the power of that role requires that field instructors take the initiative. They can do this by being particularly sensitive to what is left unsaid, to what is conveyed by attitudes or body language or behaviour. It is important to respond to these cues in a tentative, non-threatening manner that conveys genuineness, curiosity, and openness to mutual disclosure. Unexamined assumptions and stereotypes about cultural differences interfere with open-mindedness. Obvious visible differences, such as race, age, gender, or disability, are easier to acknowledge because one cannot pretend they do not exist. Differences such as ethnicity, sexual orientation, social class, or religion are not so obvious and may or may not be barriers to establishing a good teaching and learning relationship. Confronting power issues in cross-racial and cross-cultural dyads may have historical and personal meaning for students (Marshack et al. 1994). As judged on the basis of their experiences with systemic and interpersonal racism, the open discussion of issues may involve a level of exposure and risk that they have learned is best to avoid.

The field instructor has to 'play it by ear,' mindful of unwanted and unnecessary intrusion into what should properly remain private space. This may occur because the issue is not germane to the work of the practicum or because the student responds to a tentative opening from the field instructor with an indication that a boundary must be respected. The test to be applied is to what extent does the particular issue relate to the work of the practicum by being connected to the social reality and needs of the clients served or to the quality of the learning and teaching relationship being negatively affected and impaired.

It has been observed that practice is an interface between the meanings or theories of the worker and clients' stories, narratives, and cultural myths (Saleebey 1994). Human beings can create their worlds or realities by creating meanings and using symbols to make sense of the world. This world-view is built on cultural patterning, which is learned early and often expressed in story and narrative. No culture has a monopoly on truth, and even a relative truth of a specific culture can change and shift with time and with exposure to other cultures. In addition, when we take into account the consequences of majority or minority membership, and the uniqueness of individual and family psychosocial processes, it is clear that each narrative or life story is both collective and specific to the individual. Each person's narrative reflects the components of the ITP Loop Model: contextual, organizational, psychosocial, and interactive. The field instructor–student relationship may be enriched through some relevant sharing of personal narrative. It may be that through the use of narrative, field instructor, student, and clients can be empowered to restructure or reshape a constricting narrative by confronting diversity and reaching for new levels of understanding of context, interpersonal function, and organizational response.

Organizational Context

At the beginning of this chapter, we asked you to retrieve your own experience as a student in the practicum and reflect on its positive and negative factors. We briefly discussed the effect of contextual issues arising from the agency and the school. In concluding the discussion in this chapter on the student–field instructor relationship, we are returning to the theme of context and will focus on aspects of the organization and their impact on the relationship, your role as field instructor, and ultimately the student's learning.

We use the metaphor of a small row-boat bouncing on a turbulent sea to capture the dynamic between the instructional relationship and the organization in the current climate of instability and change. The field instructor and student can successfully address the many issues presented in this chapter with respect to the development and growth of a highly productive and effective working alliance. However, organizational issues may be beyond their control and may have a powerful effect which can undermine the work they have been doing. Conversely, organizational factors can be positive, or at least provide an opportunity for new or enriched learning.

Since practicum learning occurs through delivering a social work service, students do in fact contribute a resource to the setting. When an agency finds itself under-resourced, the balance may shift between the resources it contributes to student education and the resources students provide to the setting. Students may find themselves asked to do a range of secretarial and clerical tasks not typically associated with the role of social work student. A student may comply with a request for fear of alienating staff colleagues but may still feel exploited by the setting. In some instances, students will refuse to do the task and find themselves in a conflict with team members. For example, when a student in a residential treatment centre for children was asked by a child-care supervisor to drive a child to a dentist appointment, the student objected to being used as a 'chauffeur.' Situations such as this one are not clear-cut. Although the child was not a client of the student, the student could have learned a great deal about the behaviour of children with emotional difficulties through accompanying the child outside of the residence, but only if observation was required of the student and then reviewed in the instructional session, with some information supplied about the child and his family situation. Spontaneous requests can be fine learning experiences if the field instructor can shape them as such. In this instance, the request, without involvement of the student's field instructor, felt exploitative to the student.

When the agency's management and the field instructor disagree on appropriate assignments for students, field instructors face an uncomfortable situation. Since they are responsible for the students in the agency, they need to advocate on their behalf. In some situations there is a cost to disagreeing with the authority in the agency. Ideally, a clear understanding of the role and expectations of students in the agency is agreed upon before students arrive. However, even with thorough planning, in the current climate of rapidly changing organizations previously arrived at agreements may give way to pressures of the moment. Again, the impact of resource cutbacks may see the erosion of a careful learning plan in which education is primary. Field instructors who find themselves caught in such dilemmas can consult with their faculty-field liaison for assistance. It may be that renegotiation of the agreement between the school and the setting is in order.

Students' roles and responsibilities in informal settings – for example, residential treatment centres, community centres, and grass-roots organizations – may be less structured than in large organizations such as hospitals, school boards, and child protection agencies. Division of labour and staff roles may be less formal and there may be a prevailing ethos that emphasizes collaboration and everyone 'pitching in to do what is necessary.' This may include, for example, a range of clerical and reception tasks, arranging furniture, and preparing food for special meetings. Field instructors need to work with both staff and students to, on the one hand, help students learn in this informal atmosphere and, on the other hand, ensure that students are not being used to perform tasks not appropriate to their role.

Previously, schools of social work would strive to provide practicum experiences for students in agencies that were stable. If an agency was undergoing a major reorganization, the school and the setting might decide to suspend student practica for a brief period of time. This is no longer a reasonable approach. Organizational change has become the norm, and students need to learn about organizations, their structures, dynamics, and change processes. Students need to learn how to survive and thrive in agencies undergoing change as this is likely to be the employment environment they will enter. Field instructors can use the ITP Loop Model with students to retrieve experiences in daily interaction in staff and team meetings, in informal conversations with staff, in observations at board meetings, and in implementing program and policy changes. Reflection can be used to examine their reactions and feelings about these issues as well as the macro issues facing organizations. Organizational theory provides concepts to link these phenomena to a knowledge base. Effective strategies to manage stress and avoid worker burn-out provide useful knowledge to prepare students to learn in changing agencies and to function in the real world of social service and health organizations.

5

Guiding the Learning Process

Using the ITP Loop Model

With the assignment of clients and projects, the core of teaching and learning in the practicum gets under way. The ITP Loop Model provides a comprehensive process for retrieving practice data, examining the data for subjective meanings, linking it to a conceptual base associated with the profession of social work, and finally converting this knowledge and understanding into concrete intervention planning. The ecological and multi-factorial perspective should serve to focus the attention of the student and the field instructor and guide discussion, analysis, and selection of intervention priorities. In chapter 1 the phases and content focus of the ITP Loop Model for field instruction were introduced. This chapter will examine how a variety of teaching and learning methods can be used in conjunction with the loop model.

The first stage of the ITP Loop Model, retrieval, requires the practitioner, be it student or social worker, to access and present practice data. Many methods are available: direct observation, audio- and videotape, written records, and verbal reports, each with strengths and weaknesses. Most methods capture events and interactions in a single interview, committee meeting, or professional interchange and provide data for an in-depth focus on interactive processes. The content framework of the ITP Loop Model directs attention to data at multiple levels – psycho-social, interactive, contextual, and organizational – to gain as full an understanding as possible of the situation.

Particular retrieval methods lend themselves more or less readily to particular teaching approaches. For example, live supervision tends to promote feedback about specific practice skills and interventions, while written records tend to promote discussion and tentative conceptualization. If field instructors adopt the comprehensive perspective provided by the ITP Loop Model, they may be able to extend a specific method to consider other phases in the loop. For example, while reviewing data retrieved on videotape lends itself to feedback and role play of intervention skills, the field instructor or student can just as easily use a segment of tape to reflect on the student's subjective experience of the recorded events or to formulate hypotheses linked to a particular conceptual base. Similarly, this data can provide a stimulus to a focused discussion that examines the data from a structural or organizational perspective.

Since focusing only on segments of interactions may miss the totality of the session, the overall gestalt of the case or project, sometimes it is important to stand back from the work and monitor and plan progress toward client or project goals. The linkage phase especially benefits from sifting through data which has emerged over time so that the student and field instructor can consider a variety of theoretical perspectives or frames to determine which will be most helpful. As with a camera lens, a sharp focus on the details of practice provides one picture which may be different from the view seen when using a wide-angle lens. Multiple perspectives enhance understanding and learning.

The second phase of the ITP Loop Model, reflection, can be used with all retrieval methods to help the student gain access to personal subjective reactions to practice phenomena. The following guidelines are suggested:

1. Start with students' life experience associations when these associations occur spontaneously, and help students to compare and contrast their personal experience with that of the situation, using psycho-social, interactive, contextual, and organizational perspectives.
2. Encourage students to identify their feelings, thoughts, and assumptions regarding the practice data.
3. Encourage students to consider their behaviour as a factor that affects the practice situation.
4. Give feedback regarding students' behaviour as it affects the practice situation. Feedback should be empathetic, timely, clear and direct, systematic, balanced, reciprocal, and based on learning objectives.

The third phase of the ITP Loop Model, linkage, is used to identify and label knowledge that will help explain the practice data and the subjective reactions that have been evoked; ultimately this knowledge will be used in planning professional responses. The following guidelines are suggested:

1. Start with students' cognitive associations and understanding of the practice situation. As in reflection, psycho-social, interactive, contextual, and organizational factors are considered.
2. Give your own cognitive associations. You can identify the theoretical concepts you are using to explain, examine, and analyse practice phenomena.
3. Encourage students to look for the fit or lack of fit between the theory and the specific practice situation.

The fourth phase of the ITP Loop Model, professional response, is used to select a plan that will inform the next encounter with the client or situation. The following guidelines are suggested:

1. Field instructors and students use the insights uncovered in reflection to plan the next professional response. Students are encouraged to examine possible responses at psycho-social, interactive, contextual, and organizational levels.
2. Field instructors and students use the relevant theories discussed in linkage to form the next professional response, by setting priorities demanded by a particular situation and selecting appropriate responses.
3. Field instructors and students contrast approaches to anticipate the possible effect of a specific intervention. Field instructors and students can examine possible responses at psycho-social, interactive, contextual, and organizational levels, and consider the relative effects of actions directed at one, several, or all levels as appropriate to the situation.
4. Field instructors prepare students, as needed, to carry out the plan through such methods as observation, role playing, co-working, live supervision, and assigning reading materials.

Examples of applying the ITP Loop Model in field instruction can be found in chapter 1.

Field teaching based on any assignment can begin by guiding students to identify and acknowledge what they know at the outset that can help them understand a situation and then to discover what they need to learn in addition. This is a variation of partializing, useful to give clients a sense of manageability and also useful to give students a sense of how to approach complexity. It is especially reassuring to tap into already acquired knowledge. For example, applying the ITP Loop Model, a young student anxious about meeting a young nineteen-year-old woman in hospital with diabetes, a serious illness which will become chronic, was encouraged to think about her own knowledge of the life goals of young adulthood, and to use her personal experience and her knowledge of developmental theory and the impact of illness, to inform her initial approach to her client. A plan for obtaining additional knowledge and skills needed for effective work can then be developed. Additional knowledge and skills might include greater understanding of the illness, its incidence, aetiology, symptoms, treatment, and prognosis, knowledge of appropriate community resources, as well as interviewing techniques and skills of accurate interpretation. A plan to acquire this knowledge and skill might include reading, anticipation and skill development through role playing, observation, and searching for and contacting relevant resources.

Developing a Strategy for Teaching

It is useful for field instructors to think about developing a teaching strategy or plan for teaching in the field. First, which modes of presentation will be used by students to present their practice; and second, which teaching approaches will be used to promote learning? Modes of presentation refer to both direct and indirect methods to access the student's actual practice with clients, committees, and projects. Direct access is achieved by observing a student's practice, listening to audiotapes, or watching videotapes; indirect access, through verbal and written reports. Teaching approaches refer to discussion, modelling, live supervision, and role play.

The choice of method depends on many factors: the agency context, educational objectives, the student's needs and the field instructor's abilities as expressed in the learning contract, as well as the immediate needs of the clients or community. Different approaches may achieve the same educational outcome, and one approach may achieve a number of objectives. Many writers suggest that multiple methods be viewed as a way to enhance learning, rather than simply as a competing set of options, with the choice among them depending primarily on the field instructor's teaching style and orientation and the student's preferred learning style (Goldberg 1985; Hawthorne 1987). We suggest experimenting with a variety of methods in the spirit of finding the most effective approaches for the student and the field instructor in the particular setting. Since each method has strengths and limitations, combining several approaches may be the best course of action.

Agency Context

The agency context and the type of practice will affect the modes used for data presentation as well as teaching methods. Many approaches depend on the availability of technological resources such as built-in one-way mirrors, microphones, and listening devices. Where the setting does not have these facilities or video equipment, students may have to supply their own audiotape recorders if they and their field instructors wish to use this medium. Practice in the community, with people on the streets, and in hospitals, where patients cannot leave their beds, does not easily lend itself to recordings. In some settings, accountability expectations and procedures or research protocols will determine what methods must be used to gather and present client data.

Learning and Teaching Styles

Students' learning-style preferences and field instructors' teaching styles influence the techniques chosen for data presentation and teaching. In chapter 4 we discussed learning and teaching styles and noted the work of Kolb (1984). To briefly review, Kolb developed an experiential learning model consisting of a four-stage cycle: concrete experience, observation and reflection, abstract conceptualization, and active experimentation. By using these concepts, learning-style preferences can be identified which represent an individual's emphasis at each stage of the learning cycle. A group of field educators in Australia linked each learning style with preferred educational methods (AASWWE 1991).

Students whose preferred learning style is concrete experience prefer to begin with personal practice experiences. Recommended educational methods for these learners include immediate activity with cases or projects, receiving feedback in the context of a collegial relationship, sharing feelings, and self-direction. Students whose preferred learning style is reflective observation prefer learning environments which provide the opportunity to think about the data and emphasize understanding concepts. Educational methods recommended for these learners include observation, expert interpretations, discussions guided by the field instructor, and performance judged by external criteria. Students whose preferred learning style is abstract conceptualization prefer learning environments which emphasize logical thinking. Educational methods such as case studies, thinking alone, and reading and discussion of theory are recommended, though these methods should derive their questions from a practice situation. They should be based on the immediate situation, not a hypothetical one. Students whose preferred learning style is active experimentation prefer learning environments which emphasize the application of knowledge and skills and in which they can try out new ideas. Educational methods recommended are small group discussions, projects, peer feedback, and modelling by the field instructor. If field instructors and students have not yet identified their respective learning styles, they may wish to do so now and give some thought to initially selecting teaching techniques that support preferred learning approaches. Methods which require new approaches to learning can supplement the dominant style. For example, a student learning direct practice who prefers concrete experience may be comfortable producing audiotapes and receiving his instructor's feedback. To extend his learning style, this activity might be supplemented with written process recordings, with an emphasis on conceptualizing the themes in the interview and linking themes to a comprehensive assessment. A student learning administrative practice who prefers abstract conceptualization might be working alone to develop a new procedure for the agency's information system. The field instructor might supplement this activity by assigning the student to work with a group of social workers who will ultimately be expected to use the new procedure. The student might be asked to tape-record the meetings with the social workers for retrospective analysis of how she dealt with their expressed and veiled concerns.

When choosing teaching methods, field instructors' own preferred learning and teaching styles will play a part, but field instructors should not assume that their preferred learning style and educational methods are universally helpful to students. As stated earlier, it is important to differentiate between what is unique to the particular student and what are universal principles in teaching. For example, a field instructor who did not find process records helpful may not value this tool. It may be useful, however, to students who learn from written reflection and from the conceptualization gained as a by-product of this method.

In some instances, the fit between the student's preferred learning style and the field instructor's preferred teaching style may be less than ideal. For example, a student who benefits from observation of practice followed by linkage to theory may pose a challenge for a field instructor who prefers to give direct feedback during an interview and is uncomfortable with discussion of concepts not closely related to the immediate needs of the practice situation. Obviously field instructors, committed to providing the most optimal learning environment for their students, will search for ways to meet their students' educational needs. Flexibility and willingness to use new approaches to supplement their preferred teaching style are recommended. Staff with teaching approaches more congruent with the student's may also be enlisted. As well, use should be made of a range of educational activities in the setting. In this way, the student will be involved in multiple educational activities and exposed to many teaching methods which stimulate the use of a range of learning styles.

Educational Objectives

Social work students need to learn, through reflection, to critically appraise how aspects of their personal self are present in their professional roles; through linkage, how to conceptualize their practice; and through selecting and implementing a professional response, the skills of a variety of social work methods. Each retrieval method provides a different type of data, so that differential selection of a retrieval method will promote a specific type of learning. For example, videotaping a cross-cultural family interview can promote a discussion about the student's thoughts and feelings, which may stimulate critical self-reflection; writing a draft of a program proposal for a community-based health promotion program can promote conceptualization and linkage to concepts drawn from community development and empowerment theory; and an audiotape of a group meeting provides data for an evaluation and discussion of group leadership skills.

Specific educational objectives for the student can also help determine over time the most desirable mode of presentation and best teaching method. Insofar as possible, teaching should be sequential and move to greater degrees of complexity. As a result, data retrieval and teaching methods may vary even within the same assignment. In the contracting phase, the student and field instructor will have assessed the student's educational needs and identified areas for learning. The field instructor can use these objectives to decide which one should be given priority and focus at a particular point in time. For example, a beginning student in direct practice is likely to need to learn interviewing skills, while at a later stage the priority may be to complete a family assessment for a multi-disciplinary team. A beginning student in community practice may need to learn how to take minutes in a committee meeting, and at a later stage how to lead a community meeting confronting a contentious local issue. Given a specific educational objective, the field instructor determines the kinds of data that will be most useful to track the student's practice and ongoing progress in learning. To continue with the previous examples, if developing interviewing skills is the learning objective, the field instructor might ask the student to audiotape and analyse an interview; if conducting a family assessment is the learning objective, the field instructor might ask the student to videotape a family interview and submit a draft of a family assessment; if understanding group process is the learning objective, the field instructor might ask the student to provide a process record of a community meeting; and if skill in leading a community meeting is the learning objective, the field instructor and the student might co-plan and co-lead a community meeting, and follow up the meeting with a debriefing session. Finally, the field instructor needs to determine which teaching methods will be most helpful. For example, to teach interviewing skills the field instructor might have the student observe experienced workers and role play with the field instructor; to complete a family assessment, the field instructor might use live supervision to coach the student, so that important missing information about the family is elicited; to help the student learn minute taking, the field instructor might review the process record with the student, discuss the central issues, and provide a guide for turning the record into draft minutes; and to learn to deal with contentious issues in the community, the field instructor might co-lead meetings with the student.

These examples also illustrate how learning experiences can be selected to provide opportunities for students to master specific skills and how successive assignments can build on previous ones. Using the community practice example, the student learned how to work with a small committee of local residents before being expected to conduct a large meeting. Through written reports and discussions in field instruction, themes were identified in the student's practice. The student and field instructor agreed that the student had trouble maintaining group focus when there was conflict between committee members. The student was planning to chair a community meeting at which it was expected there would be considerable disagreement about plans to locate a residence for people on parole in the neighbourhood. The field instructor used preparatory discussion and role playing as an additional method to guide the student's learning. As well, the field instructor accompanied the student to the community meeting with the mutual expectation of co-leading as necessary.

These examples show how the contract can be used to make field instruction systematic, organized, purposeful, and educational. Hawthorne (1987) contrasts this approach with reactive teaching, in which the focus in field instruction is on the student's questions about how to handle the assignment. While field instructors will certainly be concerned with case management, a primary focus on specific instructions may promote random and fragmented learning more characteristic of an apprenticeship approach. An educational approach should help students learn those generic principles which are transferable to similar situations, so that a sense of professional competence begins to develop. Students need to learn to recognize situational similarities and differences.

Service Needs

Finally, teaching approaches will always be secondary to the immediate needs of the client or community. While we have recommended a planned approach to field instruction, emergencies, crises, and a multitude of unpredictable issues arise in any human service activity. Students find themselves in situations in which an immediate response is necessary or in which they must seek 'on the spot' advice from the field instructor or other staff. Data is exchanged verbally and direction sought. However, learning from crises can be maximized by using the ITP Loop Model retrospectively. The actions taken in the crisis can be retrieved, reflected upon, and linked to the knowledge base used, as well as to other perspectives, to fully illuminate the situation; finally, alternative professional responses can be examined.

Feedback

In chapter 4, on the instructional relationship, empirical studies of student satisfaction in the practicum were reviewed, and the student–field instructor relationship was highlighted as the critical factor. The studies identified the important components of the relationship: availability, support, structure, promoting student autonomy, feedback, and linking theory and practice. Feedback is one of the major features of the middle phase of the practicum and of the actual process of teaching and learning. In numerous studies, students reported that they valued instructors who observed their practice and gave them systematic and critical comments about the skills they were acquiring (Baker and Smith 1987; Barth and Gambrill 1984; Fortune and Abramson 1993; Freeman 1985; Urbanowski and Dwyer 1988).

'Feedback' is a term borrowed from rocket engineering by Kurt Lewin, a founder of laboratory education. It has been defined as a 'verbal or non-verbal process through which an individual lets others know his perceptions and feelings about their behaviour' (Hanson 1975, 147). It is a critical aspect of field instruction which must be utilized in the service of mutual understanding and is the essential fuel of the ITP Loop Model. Feedback, as with the application of any skill, is an art. It can either facilitate learning or retard change (Freeman 1985). Feedback contains elements of empathy and support, but it must provide more than these because the aim of field instruction is to guide change in the student's knowledge, attitude, or behaviour in a desired direction. Timing is crucial in giving feedback; it has been found that feedback is most effective when it is given immediately after the event (Freeman 1985).

In her paper on feedback, Freeman (1985) outlines a four-step plan to ensure optimum learning through feedback. The steps are: (1) clear specification of performance criteria; (2) reliable observation of the student's practice; (3) provision of effective feedback; (4) monitoring the student's use of feedback. The first step is part of developing the learning contract and includes stating learning objectives in behavioural terms and indicating in advance the criteria that will be used to assess progress. Next the student and field instructor will find ways for the instructor to observe the student's practice so that feedback is based on data which is accessible to both of them. Thirdly, effective feedback has the following attributes: it is timely, given regularly, is systematic, and given in a concise, direct manner. It is important to check with the student that the feedback is understood. Balanced feedback contains both positive and negative comments, though not necessarily in equal portions. The fourth step is following up on the student's use of feedback in a regular way, so that tracking the student's progress is done continuously and not left solely to a final evaluation.

In general, presenting feedback in this way makes for greater acceptability. There is no substitute, however, for judgment regarding which students are more sensitive to negative criticism. Students frequently report that they do not know what they are doing right because they are never told by their field instructors or they receive global praise such as 'That was a very good interview.' In the absence of specific positive feedback, negative feedback can be experienced by some students as a total attack on their competence to function. These students, in particular, need to be told what they can do well, no matter how slight that accomplishment might be. Balanced feedback is a key concept.

Feedback is more acceptable when the student perceives the field instructor to be qualified and to possess knowledge of the student's concerns derived from direct observation or from information shared by the student. The way the field instructor expresses this concern and expertise is critical. If the student feels that the field instructor comprehends the student's frame of reference, that is, the way the student might view the world, then the chances are good that the student can accept whatever pain the feedback might provoke and work toward change. Additionally, feedback must be reciprocal, so that the student feels able to indicate when a message is not understood or is unacceptable. An authoritarian tone taken by the field instructor is not likely to encourage reciprocal feedback and can produce angry silence, begrudging compliance, or open resistance.

The field instructor is cautioned to check on whether the student is receiving any conflictual feedback from others; for example, from someone in another discipline, such as a psychiatrist or psychologist in the setting, from the faculty-field liaison, or from a classroom teacher at the school. Unless the student can discuss these differing messages openly, the student will be confused and in danger of being drawn into a power struggle. Finally, modelling clear and open feedback for the student will encourage the transfer of this technique to work with clients.

Feedback takes place in the context of the relationship between student and field instructor. The interpersonal dynamics and issues discussed in chapter 4 can either support the acceptance of feedback and the promotion of learning or block them. It is in the daily instances of give and take in this important middle phase that the field instructor's and student's commitment and ability to maintain a productive partnership are truly tested.

Methods of Guiding the Learning Process

About Methods Involving Direct Access to Practice Data

Technological advances in audio- and videotape and one-way mirrors have revolutionized teaching and supervision in the human service professions. No longer do classroom and field instructors and students have to rely on descriptions of practice. They can now actually see and examine the details of practice.

If you are a field instructor in a community practice setting or if you are teaching administration, planning, or policy, resist the temptation to skip over this section. While many of the techniques to be discussed have been derived from direct practice, with imagination they can be adapted to augment field instruction for students in a wide variety of settings. Interpersonal exchanges are a core component of professional social work activity, and responsibility for their development must be accepted by both students and field instructors. This means that regardless of setting, students must learn how to engage with others, how to focus, how to listen, and how to resolve conflict so that the desired outcome can be achieved, whether that be a therapeutic exchange, facilitating the development of a community program, or reaching consensus around a policy position. Therefore, the succeeding section will present a summary of the literature on techniques for monitoring and teaching using direct access to practice data. This literature is overly representative of direct practice. The need for reports on the direct access of work from a broader range of settings is apparent, for it is just as important to know what the student is actually doing and saying in community or policy and planning settings.

Numerous studies have demonstrated that students acquire interviewing skills through learning activities that include demonstration, role play, focused use of audio- and videotape, feedback, and reinforcement (Collins and Bogo 1986; Magill and Werk 1985; Mayadas and Duehn 1977; Schinke, Blythe, Gilchrist and Smith 1980; Sowers-Hoag and Thyer 1985; Star 1979). Barth and Gambrill (1984) conducted a study to identify the amount and type of interview training students receive in field learning. They studied chances to observe, to be observed, and to gain feedback as key indicators of training quality. They found that supervisors rarely served as a model of interviewing, supervisors rarely provided feedback on students' performance during actual interviews with clients, and students' interviews with clients were rarely recorded on audiotape or videotape. They concluded: 'Trial and error is a slow, frustrating and ineffective instructor. Boosts to interviewing effectiveness are less likely to result from repeated but solitary practice, or even from supervisors' critical responses to after-the-fact reports of interviews, than from specific feedback based on observation of students' performances' (Barth and Gambrill 1984, 9). More recently, Rogers and McDonald (1995) investigated preferred teaching methods of field instructors in one school of social work and found that the more direct teaching methods, such as observation of students, reviewing students' audio- and videotapes, or co-working, were used least frequently and less consistently than written material or verbal reports.

Several reasons are presented by these researchers to explain the reluctance of field instructors to promote observation, modelling opportunities, and feedback, among which was the fact that prominence of such methods was not part of the experience of most field instructors during their own social work education. They also note other factors that may be significant, such as time constraints and lack of training materials. Time can be utilized in different ways, and modelling and role play take no more time than other methods of field instruction that rely more heavily on after-the-fact reports. Field instructors or other staff can arrange direct observation or the reviewing of tapes of interviews by obtaining the informed consent of clients and by giving assurances about the purpose and use of such observation and taping.

Traditional field instruction consists of discussion of past events and feelings. Rhim (1976) notes that conscious and unconscious selection, sifting, and perception will affect what is presented to the field instructor. Much of the student's non-verbal behaviour will not be accessible as it may be beyond the student's awareness. The field instructor is then faced with the task of 'interpreting, commenting upon, and attempting to elicit the underlying meaning based on his assumptions as to what he thinks might have occurred' (Rhim 1976, 644). As actual behaviours of the student and client system are not accessible there may be a tendency to focus on intentions and to attribute meanings not intended.

Use of an ecological framework and systems theory directs attention to the complexity of multiple transactions at various levels of communication. This focus may overwhelm students in their attempt to keep up with the volume of information evident in any practice situation. Audio and video technology may be a more appropriate medium than print to record data based on systemic concepts. Commenting on supervisory developments in the related field of family therapy, McCollum and Wetchler (1995) state that with direct access to the raw material of therapy '... no longer was supervision a largely inferential process wherein the supervisor tried to ferret out what "really happened" through the scrim of the therapist's later reconstruction of it' (155).

Field instruction based on direct access to an interview or meeting, or on access to an audio or video record, is more objective and concrete than instruction based on recall. Viewing or hearing the student's actual practice interventions enables an accurate and realistic assessment of learning needs and assists in contracting educational goals and evaluation of goal achievement. In their study of teaching methods used by field instructors, Rogers and McDonald (1995) found that the more field instructors obtained direct access to students' actual performance through reviewing taped interviews or through direct observations, the less likely they were to answer affirmatively the researchers' question whether the students were ready for a professional role. In training new field instructors, we have often encountered the situation of field instructors who, based on students' verbal reports, believed that the students were performing quite well. When they finally had access to practice on an audiotape of an actual interview or observed the student in a community committee meeting or giving a presentation, these field instructors were surprised and dismayed at the lack of skill that was demonstrated. This is probably a manifestation of inexperience and a reflection of the fact that intellectual understanding is easier to acquire than the complex art of application.

Methods which involve access to actual practice data expose students' work and their immediate emotional reactions. As a result, observation and videotaping can be anxiety-provoking. This anxiety can be diluted by viewing the work of other students, workers, and the field instructor, replete with the mistakes inherent in any practice endeavour. Seeing experienced practitioners' work, with the normal confusions, repetitions, and even tedium, tends to de-mythologize practice as a logical sequence of activities following a theory and plan. Observation of others' work helps students gain a realistic picture of practice, and may help them become comfortable with mistakes and open to the risk of exposure in the service of learning.

MODELLING AND OBSERVATION

Modelling and observation require that the student have the opportunity to observe the field instructor or other staff as they work. Considerable research has shown that a major source of social learning occurs through observing the behaviour of others (Bandura 1969). Mayadas and Duehn (1977) found that such vicarious learning, framed in an educational context, was an effective, reliable, and rapid technique for developing new interpersonal responses and strengthening or weakening previously acquired social skills. They concluded from their research that modelling provides students with more relevant cues than verbal description and facilitates the imitation by students of an array of complex clinical skills, while eliminating much of the inefficiency of trial-and-error learning. Modelling was most effective in teaching affect dimensions of reflection and expression to students who have difficulty with complex interpersonal discrimination. In another study, Schinke, Blythe, Gilchrist, and Smith (1980) found that a teaching method consisting of didactic presentations, supervisor modelling, student role playing, and concurrent feedback and coaching resulted in increased basic interviewing skills.

The only study comparing two teaching methods in the field practicum was reported by Larsen and Hepworth (1980), who randomly assigned students to one of two training methods. The first method consisted of modelling, taping interviews, and receiving feedback about students' interviewing behaviours. The second method, called a traditional field approach, consisted of discussion of process recordings and was more focused on case dynamics than students' skill levels. They found that students taught in the former method performed at a higher overall level of competency and had more confidence in their skills than those taught in the traditional approach.

Since there is little empirical evidence to give field instructors clear directions about the most effective teaching approaches, the results of these well-designed studies are instructive. Together they support the conclusion that students most easily acquire skills when these are clearly defined and when students observe skilled models in action. Our own experience strongly supports this conclusion. These skills must be sharpened by practice, and students must also receive feedback on their practice, including suggestions for improvement. The principles of effective feedback, that it is empathetic, timely, clear and direct, systematic, balanced, reciprocal, and based on learning objectives, contribute to the success of this approach.

CO-WORKING

Co-working is another way to guide student learning as well as monitor progress. Co-working occurs when the field instructor and the student arrange to share the work, whether it involves an individual, family, group, or project. It is not observation or participant observation, but is an arrangement wherein both field instructor and student play an active role, assessing, planning, and implementing intervention together. The content of field instruction meetings is concerned with joint planning and evaluation, and they can be infused with a lively investment of energy. In utilizing the ITP Loop Model, both field instructor and student retrieve the same information, but reflection is unique to each. Linkage and planning the professional response become joint efforts.

There is a reservation that attaches to co-working. Differences in skill level and experience can create an imbalance that can undermine the 'co' in co-working. Most writers stress the need for co-therapist egalitarianism as a requisite for successful co-working with groups (Schlenoff and Busa 1981). Indeed, Yalom (1969) has stated that use of co-therapists of unequal status was not advisable under any circumstances. The authority and status of the field instructor in relation to the student reinforce the hierarchy of learner and instructor roles. The inequality of the relationship cannot be denied. However, if the field instructor and student, starting from this point, still feel they can collate their skills and use the experience to enhance the process of learning and teaching, it can be a productive approach for both. It is not an appropriate method for all situations, nor for all students or field instructors.

The literature contains an interesting report on the use of student and field instructor as group co-therapists (Schlenoff and Busa 1981). Though the report acknowledges the unequal nature of the relationship, this disadvantage can be overcome by taking steps both to build a relationship of mutual acceptance and to incorporate techniques that will help less experienced students increase their activity. Mutuality is seen as dependent on both student and field instructor developing comfort in exposing their work to comment and evaluation. Students can be encouraged to voice their opinions first, in order to minimize their reluctance to disagree with the field instructor. Competitiveness is another concern because it can create problems if the student appears to side with group members in opposition to the field instructor co-therapist. Schlenoff and Busa (1981) stress the absolute importance of pre- and post-session discussions, in which the process can be reviewed in a way that utilizes the fact that it is the live experience of both student and field instructor. Finally, the authors recognize the problem of a student remaining steadfastly resistant to taking a more active role in the group and, alternatively, consider the problems created by an overly assertive student. Field instructors might consider that the resistant student's performance anxiety may be related to unclear expectations, while the overly assertive student might be encouraged to reflect on the effect he or she may have on the group participants.

Students may sometimes co-work with another staff member, but the immediacy of the experience will not be available to the field instructor, who will have to depend on feedback from the staff member who is directly involved with the student. Learning from other social workers and staff provides additional perspectives and approaches for students. A task-focused approach in communication with students which centres primarily on 'what should be done next' does not fully capitalize on the educational benefit of multiple teachers. Rather, efforts should be made to orient these agency workers to the merits of promoting critical reflection and articulating the concepts underlying their work as they debrief with the student.

Schur (1979) has described co-worker teams of two students assigned to work with individuals, families, and small groups. It was felt that this model facilitated learning co-working approaches and promoted self-awareness. Role playing was utilized by both students in field instruction sessions, and peer learning seemed to produce less defensiveness on the part of the students. Schur cautioned that close supervision was essential and that one had to remain alert to the tendency for the co-working students to reinforce weaknesses, particularly in pairs that may have similar gaps in knowledge or similar problems.

LIVE SUPERVISION

Live supervision is a method of training which has developed in family therapy and training (Liddle 1991; Liddle and Schwartz 1983; Montalvo 1973). Using two rooms separated by a one-way mirror, an instructor, supervisor, or team of experienced workers guides the student or worker, who works directly with the family. Supervision has an immediate impact on the action occurring between student and family during the session. Rather than describing preferred or alternative interventions after the fact, when the opportunity to try them has passed, live supervision allows the field instructor to see what the student is doing and provide immediate direction and coaching. Other students and workers can observe from behind the mirror at the same time. Planning and debriefing sessions can be held before and after the family interview.

The actual communication between student and field instructor can take place via telephone, earphone, consultation, or walk-in. Telephone communication consists of phoning into the session and delivering a suggestion or message, which is received without discussion. If the student is unclear about the directive, clarification can be requested. Short, precise suggestions are most appropriate. As this method is uni-directional, the student cannot respond to the field instructor during the session. Consultation, by contrast, occurs when a discussion between the student and the field instructor takes place and can be initiated by either party. It allows for reciprocal interactions and some opportunity to briefly discuss proposed interventions. 'Walk-in' communication refers to the field instructor's entering a session and leading or partici-pating in the session. This technique may undermine the student's posi-tion of responsibility with the family and is used primarily in client situations that require an immediate therapeutic response that would be too complicated to convey by telephone. The technique chosen depends on the complexity of the intervention, the student's skill level, and the current issue being addressed by the family.

This approach assumes that learning is maximized through experi-encing the positive effect of successful intervention in a client system. The instructor observes the client situation directly, becoming aware of both verbal and non-verbal data, as well as of interactions between fam-ily members that may go unnoticed by the student. The instructor does not have to rely on the student's self-report, with the selective percep-tion that may accompany that method. Unlike tapes viewed after the event, the observation is simultaneous with the event, providing the opportunity for the field instructor to give feedback to the student, which can then be used to alter the course of intervention with the fam-ily. Student and field instructor can work specifically on areas identified in contracting. Through direct observation, new learning objectives are formulated and recontracting flows out of the work. If this method is used in the agency, students can observe other students and workers during their family interviews and learn from modelling.

Since this model focuses primarily on formulating professional responses, field instruction conferences need to provide opportunity for reflection and linkage. Pre- and post-interview sessions are important to assist students to retrieve the interview, reflect on their experience, and link the field instructor's in-session interventions to the knowledge base used and the particular way of conceptualizing practice. If this step is omitted there is the danger of training technicians who remain depen-dent on co-workers or teams, and are less able to practise autono-mously. For students who are observing, however, the field instructor can highlight phenomena, make linkages to a knowledge base, and dis-cuss professional responses. The field instructor's ability to be both in and out of the same session provides a unique chance to demonstrate and comment on what Schon (1987; 1995) refers to as reflection-in-action – intentionally thinking about our actions while we practise. The challenge still remains, however, to help the student being supervised to link theory with her or his own professional behaviours. The field instructor and student together can review periodically a videotape of the live session to focus on integration of theory and practice.

Agencies using this methodology have policy and procedures which protect clients' right for service should they not wish to be observed. These procedures are explained to clients at intake and may include the signing of consent forms. Some agencies introduce the team and other observers to the clients and are explicit in explaining their respective roles.

As this is a hierarchical model, it is useful only if students are able to learn through giving up some degree of autonomy and control of the actual interview. It is important that the student and the field instructor be able to establish rapport early in their relationship, and they must agree on the respective power each has to make decisions about interventions during the client session. As well, they need to agree on the procedures to be used to reach each other during the session. Feedback and monitoring of the supervisory relationship should be a regular feature in this approach. Students report a range of reactions from being controlled to feeling supported.

In an exploratory study of the important factors in live supervision, Wark (1995) found that both supervisors and supervisees reported that instruction and support were useful to skill development. Supervisees also valued supervisors who gave them enough autonomy to practise using the supervisees' framework to inform their own style. These findings highlight the challenge of the approach, the need to achieve a balance between the direction inherent in this hierarchical model and students' needs for self-direction as they learn to practise.

Live supervision has been developed and used primarily in marital and family therapy. Goodman (1985) discusses its use with individual clients. It can also be used as a means of monitoring group therapy sessions.

In settings using family therapy models, multi-disciplinary teams often provide supervision to therapists and students. Sessions are observed using the one-way mirror, and live supervision, as discussed above, or some variant of it is utilized. The reflecting team method, in which observers discuss their ideas about and suggestions for the family and the therapist in front of them, has been described by Anderson

(1987). In this approach there is also considerable discussion of the family before and after the session. Social workers and educators who have evaluated the use of family therapy teams with social work students point out its strengths (Koopmans 1995; Thomlison 1995). By observing many therapists and students at work, students report that they learn about a variety of clients beyond those in their own caseloads, and about a variety of therapeutic perspectives and techniques. Through a reflecting process with a team, rather than with only one field instructor, they see that many ways of responding, understanding, and intervening with families can be helpful. Thomlison (1995) found that the critical thinking and analysis engaged in by reflecting teams extends students' theoretical knowledge and supports the integration of theory and practice as described in the ITP Loop Model. The reflecting team members probed and questioned each other's assumptions, perspectives, and understandings. Students become part of this process and reported that by questioning their own practice and conceptualizing more frequently than in their previous field instruction experiences with one instructor, they learned to redefine themselves in light of the feedback given to them by the team.

As in live supervision, student performance anxiety is an issue, especially in the early stage of the practicum. When students recognize that the responsibility for helping the family is shared with the team, the experience is seen as supportive rather than only evaluative (Koopmans 1995). Students value teams who they perceive as caring, committed, and supportive of the team members. The major limitation of this approach is the amount of staff time needed for the team members to observe, process, and debrief the session.

USE OF AUDIO- AND VIDEOTAPE

Technological developments now allow students and field instructors to make use of audiotape and videotape recording in a range of practice situations. Both methods capture the actual client situation and practice behaviours, and they do not permit some of the omissions and distortions characteristic of verbal and written reports. Videotape is preferable in that it presents visually the totality of the worker and client system, capturing both non-verbal and verbal communication and therefore some subtle nuances that would not be captured with the sole use of audiotape. However, since videotape presents a multitude of stimuli, the viewer can become overloaded and adopt a passive stance when reviewing the tape. Field instructors and students need to focus on their specific educational objectives or practice themes. As the availability of videotaping may be limited because of cost, audiotaping is a useful alternative if its limitations are recognized, and it can be especially useful for teaching active listening and the relationship between process and content. Audio- and videotapes allow the student and field instructor to examine what is said, the way it is said, the subtleties of verbal interchange between the student and client, and the specifics of the student's skills (Goldberg 1985).

Field instructors can use tapes in a variety of ways for teaching purposes. The field instructor can watch or listen to the entire tape prior to the field instruction conference, can watch or listen to segments of the tape with the student in the conference, or can request that the student review and analyse the tape prior to the conference. Reviewing an entire tape is helpful in obtaining an initial assessment of the student's skill level and for final evaluation. For ongoing instruction, it is useful to have the student review the tape, provide a written analysis, and identify critical points for discussion with the field instructor. For example, the student can be asked to analyse a segment of tape in which she or he felt stuck, in an attempt to recapture the probable relationship between the content and the student's block. The ITP Loop Model provides a framework for analysis, using a four-column written format: the first column is used for retrieval, and the student writes key words in the dialogue; the second column is used for reflection, and the student writes his or her subjective thoughts and feelings; the third column is used for linkage to conceptualize themes or issues and record them. For the fourth column, the student might be asked to evaluate her or his interventions and write alternative professional responses. The tape and analysis can be reviewed by the field instructor prior to the conference, so that both the student and field instructor are familiar with the same data and can discuss particular segments of the tape, dynamics and issues of the practice situation, or future plans. If this four-column analysis is assigned, it is helpful to prepare the student by first jointly completing such an analysis.

It is less time-consuming for field instructors to ask students to select taped segments for analysis and review. However, depending on the student's stage of development, field instructors may on occasion review the entire tape, or themselves select particular segments. Winter and Holloway (1991) investigated the relationship between trainee experience in counselling psychology and supervisory approach. Of interest to this discussion was the finding that as the trainees' experience increased, they chose audiotaped passages to present to their supervisors that reflected less favourably on them as counsellors. The researchers speculate that more experienced students may be less fearful of evaluation, have less need to impress their supervisors, and may be less vulnerable to feedback. Whether these findings can be generalized to social work students is unknown.

Initially, students may feel anxious using audio- or videotapes. Star (1979) found that an instructor who is open to hearing about student concerns, and feels comfortable with the equipment and confident of its usefulness, can create a learning climate that diminishes the anxiety associated with taping. Students tend to relax after using the equipment.

Most agencies will have a protocol for introducing and explaining taping to clients. The client is asked for permission to tape and informed that taping is voluntary and service will not be withheld should the client deny permission. When the client is told what technology is to be used, it is clearly specified that its purpose is for supervised training. The client is also informed about who will hear or observe the tape, and when and how it will be erased. Finally, the client is asked to sign a consent form. If the agency does not have such a protocol, the field instructor may wish to use these guidelines to preserve confidentiality and the client's right to service. Involuntary clients in correctional, psychiatric, or child protection settings may fear the worker's authority, so that they may agree to taping but withhold important thoughts, feelings, and behaviours. Other clients may also be suspicious and fearful of the taping. Professional judgment will help the field instructor establish when it is inappropriate to use tapes.

Students may be helped through preparatory role plays to present their request for permission to tape in a comfortable manner. It is sometimes helpful to suggest to a client that the tape be used on a trial basis and discontinued if the client wishes. Students should be instructed to place the machine so that it is visible. They can be assured by the field instructor that both they and the clients will soon ignore its presence. Since it is not customary practice to use taping in community or administration practice, students will need to explain the educational purposes of their request to committee members. As appropriate, the field instructor may need to develop a protocol for the student to use to ensure confidentiality of the meeting.

About Methods Involving Indirect Access to Practice Data

Reporting practice events in written or verbal form provides the student and field instructor with data for field learning. In using these methods, one is aware that the actual events are not being reported. Rather, students' perceptions of those events are conveyed, with all the omissions, distortions, and self-corrections inherent in recalling and describing past events. Field instructors are faced with a twofold task: to determine from such reports what might have happened; and to assist students to reflect about themselves and their practice, make linkages to theory, and plan new professional responses. Reporting, therefore, can be as time-consuming as using electronic methods. Methods used for reporting are the process record, summary reports, and verbal reports.

PROCESS RECORDING

Process recording is a written description of the dynamic interactions between a student and persons involved in a social work interaction. Its primary intent is to retrieve the practice experience itself and communicate that experience to the field instructor.

Unlike methods which provide direct access to practice data, process recording allows students the opportunity to control, consciously or unconsciously, what and how much of their practice is included and exposed. In writing, students may unwittingly impose meanings, structure, or sequences on the data. While distortions and omissions in themselves are revealing, the field instructor will be hard pressed to sort out facts from perceptions. However, writing process records does provide students with time to recall and reflect on their interviews, the feelings it elicited in them, and the possible effect of their interventions on the client system. Analysis may begin to occur through writing process records.

Field instructors will find that focus can be provided by the reflection phase of the ITP Loop Model, in which students access those factors which underlie their retrieval and interpretation of practice situations. Subjecting the process record to focused reflection can assist students' development of greater self-awareness. Nonetheless, for an accurate picture of practice, field instructors need to use other methods. We concur with Witkin (1982) that the process record is vulnerable to errors in interpretation.

Generations of social work students have laboriously struggled to recall the details of practice encounters and prepare a process record. Considerable discussion has taken place regarding the inclusiveness of the record. Wilson (1981) expects students to communicate everything they can remember, including verbal and non-verbal actions, and their 'gut-level' feelings. Urdang (1979) also favours total written communication of content as an aid to developing students' ability to recall and reflect on practice. Dwyer and Urbanowski (1965) are critical of this detailed approach and argue for structured recording.

Process records are generally submitted to the field instructor in advance of the conference, with some indication from the student of issues and concerns she or he would like to discuss. In reading the record, the field instructor will also note specific areas for discussion. Some field instructors go through the entire record, while others select segments for discussion, analysis, and possible role play. Since students usually spend considerable time producing a process record, they expect their field instructors to have read it and to use it in the conference.

SUMMARY RECORDING

A number of social work educators and practitioners have been critical of the detailed method of process recording described above. They argue that it does not promote a disciplined and structured approach to practice and is poor preparation for autonomous professionals (Kurland 1989). Dwyer and Urbanowski (1965) developed a structured approach that helps the student record and conceptualize the sessions in terms of purpose, observations, and selected content. They suggest that the student include pertinent facts and the responses of the client and the student to those facts, the feeling content of the session, client preparation for the next interview, and endings. The record should conclude with impressions, student role, and future plans. After more than twenty years, they still find this structure useful (Urbanowski and Dwyer 1988). More recently, Tourse (1994) has added two dimensions to the approach for teaching clinical social work: themes and defences. 'Themes' identifies issues that cut across segments and topics in an interview and that reoccur over a number of sessions. 'Defences' uses ego psychology to assess an aspect of the client's functioning; it is useful if field instructors and students are familiar with and use this theoretical knowledge base.

In a review of formats for process recording, Graybeal and Ruff (1995) report on an unpublished five-category system developed by Cohen

(1988). The categories include: (1) pre-engagement, where the student records affective and cognitive preparation; (2) narrative, where the student describes what transpired, providing a summary of the interaction; (3) assessment, where the student evaluates what occurred; (4) plans, where the student describes the next steps; and (5) questions, where the student poses any questions about the content or process of the interview for the field instruction session.

Videka-Sherman and Reid (1985) point out that a number of summary recording guides exist which address the issue of accountability in social work practice by focusing on evaluation of practice interventions, rather than on the interactions that have taken place between worker and client. Since these summary recordings are limited for educational purposes unless they include what the student did and how the client responded, Videka-Sherman and Reid have developed the Structured Clinical Record, a clinical teaching tool 'to assist field instructors to monitor the clinical learning of social work students, and to give the student experience in organizing and reporting on practice which is accountable, systematic, and which links practitioner interventions with client responses' (1985, 47). The recording guide consists of a face sheet with referral and contextual data; problem formulation; goal statements; and principal interventions. Students are instructed to record their interventions and client responses in specific terms. The goal is to help students reflect on their actions and their effect on the client, in order to determine which interventions are effective and when alternative interventions should be used. The authors state that this form of recording preserves the advantages of process recording by retrieving examples of specific interventions and client responses for consideration. Further, it requires students to think systematically about a case, and to link a generic problem-solving practice theory to intervention and goal attainment. The authors note it has limitations outside of direct practice with the problem-solving model.

Summary recording provides field instructors with students' thinking about their work after it has undergone a reformulation. It is subject to the same critique as process recording, so that the field instructor may find actual practice data is difficult to retrieve. Recognizing this limitation, field instructors may need to supplement the summary record with verbal inquiries about the practice experience. They will then be able to use the summary record to help students reflect on their practice and their feelings regarding the situation, to link practice phenomena to a knowledge base, and to plan professional responses. The summary recording systems described above provide some direction for students to begin this work prior to the instructional conference.

VERBAL REPORTING

Verbal reporting of practice situations happens frequently. It is spontaneous, immediate, and may be time-saving. The student with good verbal skills may prefer this method to the more time-consuming analysis and writing required by other methods. There is a tendency in verbal reporting to present practice data in an unsystematic fashion, rather than to engage in more focused retrieval. As well, verbal reporting may lead to a consideration of professional responses in a manner that converts field instruction into case management. While this method may be appropriate in crisis situations, integration of theory and practice necessitates that the practice data presented be subjected to reflection and linkage in forming professional responses.

ROLE PLAY

It is an aphorism that all the world is a stage. Because this is so, field instructors and students can join in holding 'a mirror up to nature' in order to replay or rehearse the feel of a real situation. The 'as if' nature of this technique ensures a feeling of safety and permits the student to take risks, and to try out or play out ideas.

Role play can be either anticipatory or a replay of a past occurrence. It can be utilized when the field instructor and student wish either to experience actively the retrieval of a part of an interview that has already occurred or to anticipate a responsive exchange. They can try on possible ways to develop a theme or cope with an expected or unexpected response. Role play can also be effective in that part of the reflective phase of the ITP Loop Model when student and field instructor search for answers to why a particular strategy was not successful. Role play permits the rehearsal of a specific skill which may have been identified as a learning objective, such as the use of open questions, or focusing, or confronting a client around a specific concern. As discussed above, role play, in conjunction with observing models and feedback, is a highly effective method for mastery of interviewing skills.

The field instructor may assume the client's role or that of the worker with the student as the client. The assumption of the client role can provide the student with an expanded perspective of the work as the client perceives it. Through role play, students can more easily empathize with the client and may discover, in an experiential way, aspects of the client's affect of which they were previously unaware. Similarly, the student can experience the impact of the field instructor's approach in a direct way different from that gained through observation (Sterling 1990). Experiential educational methods such as role play are incomplete unless followed by debriefing. Field instructors and students reflect on the exercise and share their respective insights. Knowledge derived from this experience needs to be examined, however, in light of the actual client's experience to determine to what extent new knowledge is a product of empathizing with the client and to what extent it is a reflection of the student's and field instructor's personalities and theoretical orientations.

While role play has been discussed for direct practice with clients, field instructors have used role play successfully with students for work with committee members and to prepare students for presentations and advocacy efforts aimed at individuals and groups who are indifferent or hostile to the proposals. Role play is an indispensable tool limited only by the field instructor's imagination. For the field instructor and student who learn best by active experimentation and concrete experience, it is an important technique.

Group Supervision and Student Seminars

Many writers have discussed the usefulness of group supervision as a method for providing field instruction where there is more than one student in the setting (Abels 1977; Cowan, Dastyk, and Wickham 1972; Mayers 1970; Shulman 1982; Tebb, Manning, and Klaumann 1996). Presenting cases, projects, tasks, and concerns for discussion to a student group supervised by the field instructor provides students with an opportunity to expand their learning as they hear about assignments other than their own. In this way, they are exposed to a wider range of practice situations than that provided by their assignments. Through group instruction, more ideas are generated and multiple perspectives shared.

The group medium can provide significant affective learning if students are encouraged to express and work on emotional concerns connected with learning to practise. The field instructor can help students identify and express the various issues or conflicts characteristic of student learning; for example, feelings of inadequacy, fear, and being overwhelmed, and concerns with professionalism, use of authority and social control, and self-determination. Well-functioning student groups provide mutual aid and emotional support (Kaplan 1991b). As students perceive their peers struggling with similar issues about practice and becoming a professional, they appreciate the universal nature of their private concerns. In groups where students can listen to and respect each other, exchange different perspectives, and give each other positive and negative feedback, a rich resource for learning is being developed.

The literature notes that the effective functioning of the learning group is dependent on the expectations and patterns of interaction that develop in a particular group (Abels 1977; Cowan et al., 1972). Knowledge of group dynamics and skill in group practice enable the field instructor to focus the group process productively. Field instructors are cautioned that some groups may become too introspective and overly focused on self-awareness, while others may avoid dealing with affect and focus exclusively on case management. Some group members may engage in competition and rivalry with respect to the field instructor. While group supervision may be less resource intensive for staff, there is merit in offering both group and individual field instruction (Cowan et al. 1972; Thomlison 1995).

Field instructors can use the phases in the ITP Loop Model to structure the group's learning. Any of the methods discussed above for retrieving practice data are appropriate. If the group uses verbal reporting, an additional opportunity is available for students to learn about the structure and skills of effective professional presentations. In reflection, the field instructor can encourage the expression and exploration of each student's unique way of understanding and responding to the practice data presented. Students will become aware of a range of underlying assumptions, world-views, and values.

Student groups offer an excellent opportunity to link a specific body of knowledge to client or project issues. The field instructor may provide the knowledge base or have the group members present concepts from the practice and research literature. The small group provides the opportunity for students to actively participate in the analysis, discussion, and linkage of concepts to the practice situations they face. Knowledge necessary for all students to learn in a specific field setting can be structured so as to complement field experiences. For example, students in a setting serving involuntary clients can have a group session which provides a conceptual base for engagement with such clients; students embarking on a community action project aimed at changing housing by-laws can learn about the relevant legislation in a group presentation. New practice responses can be formulated and rehearsed through role play until students feel comfortable enough to transfer new learning to actual practice situations. Peers as well as the field instructor can provide feedback as students attempt to master new behaviours.

Some settings organize student seminars, offered by a variety of staff members, to supplement individual field instruction. This is an effective device to systematically present a broader perspective of the service field, the complexity of multi-function settings, and the specialized knowledge used in addressing the needs of the population served. An interesting extension of this method has been reported in which a number of university teaching hospitals collaborated on a student seminar series for all social work students in their institutions (Bogo and Globerman 1995). In some settings, student seminars are designed for students from multiple disciplines and may include teaching the dynamics and skills of interprofessional collaboration.

Where there are a large number of students, a student team may be organized that is led by the educational coordinator or a staff member other than one of the field instructors. In a manner similar to group supervision, the team is used for peer support through discussion of difficult cases, projects, or situations in the setting. Students are expected to learn how to present material for critical review, and to give and accept critical feedback in a professional manner (Bot, Lackstrom, McNamee, Urman, and Hutson 1995).

On Writing Skills

Developing competence in writing is an aspect of the practicum that is frequently neglected. This is surprising since the importance of such competence is obvious in meeting the demand for a whole array of written communications and presentations, including assessments, court reports, hospital chart notes, special program designs, project reports, policy statements, personnel policies, training manuals, and professional letters.

It must be admitted that students, and field instructors as well, vary widely in their abilities to spell, to construct proper sentences, and to organize thoughts and information in written form. Learning to write well, whatever the requirements of a particular agency or setting, should be a primary goal of all field instructors for every student.

Students need to learn to write concise and informative summary recordings to reinforce accountability for professional practice in agencies. These records are the end product of considerable thought; they represent a cognitive process that involves retrieving information, sifting through it to select the most important and relevant facts, and formulating assessments and plans made in collaboration with the client, team or committee members, and personnel from other involved settings.

Writing is a requisite skill of every university program; however, researching and writing papers for courses does not seem to provide adequate preparation for the special skills required for professional writing of the kinds listed above. These skills include selection of the relevant data to be included, on the basis of both the purpose and the anticipated recipient of the document, report, record, or letter; and the ability to synthesize the information so that it appears organized, logical, and clear.

Most agencies attempt to facilitate the organization of assessments by providing an outline form of the required information. If such a form is not available, field instructors should develop an outline together with the student. Modelling can be helpful by making available to the student sample assessments, reports, or letters that have been written by others in order to give the student an idea of composition, form, and style. However, the best learning occurs through the student's own efforts at writing, followed up by thorough and specific feedback, including actual suggestions for strengthening the written work.

It is strongly recommended that learning objectives include developing professional writing skills and that specific learning activities should include writing a particular kind of report or record required of workers in the setting.

6

Special Situations

This chapter will explore specific characteristics of students who differ from the average or normative type of student. An underlying precept of the ITP Loop Model stresses anticipation and preparation using the looping scheme. Special situation students may provide field instructors with a challenging exercise in its use. Factors such as age, life experience, work experience, racial, ethnic, and cultural diversity, and physical disability present a unique challenge to field instructors to maximize individual potential and talents and to convey affirmation and respect. This is a constantly evolving process of trial, reassessment, and retrial. The objective, as always, remains the provision of an optimum practicum learning situation.

Age and Experience

In general, age and life experience are variables that influence both the field instructor–student relationship and the student's approach to work within the agency. The young student, generally under twenty-five years, usually expects to be seen as a learner willing to enter into a more traditional student relationship with the field instructor, who can teach the desired expertise. It follows that field instructors generally feel flattered and challenged by young students who are enthusiastic learners.

Mature Students

Many social work programs attract students who may be considerably older than twenty-five years and are returning to school after years of work and life experience. These students may have relevant social work experience and are returning to school for advanced study or for a first-level degree after having worked in a social agency. Some students turn to social work as a mid-life career change or after many years of volunteer experience. Mature students may be older in years than the field instructor, and they can react to the practicum in ways that may stress the field instructor and impede learning. In general, mature students are apprehensive about entering university well beyond the usual age of entry. They are concerned about their capacity to study, to integrate new knowledge, and to refute the caveat that 'you can't teach an old dog new tricks.' They may feel that younger students and faculty will expect them to possess knowledge just because they have been around longer or that younger students will laugh at them. Whatever the combination of fears, it must be accepted that they feel somewhat uneasy about assuming the student role.

If the field instructor is younger than the student, the initial discomfort of both student and instructor may be increased. It is the instructor who can best initiate discussion of the mature student's concerns and thoughts about being a student in a social work setting, undertaking social work assignments, and being expected to submit work to the scrutiny of the instructor. It is helpful to acknowledge the value of the mature student's life experience and employment experience in another field and to encourage the student to draw upon that experience. The focus is always to help the student to keep a balance between relying on maturity and experience, on the one hand, and the necessity, on the other, of suspending old and fixed ideas that may stand in the way of growth and learning.

The mature student who enters the social work practicum with work experience in a field unrelated to social work has made a significant career change. This student may have been quite competent in the former work role and now feels like a 'rookie' confronting an unknown set of expectations and skills. For such students, the career change may create problems because frames of reference and accustomed patterns of behaviour are difficult to shift. Former careers and professional experience in nursing, teaching, or fields such as commercial public relations may create conflict as the student struggles to define the differences and similarities in the approach to persons from a social work perspective. Nursing and teaching demand far more structured professional behaviour, which can serve to contain performance anxiety. Routines and procedures learned and repeated from situation to situation promote task competence and decrease anxiety. Social work, however, rarely proceeds within a detailed lesson plan or precise medical procedure but rather emphasizes openness and use of the perceptions processed in the ongoing interchange between worker and others. If instructors are not aware that students may have difficulty with the differences in professional approach, the discomfort, confusion, and mounting anxiety can affect teaching and learning and the success of the practicum. When these differences are acknowledged, both the instructor and the student can avoid a struggle of wills and instead can focus on identifying the ways in which social work practice differs from past professional experience and behaviour.

The mature student who has worked in a social work setting before entering a social work degree program presents a different challenge to the instructor. Students who have work experience as social workers may feel quite defensive about revealing what they know and do not know. They may give the impression that there is little they really have to learn and may indicate that the field instructor should function more as a colleague and let them get on with their work so that they can obtain the degree that they lack. It may be tempting for the field instructor to go along with the collegiality and collude in giving the student autonomy with minimal monitoring, but this would be a disservice to the student. Both student and field instructor need to take the time to set appropriate learning objectives based on observation and the formulation of the student's baseline level of knowledge and skills, with open discussion of the student's maturity and relevant experience (Vayda 1981). The student may feel that competence is expected and so hide behind an aura of competence that may mask a fear of exposure of a lack of sufficient skill and knowledge. Conversely, the student may deny the significance of experience, skills, and knowledge in an attempt to minimize performance expectations from the field instructor. A discussion of the special situation of being a mature student with more experience than a young student and more uncertainty about assuming the role of a student and about what will be expected by the field instructor should occur as early as the initial interview. Recognition can be given for experience and status, but also there can be an acknowledgment of the possibilities for growth in achieving new levels of understanding and performance.

The Exceptionally Good Student

The exceptionally good student possesses competence beyond the general expectation of a student at a particular level of education. This student may be naturally suited to social work and may possess strong interpersonal skills, good organizational abilities, a critical and lively intellect, and strong commitment to helping. Such a student appears able to practise with little guidance from the instructor, is able to relate theory to practice, and completes work in a timely and competent way. Faced with this kind of student, the field instructor may feel both pleased and threatened, and may question what she or he is able to teach that will provide challenge and stimulation. Exceptionally good students often have a history of situations in which they are expected to work well and independently, and so they do not expect intensive teaching. Field instructors may feel less inclined to challenge the student by setting learning objectives that are based on ongoing critical assessment.

Exceptionally good students may have difficulty admitting the need for some assistance from the field instructor. Accustomed to being competent and knowledgable, the state of not knowing may be uncomfortable to their self-image. The student may struggle alone in attempting to maintain a sense of self as a competent person. These students need an instructor who will reach out to student concerns, as well as give permission to be less than perfect, to risk and make mistakes, out of which can grow enhanced learning and performance.

Exceptionally good students have to find their way when in a group with other students. They may be helpful to peers, giving assistance and advice, thus neutralizing feelings of competitiveness that could isolate them from the other students. Some, however, may be critical of others' work and give negative feedback that can serve to heighten competitive tensions in the group. Some very competent students may choose to avoid standing out as special by withholding their thoughts and limiting their participation in the group sessions. Field instructors will need to help students develop awareness of the effect of their attitudes and behaviour on others in the group.

The Resistant Student

The resistant student can be characterized as the student who gives evidence of competence and knowledge but who seems intent upon keeping the field instructor at arm's length. The objective of the student seems to be to avoid engaging with the instructor. It is a defensive armour that can be difficult for the instructor to penetrate. In a classic article, Kadushin comments that 'the supervisory situation generates a number of different kinds of anxieties for the supervisee' (Kadushin 1968, 27). Kadushin believes that this anxiety is generated by the field experience because of the expectation that the student must make changes in behaviour and, in some cases, in personality. The demand for change threatens long-standing patterns of thinking and believing, and may be perceived as a betrayal of earlier role models, such as teachers and peers, whose behaviour and beliefs the student may have incorporated but which now need to be re-examined (Hawthorne 1975; Kadushin 1968). Three examples of the resistant student are suggested in which the competence base is the variable. The first is the student who is fearful about possessing no theory of practice and few skills, who fears that this lack will be exposed, and who avoids engagement with the instructor. The second example is the student who is comfortable with a minimal level of competence and uses a pleasant personality to establish a façade relationship. The student is afraid to let go of the comfort of an easy relationship and resists the demand for more substantive evidence of analysis and performance. It is easy for such students to collude with clients, who may also be resistant to a demand for change and movement. The third example is the student who does not accept the learner role and wishes to operate quite independently of the field instructor. Case management decisions, for example, may be readily discussed, but there is reluctance to focus on student and client transactions.

Field instructors can turn to the ITP Loop Model to help such students recognize the resistant nature of their behaviour. By retrieving the content of what is brought to the teaching sessions, the field instructor can reflect on what has been omitted from them, and how this incompleteness inhibits the process of teaching and learning. The field instructor could raise the issue that the student may be feeling anxious and acknowledge the difficulty most persons experience when their behaviour and assumptions need to be re-examined and possibly changed. This process can be linked to learning theory, which demonstrates how the universal process of conceptual and behavioural change occurs through the use of critical analysis of experience, observation, and knowledge.

The Student with Disabilities

The student with a specific disability can present a special situation for the practicum instructor. Until recently, social work literature has had too little to say about the practicum aspect of their education (Hawthorne 1985; Romano 1981). The challenge for both school and agency social work educators is to keep the quality standards of programs in a delicate balance with the rights of students with disabilities to participate in these programs. In effect, the issue becomes that of determining the reasonable accommodations that social work programs can make that will preserve the program's integrity but will also meet the special needs of the student with a disability. The Americans with Disabilities Act of 1990 (ADA) has defined a qualified individual with a disability as a person who 'with, or without reasonable modification to rules, policies, or practices or the provision of auxiliary aids and services, meets the essential eligibility requirements for the participation in programs' (sec. 201, Stat. 327, Americans with Disabilities Act of 1990, Pub. L. 101–336, 42 , U.S.C., Stat. 327). In Canada, the Charter of Rights and Freedoms includes in equality rights a proscription against discrimination based on mental or physical disability. These rights do not preclude governments from initiating special programs to improve the circumstances of special groups or individuals, such as special provisions for the blind or for persons with a physical disability (Canadian Charter of Rights and Freedoms, Part I of the Constitution Act, 1982, being Schedule B of the Canada Act, 1982 U.K.). It has been observed that increasing numbers of students with disabilities have been entering postsecondary education, and among those are increasing numbers of students with learning disabilities. This group accounts for 30 to 50 per cent of the postsecondary disability population (Cole and Cain 1996). Other disabilities include visual impairments, hearing impairment or deafness, speech and communication disabilities, and orthopaedic impairments.

The interpretation of legislation to secure the rights of persons with disabilities generally recognizes the right of educational programs to set their requirements, but when reasonable accommodation to the needs of the person with a disability would permit that individual to perform essential job functions required by professional practice, it is expected that the program will provide or make such accommodations. Such an expectation can serve as a guide for negotiations between the school and the agency regarding the practicum (Cole and Cain 1996; Crist and Stoffel 1992), but in order to begin the process, a student with a disability must accept the responsibility to request accommodation because of a specific disability. For some students with disabilities, this may be difficult because they wish to be treated as all other students and to avoid the risk of putting themselves at a disadvantage. Many schools have student advisors who are prepared to advocate for accommodations that would meet the needs of specific students without sacrificing educational standards or violating the student's right to fairness. These persons can also access campus resources and services that can facilitate off-campus accommodations that may be required to meet the needs of the practicum.

Several studies have been reported that investigate the experiences of social work students with disabilities. In one study, a questionnaire was mailed to BSW field work directors (Alperin 1988). Out of 197 respondents, 113 programs reported having students with disabilities in the practicum sequence. Reported problems included special transportation requirements as a significant limitation for physically disabled students in regard to their ability to get to and from the agency as well as to meet some service needs of the agency. Another frequently cited concern was the reluctance of some agencies to accept students with disabilities. Other problems cited included recording difficulties, difficulties with reading and keeping records, personal problems such as immaturity and lack of acceptance of the limitations of the disability, inability to function independently, and unwillingness to take responsibility for personal care. The least frequently cited concern was client acceptance. The author concluded that students with a broad range of physical disabilities are preparing to become social work practitioners and, according to the practicum directors who responded, are choosing professional career paths that do not differ from those of non-disabled students. Students with disabilities who completed social work programs were reported to be able to secure social work employment at the same rate as did graduates who were not disabled. The percentage of students with disabilities proceeding to graduate schools was double that of the non-disabled (Alperin 1988). Of interest is a study that found that students with disabilities tend to be older than the usual college student. This may be the result of a delay in the awareness of students with disabilities that they might succeed in university studies with accommodations that are now secured in legislation (Thompson and Dickey 1994).

In another study, fourteen students with disabilities were interviewed as well as twelve field instructors (Reeser 1992). The investigation looked into the advance preparation required when agencies were asked to provide practicum settings for students with disabilities; what might constitute reasonable requests from the school to the agency regarding accommodations to meet the specific needs of these students; as well as the extent of the students' willingness to make their own accommodations to agency requirements. The most frequently reported considerations of field instructors regarding student placement were the following: students' acceptance of their disabilities; likelihood of clients' accepting the students; sensitivity of the agency's staff; time flexibility, and geographic and physical accessibility of the setting; special needs of persons with disabilities, such as telephone arrangements for deaf students, recording and writing arrangements, and wheelchair accessibility of the agency; use of agencies serving persons with disabilities; and concern about possible danger to the clients served by the agency, although this concern was rejected by the student interviewees. In the responses of both students and field directors, the most frequently reported factors promoting acceptance of students with disabilities were the following: placement with a field instructor who has a disability or has experience with disabilities; situations in which students can link with campus services for students with disabilities; schools that can count on many agency resources; the existence of school-sponsored practicum days; practicum directors willing to advocate for students and provide guidance to faculty and field instructors; and early practicum preparation, including consideration and planning of how best to inform the agency about a student's disability. Students interviewed tended to believe that their placements should be arranged before those of other students; that they could educate the agency during their initial interviews in order to dispel stereotyping; and that students needed a realistic acceptance of their disability, as well as reasonable expectations concerning the accommodations that could be made by the agency (Reeser 1992).

The more complex issues regarding students with disabilities are the psychological ones. Although all students approach the practicum with heightened concern regarding how well they will be accepted, for the student with a disability this acceptance factor is critical. In the initial interview, the field instructor is well advised to look beyond the disability and to consider the whole person, including his or her knowledge, attitude, and experience. The instructor should encourage the student to address specific accommodations and needs relevant to the disability, but should take care not to let the disability become the sole focus of the interview. The disability should not be used by either student or instructor as a reason to go easy, to shrink from making demands for learning, developing professional behaviour, and adhering to agency procedure. Adjustments with regard to time needs and assignments, if they are required, must be disability specific; for example, if the disability means that more time is required to get from place to place, or if the student is dependent on special transportation, then work assignments should be adjusted accordingly.

The formulation of a learning contract is of particular importance for the student with a disability. Through developing a learning contract, both instructor and student are able to articulate clear goals and the means by which they can be achieved. The faculty-field liaison can be helpful in this process by sharing with the field instructor the strategies used in facilitating classroom work which have been especially useful (Weinberg 1978). The issue of confidentiality may arise when a student with a disability requires an attendant or an interpreter to be present during contacts with clients. Clients should be prepared for the presence of another person, and the attendant or interpreter needs to be briefed about the importance of confidentiality.

The question of whether to arrange a practicum for a student with a disability in a disability-focused setting is often troubling. The short answer is, it depends. Some students and practicum coordinators are strongly opposed to such settings, which are seen as a strong statement that students with disabilities have only limited options and must be restricted to work with similar persons. This may be an accurate assumption of prejudice if the selection is made without thought and solely in response to the disability factor. However, in a disability-focused setting, acceptance and understanding can be mutual and can work in the service of both the students and clients. Students in such settings are expected to learn to work with non-disabled staff, families of clients, and other non-disabled persons in the community. An important factor is the possibility for employment opportunities which may arise for the student with a disability.

Sensitivity and openness in communication are of particular importance in helping instructor, student, and agency staff make the practicum a successful one. Modelling of these qualities by the instructor can encourage the student to relate to clients and co-workers in a similar manner. The goal for all parties is to cope with the disability, using whatever accommodations are required and possible that will not jeopardize learning or the quality of service.

7

Legal Aspects of Field Instruction

This chapter is cautionary. It deals with some of the legal issues which may arise when a student who is not an employee of the agency enters into a practice and learning relationship with the agency, the field instructor, and clients served by that agency. Legislation differs from province to province in Canada and within the United States. The extent and nature of insurance liability coverage also vary among universities, practicum agencies, and institutions, for example, between a small neighbourhood agency and a large metropolitan hospital, and among professional social work associations. It is advisable for agency directors to clarify questions of legal liability with the practicum coordinator. It may be necessary for practicum coordinators to consult with the university's legal department and the agency's administration in order to clarify the precise nature of the coverage provided in situations of off-campus education. In the case of a university teaching hospital that trains students from many health-care disciplines, an umbrella contract between the hospital and the university will include social work students.

Liability Issues

Social workers, regardless of their level of training, present themselves to the public as possessing particular knowledge and skills, whether there is a direct contractual relationship as a result of a fee for service or whether that service is provided by a publicly mandated, publicly funded agency (Vayda and Satterfield 1989). In general, students in training and volunteers will not be held to the standard of care expected of fully trained professionals, but, rather, to what can be reasonably expected of a student or volunteer. They will be expected, however, to be competent for their assigned position and to possess more skills than a lay person. In addition, they will be expected to be aware of their limitations in knowledge and skill, and to seek help from staff or supervisors or, when appropriate, to refer the case to qualified persons. It follows that professional staff may be held liable for negligence in regard to inadequate screening, placement, or supervision of students or volunteers. The legal accountability of social workers and students to their clients and of field instructors to their students is a legal reality, but actual civil or criminal charges brought against them are rare. In one study completed in 1985, questionnaires were mailed to 429 deans or directors of accredited social work programs, of which 276 responded. Four respondents reported that students had been named as parties in four states (Gelman and Wardell 1988).

Formal arrangements between school and agency, in most social work programs, have now replaced informal agreements as another response to the current litigious climate in North America. Letters of understanding or contractual agreements which formally recognize mutual expectations and responsibilities have become standard practice in some social work educational programs. In the same study, 86 per cent of the responding schools reported some type of formal contract, and 30 per cent of the respondents reported provision of blanket liability coverage to their students. Those reporting blanket coverage, however, also indicated that they were uncertain about the specific terms of the coverage (Gelman and Wardell 1988).

Subsequent to the 1988 study, Gelman, Pollack, and Auerbach (1996) conducted a follow-up study in which a fifty-item questionnaire was mailed to deans and directors of 466 graduate and undergraduate programs in the United States. There was an overall response rate of 65 per cent. The questions asked for information concerning program relationships with field practicum agencies and experience with affiliation agreements as well as litigation involving practicum students. They reported in their findings that 95 per cent of the respondents had some type of written affiliation agreements or contracts. More than half the respondents (62 per cent) reported that they provided malpractice insurance for students, while 35 per cent said they required students to purchase such insurance. Six programs reported that one of their students had been named in a lawsuit brought against an agency practicum site, with a field instructor named as a party in five of these cases. Charges involved sexual misconduct or harassment, personal injury of a client, breach of confidentiality, and failure of a mandated reporter to report.

Malpractice is a specialized form of negligence that must have certain characteristics for there to be a legal basis for action. These have been summarized as follows:

1. A duty or obligation, recognized by law, requiring the actor to conform to a certain standard of conduct.
2. A failure on his part to conform to the standards required.
3. A reasonably close causal connection between the conduct and the resulting injury.
4. Actual loss or damage resulting to the interests (health, finances, and emotional or psychological ability) of another. (Prosser 1971)

Though malpractice litigation has captured public attention because of the escalating cost of liability insurance, malpractice charges made against social work practitioners are still relatively uncommon events. A review of the literature reveals that there is little case law involving malpractice suits brought against social workers, but the risk is always present (Besharov and Besharov 1987). In a New Jersey study, 105 social workers responded to a questionnaire that was designed to elicit the respondents' awareness of existing malpractice litigation, the steps social workers could take to protect themselves, and knowledge about conditions that could lead to successful malpractice litigation. The survey revealed that bases for reported litigation against social workers include a client's suicide, a poorly handled child abuse case, and a breach of confidentiality, but none of the cases succeeded in court (Gerhart and Brooks 1985). These findings notwithstanding, some agencies require that students carry their own malpractice insurance. When students are in settings where psychotherapy is the dominant mode of intervention, malpractice insurance, whether paid for by the school, agency, or student, may be a wise precaution. Practicum preparation could include the introduction of issues of practice liability and an opportunity to discuss with students strategies for ensuring protection, not only as students but as future social work practitioners.

Student-client situations that have the potential basis for criminal or civil action include 'the failure to inform the client of student status; providing treatment without obtaining proper consent; keeping inaccurate or inadequate records; administering inappropriate or radical treatment; failing to consult with or refer to a specialist; failing to seek proper supervision; failing to take action to prevent a client's suicide; and failing to warn third parties of potential harm [as well as] ... breaching confidentiality; exhibiting professional misconduct, such as engaging in sexual relations with clients; ... failing to report child abuse or neglect; and abandoning clients or failing to be available when needed' (Zakutansky and Sirles 1993, 340). The rights of clients that must be protected include the right to self-determination; the right to the least intrusive intervention; freedom from physical harm; and freedom from actions that may be prejudiced by the client's race, ethnic group, gender, national origin, age, or sexual orientation (Cobb 1994).

Finally, given that if a client should launch a malpractice suit it will likely extend to supervisors as well as to administrators and sometimes the board members, field instructors should be aware of their own liability in regard to students. A client who consents to service from a practicum student has not agreed to receive inferior or harmful service; therefore, the field instructor can be held responsible for inadequate supervision, either directly through inappropriate supervision or vicariously through lack of proper monitoring (Bonosky 1995).

Informed Consent

Field instructors should be certain that students understand the meaning and importance of informed consent. Technology has made possible computer-stored information banks, audio- and videotaping, and interviews conducted before a one-way vision mirror behind which may be persons unknown to the clients. Consumer protection activity has increased sensitivity to the vulnerability of clients, who may feel powerless in a bureaucratic service agency or even in a therapeutic relationship. Informed consent procedures, while usually required in all service organizations, may be presented in a hasty or perfunctory manner. Field instructors should discuss with students the importance of ascertaining that clients truly understand procedures, the nature of a request for information and its limits, and whether any consequences might ensue if they should choose not to give consent. Care should be taken to ascertain whether clients truly understand because anxiety may interfere with the ability to know what is being asked or explained. Written consent forms may be required in some situations, and these should have the necessary information filled in before a signature is requested. Most agencies have policies regarding informed consent procedures, and, in some jurisdictions, patients and clients have legal recourse if their right to be informed and to give proper consent has been violated.

The general principles of consent under common law require that a counsellor must obtain the client's consent to initiate any test, procedure, or counselling. The consent should be obtained in advance; it should be clear about the specific treatment proposed, as well as about such related matters as how records will be kept and any other disclosure of information. The consent of next of kin is only required if the client is incapable of consenting. A consent is valid when it is given voluntarily, that is, when the client is truly able to understand the nature of the intervention, its risks, and the consequences that might occur either with or without the intervention. Consent may also be implied by the fact that a client comes for counselling. Finally, it must be noted that a counsellor cannot ignore expressed prohibitions or limits that a client wishes to place on the intervention. If such conditions are deemed by the counsellor to be harmful or too limiting, the counsellor may choose to withdraw from the relationship and suggest that the client seek help elsewhere. Consents may be verbal as well as written. Written consents should be clearly stated in a language that is understandable to the client. Some services supply pamphlets written in languages common to their clientele. Finally, the consent must be personally requested from the client because a clerk or third party cannot answer questions the client may ask. It is not necessary that a consent be witnessed (Solomon 1997).

Single subject research is sometimes built into a practicum as an assignment or a project. When data is being gathered for research purposes, the student must be required to tell the client why the information is being gathered, how confidentiality will be insured in regard to personal identification, and what will happen if the client chooses to refuse to participate. In some instances, written consent should be obtained (Loewenberg and Dolgoff 1992).

Students frequently are expected to present practicum experiences in their classroom to serve as a basis of discussion and analysis. In making such presentations, they should be advised to change any identifying data, for example, of individuals or specific communities. They may wish to advise clients about how such a presentation will be made to the class to reassure them about preserving anonymity. Videotapes of client interviews are the property of the agency and may not be used for any purpose other than the purpose agreed to in the consent forms signed by the client permitting an interview or meeting to be videotaped.

There are instances when facilitators of field instruction training seminars have requested that field instructors bring in tapes of student interviews with clients. Concern has arisen about informed consent procedures in these instances since these tapes are removed from the agency. It may be prudent to add a description of this potential use to an informed consent form and to explain its meaning to clients.

Record-Keeping

Field instructors may find that students do not always understand the importance and legal implications of keeping records. An adequate record can be defined in general terms as a record in which the worker's activity and plan of care can be understood by another worker who might take over with that client or situation. The record of a social worker is admissible in legal proceedings and can be subpoenaed. When in court, a social worker can use the record to refresh his or her memory in giving testimony. Entries must be dated, signed, and legible. Information must be based on fact and observed behaviour. Opinions or impressions are admissible as long as they can be supported by the facts and observations already recorded. It is important to note that records cannot be altered; if additions or changes are made, they should be made openly with the original record always remaining intact. While it is permissible to keep private notes, these notes should reinforce the official record, as notes too can be subpoenaed. Inadequate records that can be proven to have contributed to the injury of a client may be the basis of a civil suit in negligence (Solomon 1997).

Privileged Communication and Confidentiality

It is important for field instructors and students to be aware of issues regarding confidentiality and privileged communications because social workers are asked to testify on such matters as adoptions, child custody, welfare support, or a client's mental state or competence. They may be compelled by the court to reveal information they have gained during individual or group counselling sessions (Bernstein 1977).

Confidentiality as a legal concept must be distinguished from privilege. Social workers and other mental health professionals need to recognize that patients and clients have important rights to privacy and confidentiality, but those rights are limited. Generally, these rights should be protected in compliance with legal and ethical codes of behaviour. Since third parties have legitimate interests in some confidential information, mental health care-givers should inform clients at the outset about the limits to confidentiality that will pertain to them and their situation. This openness will help to establish and preserve a more honest therapeutic relationship by setting realistic limits to confidentiality. Unlike confidentiality, privilege is a totally legal concept. It has been defined as 'an exception to the general rule that the public has a right to relevant evidence in a court proceeding; confidentiality refers more broadly to legal rules and ethical standards that protect an individual from unauthorized disclosure of information. Confidentiality alone is not enough to support a privilege: without a privilege statute or a common-law rule, a therapist may be charged with contempt of court for refusing a court order to testify ...' (Smith-Bell and Winslade 1994, 184). Privilege means that information told to a professional by a client or patient does not have to be disclosed.

The holder of the privilege is the client or patient, and privilege can be waived by that person. No privilege attaches to communications made by a client to a social worker. Canadian law extends privilege only to communications made to a lawyer by his or her client. Legislation differs among the fifty states; a protected communication or relationship that may be kept out of legal proceedings in one state may not be regarded as privileged in another state. Accordingly, the social worker–client relationship varies from state to state as legislatures and judiciaries have variously weighed the merits, on the one hand, of disclosure to arrive at the truth against the need, on the other hand, to protect a relationship based on trust and expectations of confidentiality.

If social workers are subpoenaed to testify in court, they cannot be held liable by the client for what they say in court. They may be held responsible to their clients, however, for failing to inform clients that they may be compelled to testify concerning the nature and content of the work with the client (Bernstein 1977). We have indicated that records and notes made by a social worker may be subpoenaed and entered in evidence if such material is deemed relevant by the judge.

Field instructors should inform students that they must let clients know in advance of interviews if the possibility exists that they may be required to testify in regard to that client's situation. It is also important that records and notes be kept up to date as the situation develops and that they be objective and based on observed facts. Students should be informed that they are not compelled to give any information by telephone to anyone, including lawyers and police. Requests for information must be in writing, and any responses should be thoroughly discussed with students by field instructors. Information cannot be disclosed to third parties without the client's consent.

Students are naturally fearful that telling clients that what transpires in an interview may not be held in confidence may jeopardize the trusting relationship they wish to establish. Conflict can arise when social work intervention is both statutory and therapeutic and it appears difficult to reconcile the use of mandated authority with social work values. In corrections or child-welfare settings, the student must establish a relationship with a client that is prefaced by the knowledge that information regarding violent behaviour or child abuse may not be held in confidence. Students must be informed that in most jurisdictions, child protection laws compel people working in professional capacities to report suspicions of child abuse to the local child protection authority. When such suspicions arise, a student should always discuss the situation with the field instructor before taking any action.

Some states in the United States and some Canadian jurisdictions have enacted special statutes whereby a judge can grant privileged communication to a professional, usually a psychiatrist or a psychologist. It is instructive to review the classic conceptual test, developed by Wigmore (1961), which is used by courts both in the United States and Canada as a standard in deciding whether a communication is privileged. As stated by Wigmore, the relevant criteria are the following:

1. The communication must originate in the confidence that it will not be disclosed.
2. The element of confidentiality must be essential to the full and satisfactory maintenance of the relationship between the parties.
3. The relationship must be one that in the opinion of the community ought to be fostered.
4. The injury to the relationship that would ensue through a disclosure of the communications must be greater than the benefit gained from the outcome of the litigation if it should succeed. (Wigmore 1961)

A Canadian case involved an application to have a youth who was charged with an indictable offence transferred to adult court. The school board, by which the youth was classified as a student with special needs, and three potential witnesses claimed privilege with respect to the youth's academic, testing, and assessment files. A *voir dire*, or special ruling by the court on a matter of law, was held to make a finding in regard to privilege of three files: the permanent record file, the coordinator's file, and the counsellor's file. The court concluded that the permanent record was not privileged and that the reports or assessments in the coordinator's file which related to physical or mental illness, emotional disturbance, or learning disability were extremely relevant and were not privileged. In making this determination, the court considered the fourth Wigmore criterion as the most important test; namely, would the injury caused by disclosure of the communications between a school counsellor or therapist and a student be greater than the benefit gained by consideration of such documentation at this hearing? The judge noted that privilege is not as important as society's concern to ascertain the truth; see *R. v M.(G.)*, 1992 125 Nfld. & PEIR 261 (Nfld. Prov. Ct.) at 131–32.

The Duty to Report and to Warn

Students should know that in most Canadian provinces and most U.S. states the law requires that a person who performs professional or official duties with respect to a child must report to a child protection agency any suspicion that a child may be in need of protection because that child has suffered or is at substantial risk of suffering physical, emotional, or sexual harm.

In regard to liability for failure to warn, the landmark case in the United States, which is also to some degree influential in Canadian courts, is the Tarasoff case, heard in 1976. A psychologist, employed by a university counselling service, was informed by a student client that he, the client, intended to kill his girlfriend when she returned from vacation. The psychologist informed the campus police, who did not detain the student, but he failed to inform the girl's parents. The girl was murdered when she returned. The parents brought a suit against the psychologist and the university, which succeeded in establishing that a duty to warn is paramount over therapist-client confidentiality. The psychologist's argument that it is difficult to predict dangerousness with accuracy was accepted by the court as a valid argument, but the court pointed out that he was being sued because of a failure to warn when dangerousness had been demonstrated (*Tarasoff v Regents of the University of California*, 17 Cal. Rptr. 3rd [U.S. 1976]).

Disclosure of Student Status

The issue of disclosure to clients regarding practicum student status and the consequent limitation on the students' time with the agency is one that has been perceived as equivocal. Social work educators have avoided taking a position, preferring to leave the decision to the agency, which may or may not have developed a policy. It is an issue, however, that has both legal and ethical consequences.

To claim professional status is to acknowledge rights and responsibilities of the parties to the professional relationship. To become a professional takes training, and the public should be as aware of the existence of a supervised practice training requirement for social work as it is for a similar phase of medical or legal education (Feiner and Couch 1985).

The consumer rights movement has exerted pressure on all professionals toward full disclosure to patients or clients of matters that affect their treatment or service. There is no doubt that a full disclosure would include the qualifications and status of the professional staff. In general, there is less question about the identification of social work student status for those doing a practicum based in a hospital, where many disciplines train students. Other settings, however, may not be so clear about this issue.

Some of the arguments against disclosure are rooted in the fear of losing clients or jeopardizing the formation of a trusting alliance, either because of lack of belief in a student's professional expertise or reluctance to invest in a relationship for which termination or transfer is inevitable when the practicum ends. These do not seem to be compelling arguments when weighed against the value of encouraging the student to establish an honest basis for relationship. The terms of a student-client relationship include the fact that a skilled field instructor is the third party in that relationship.

Liability is implied when a student establishes a relationship with a client. Both a legal and an ethical issue arises from such a relationship. From a legal point of view, it is a fiduciary undertaking because the social work student now has a duty to use professional expertise in the best interests of the client, based on the trust that client has placed on the student (Zakutansky and Sirles 1993). Marshall Kapp (1984) has written that 'the practice of misleading patients ... violates ethical principles based on respect for autonomy and the dignity of others' (143).

Field instructors should discuss this issue with their students and review with them the process of informing clients about the student-client–field instructor relationship. Students' fears and feelings about their student status can be discussed and client reactions anticipated. Students need to be reminded and reassured that they bring knowledge and expertise to the practicum. Student status does not denote incompetence but rather the need for the student to acquire additional experience and knowledge by working closely with an experienced worker in that agency. If students and field instructors view disclosure of student status as demeaning, then this attitude will, of course, be transmitted to the client.

Another disclosure dilemma is the question of whether to share information about a student's prior practicum performance with a potential field instructor or with the agency. Research on this issue has revealed no agreement among schools about whether to share information and how it should be transmitted. The majority of programs have no stated policy and tend to deal with each situation on an *ad hoc* basis (Alperin 1989). The conflict arises when the rights of students for privacy, self-direction, and an unbiased experience collide with the respect and trust that agencies and field instructors confer on schools (Rosenblum and Raphael 1991).

Questions arise, for example, about a student who had a difficult first practicum, or about a student who disclosed to the faculty-field liaison that he had been a substance abuser but has been in remission for a long period of time. Suppose this student wishes to have a practicum in a setting dealing with addiction. The answer is equivocal and in the final analysis must be based on an assessment of the specific student and circumstances. One must keep in mind that agencies, too, should be able to make an informed choice in selecting their practicum students (Rosenblum and Raphael 1991). We would argue that a student, in such a situation, should be encouraged to disclose this information to the prospective field instructor at the time of the initial interview. On the positive side, a student who has firsthand experience of addiction has the potential to form a unique therapeutic alliance with an addicted person. On the negative side, the danger always exists that the student may be unable to separate her or his experience from that of the client, so that over-identification distorts that alliance. The issue is complex because it involves both a human rights issue and the issue of therapeutic competence. The human rights issue refers to the right of the student not to feel pressured to disclose past personal information that could prejudice his or her right to be judged as a potential learner. However, lack of disclosure creates an untruthful relationship between the school, the agency, and the student. If problems arise, all parties feel betrayed. The student may feel justified in launching a complaint against the school and the agency on the grounds of discriminatory prejudgment based on past personal history. Conversely, the agency may feel that the school withheld information which was needed to make an informed decision to accept a student.

Students in Potentially Dangerous Practicum Situations

Students may be placed in agencies where there is potential risk for personal assault and injury, such as in psychiatric hospitals, child protection service agencies, residential treatment centres, or correctional facilities. Field instructors in such settings have a responsibility to discuss risk awareness and management, and procedures that the agency has developed to decrease risk in crisis situations. For example, in general, students should not be required to make home visits alone if there is any reason to believe that a potential danger exists. While Canada has universal health coverage, U.S. students need some assurance that medical or hospital costs will be covered if injury should occur. Most schools have developed agreements which clarify legal liability and cover the student who may be injured or harmed in the course of professional duty arising from the practicum. Students should not be permitted to use their own cars to transport clients unless some prior arrangement has made this a part of the agreement between the student, school, and agency. If a student or a client is injured, the field instructor may be liable for malpractice, even though the student may not have informed the field instructor that such transportation was being provided. The legal principle which implicates the field instructor, and possibly the agency and the school, is called respondent superior. This means that an employer (the agency represented by the field instructor) acts through an employee or agent (practicum student). Liability will flow to the employer, who must accept the responsibility. Implicit in this concept is the common law principle that each person has a duty to see that quality service is provided; in the case of a student as agent, through the field instructor providing adequate supervision. In the practicum situation, the necessary conditions for respondent superior doctrine are met; namely, that a professional social worker has the right to control the work of the student, and the student receives the work assignment through the field instructor (Zakutansky and Sirles 1993).

Strategy for Collective Agreement Strikes

A situation of great concern to social work educators, both within the university and the agency, is the effect on students completing a practicum when strikes of organized workers occur. Many agency employees, both professional workers and support staff, belong to bargaining units. When collective agreement negotiations break down, various degrees of work action or slowdown may occur, a strike may be called, pickets may circle the agency, and the student may be caught in the conflict. Feelings run high, and students may become politicized and identify with either side of the conflict as well as with clients whose welfare may be in jeopardy because of the disruption of service. In addition, for the student, the practicum is endangered because of lost time or a striking field instructor. If the disruption occurs near the beginning of the practicum, the school may simply help the student negotiate an alternative assignment. However, when half or more of the practicum has been completed, the school and the field instructor will have to help the student make a decision about what action to take if no resolution of the conflict seems imminent. Under no circumstances should students be required to cross a picket line or be required to substitute for striking workers.

Sexual Harassment

Sexual harassment has come into public consciousness in the last two decades, and most universities have developed policies and procedures to deal with complaints when they occur in the classroom or on campus. In general, students have sought protection from and redress against unwanted sexual overtures from faculty who take advantage of an unequal power balance between professor and student.

This issue becomes more complicated when it moves away from the campus and into the practicum environment. There may be no explicit agency policy in regard to sexual harassment, and the student may feel more vulnerable in this off-campus educational practice setting to any real or imagined behaviour which seems to make a sexual demand. Situations have arisen when a student has felt there to be a suggestion of a sexual overture in the behaviour of an agency member other than the field instructor. In some instances, this has been a director or someone who has authority over the field instructor. Such situations are complicated by the political climate in the agency as well as by the experience or maturity of the student. It is important that the student feel it is safe to bring up her or his concern with the field instructor, the school faculty-field liaison, or both, so that a response that is as informed as possible of all variables can be developed. In some instances, it may be necessary for the student to be reassigned to another setting, but that is not always necessary, possible, or advisable.

It is apparent that a sexual relationship of any kind is proscribed behaviour between student and client and must not occur within the context of a professional relationship. The same is true of the field instructor and student relationship. Both clients and students are in hierarchical positions in which they are vulnerable. Professional ethics in regard to such relationships have been clearly stated, but the number of violations of professional boundaries with both clients and students attest to the complex nature of this issue.

As we have explained, a fiduciary responsibility obtains in regard to a client and a social worker, whether the worker is the student or the field instructor. A similar relationship can be said to exist between the student and the field instructor or supervisor. 'A supervisor has a fiduciary responsibility to the student, defined as a broad obligation to act in a client's "best interests" and refrain from exploitation and harm. Although students are not generally regarded as clients, there is increasing legal awareness that fiduciary accountability can apply to any relationship that necessitates a blind trust of a professional's special knowledge or skills' (Bonosky 1995, 81).

Schools should develop policy in regard to sexual harassment through discussion among students, faculty, and field instructors so that students will feel able to consult faculty if a situation arises that they feel unable to control. Sexual attraction in a work situation, either between student and client, student and field instructor, or other persons employed in the agency may seem to be mutual, but power and authority and the primary purpose of the work situation make such liaisons dangerous for all parties while these parties are within professional relationships.

8

Evaluation and Ending

Social work educational programs have a responsibility to the profession and the people it serves to ensure that graduates can perform competently and in an ethical manner (Hughes and Heycox 1996). Professional associations and licensing bodies evaluate social workers and certify them as qualified practitioners, usually after some period of postgraduate practice. Therefore schools of social work play a gatekeeping role since students who graduate from an academic program are expected to have demonstrated at least a beginning level of professional knowledge and competence. There is agreement that the ability to perform successfully in academic courses is not an indicator of the student's performance ability in practice. In fact, the only valid evaluation of practice competence is performance evaluation in carrying out the professional social work role. Hence, schools are responsible for ensuring that faculty-field liaisons and field instructors conduct reliable and valid evaluation.

Student evaluation is the determination of the extent to which a student has achieved the objectives of a particular learning activity. Evaluation of learning in field practice identifies and describes the student's current level of knowledge and skill in relation to a desired standard, highlights the progress and difficulties experienced in arriving at that point, and specifies areas for future development (Wilson 1981). Two types of evaluation may occur: ongoing formative evaluations throughout the practicum; and summative evaluations conducted at specific points in time, such as mid-term and at the conclusion of the practicum.

Issues in Evaluation

Stress Factors

Evaluation produces stress for both student and field instructor. In a study of field instructors, Gitterman and Gitterman (1979) found 87 per cent of those surveyed experienced stress in evaluation related to defining criteria, writing the formal document, assessing student practice, and engaging the student in the evaluation process. Kadushin (1985) studied social work supervisors and found that supervisors disliked evaluation, as it reminded them of the status differential between themselves and their workers and highlighted the power inherent in their role. These supervisors further perceived the evaluation of the worker's performance as an indirect evaluation of the supervisor's effectiveness and helpfulness. There was also concern that a negative evaluation would evoke anger and would upset the balance that had been established in the worker and supervisor relationship. Field instructors, too, may experience student evaluation as a reflection of their teaching competence. Instructors question whether they chose enough appropriate assignments for student learning to take place, whether they spent sufficient time with the student, and whether they provided enough support or challenge. Field instructors question their own standards in regard to expectations, and most struggle with the scarcity of objective criteria that can be used to evaluate social work student performance. When field instructors must give negative feedback, they have concerns about whether the school will support them if the student launches a grievance or appeal.

Evaluation can produce tension between two aspects of the field instructor's role, that of expert authority and that of facilitator of adult learning. As the expert authority, it is incumbent on the field instructor to provide the student with her or his best judgment about the degree of progress the student has made, the areas of difficulty, and the possible obstacles to progress. As the facilitator of adult learning, the field instructor is attuned to the impact of negative and challenging feedback on the student's self-identity and self-confidence. While sensitive field instructors will find the best possible way to frame their messages, there still remains the awareness that the very process of evaluation may create more than optimal anxiety and threaten the student's self-esteem, all of which can interfere with learning. The challenge in giving feedback remains how to effectively balance support and encouragement, on the one hand, and the clear communication of areas needing improvement, on the other hand.

Students experience anxiety and insecurity as a normal and inevitable part of evaluation. Ongoing positive and negative feedback throughout the term will diminish apprehension about the final evaluation. Nevertheless, students tend to feel vulnerable in relation to the instructor's power in evaluation and grading. Students' reactions to identification of their strengths and weaknesses will vary according to their comfort level with receiving critical feedback and their expectations of themselves as learners and performers. For example, students accustomed to receiving positive feedback may react to the identification of problem areas with disappointment or anger. However, students who have found it difficult to learn social work skills may be pleased with the balance of strengths and weaknesses described in the evaluation.

The current climate of agency restructuring and downsizing has resulted in fewer employment possibilities for graduates than in earlier eras when expansion of social and health services created numerous jobs. As a result, competition among students for employment has increased their pressure for high grades in academic courses and for strong positive evaluations in the field practicum. In the face of this pressure, evaluation may be influenced toward compromise or capitulation. To respond to this tension, schools need to help field instructors develop clear criteria for measuring achievement of educational objectives and to apply these criteria to examples of actual student performance so that evaluation is weighted toward objectivity with a minimum inclusion of subjective content.

Evaluation as Ongoing Feedback

Since both field instructor and student experience evaluation as stressful, it is critical that ongoing discussion about the process and outcome of learning in the field practicum be a regular feature of field instruction. While it is customary for field instructors to give ongoing feedback about specific aspects of students' practice, providing feedback in an organized, systematic, and structured manner keeps the focus on incremental learning. Through numerous evaluations, the field instructor helps the student move through retrieval of practice behaviours, reflection about those events, linkage to social work knowledge, and the formulation of new professional responses. The framework presented in the ITP Loop Model articulates the key content areas in a social work practicum: psycho-social, interactive, contextual, and organizational. Knowledge and practice competence in these areas constitute the outcome objectives for evaluation.

The process of contracting can be seen as the first focused and structured feedback and evaluation activity. Re-contracting represents the continuous mutual process of clarification of objectives and outcomes of learning, feedback to the student regarding progress in meeting those objectives, and feedback to the field instructor regarding the effectiveness of the methods used for field instruction. As discussed in chapter 4 on the instructional relationship, one obstacle to achieving this degree of openness is the student's feelings of vulnerability in relation to the power of the field instructor. Students are often reluctant and fearful to express concerns or to give field instructors feedback about the effect of their teaching. In chapter 4 we have advocated that field instructors take the lead in developing and maintaining a positive working relationship by framing it as a partnership with mutual commitment to and responsibility for making it work. Furthermore, an ecological approach to social work practice incorporates interventions directed at the service organization and other significant institutions and programs affecting the lives of individuals and families. To bring about change at these levels, students need competence in advocacy approaches. Advocacy and influence processes depend on the practitioner's ability to articulate issues and present critical feedback effectively, most often to those in positions of authority who may have significant power in relation to the social worker. Learning to give and use feedback in the field instructor–student relationship can prepare the student for these important practice activities. Field instructors must take initiative and responsibility to help students learn these behaviours by encouraging feedback and demonstrating to students that their input will be heard and discussed. This reinforces the learning and teaching enterprise as a mutual endeavour.

Wilson (1981) points out that through continuous sharing of impressions, critiques, and suggestions for improvement, the student becomes aware of areas where growth is needed and can use the suggested techniques to develop new practice skill. If performance in practice is not evaluated in an ongoing and continuous fashion, both the field instructor and the student may miss the opportunity for reflection, linkage, and understanding of practice competence. Sharing evaluative feedback only at the end deprives the student of the opportunity to work on weak areas and move toward meeting objectives. In the absence of ongoing feedback, it is not unusual for the student to search for subtle cues about the field instructor's judgments of the student's work. Non-verbal behaviour, such as a frown, an irritated manner, or an off-hand comment, can be interpreted, often incorrectly, by an anxious student as a negative appraisal of the student's performance.

It is useful to structure formal review periods to examine the student's progress and practice in relation to the objectives. Monthly or mid-term reviews provide the opportunity to clarify issues and develop more focus for the next stage of learning; they also enable the student to act on the feedback and incorporate it in current practice. Though final evaluations should contain no surprises, the process of a broadened final examination of the student's work may reveal new perceptions of the student's approach to practice. Patterns may appear which are not good practice. Students must be made aware of these patterns so that they can consciously attempt to modify their behaviour in their future work. It is questionable whether field instructors should introduce these perceptions in the final evaluation if they have appeared only at the end of the practicum. Field instructors may wish to consult the faculty-field liaison about this issue, to determine whether the university has guidelines or advice about how to handle such a situation.

Objective Criteria and Expectations Regarding Competence

Evaluation must be based on clear criteria which can be used by the student and field instructor as the framework for the practicum. Reviewing empirical studies on evaluation of student learning in field education, Alperin (1996) notes that some consensus exists about what are important learning objectives for field education and that skill development constitutes the major curriculum priority. However, a national survey in the United States about methods and practices to evaluate student performance in field education found that a large number of field education directors and coordinators identified the need for more objective measures of performance as a top priority (Kilpatrick, Turner, and Holland 1994). While schools of social work do define objectives for practicum learning that reflect knowledge, value, and skill, this survey identifies the urgent need for more work to identify specific criteria.

Evaluation is aided when objectives are clear and specific, and are expressed in behavioural terms that define what it is that a student is expected to do in order to meet a particular objective. As discussed in chapter 3 on contracting, general objectives for the school's practicum provide a framework. These objectives are defined at a level of generality that allows them to be applied to field practica in a range of practice settings, such as child protection, heath and mental health, or school social services; at various levels of intervention, such as direct practice, community practice, or administration, planning, and policy development; and with specialized intervention models, such as cognitive behavioural therapy, structural family therapy, solution focused approaches, and others. The field instructor has the task of adapting the school's general objectives so that they reflect the knowledge and practice approaches used in that field setting. This includes formulating these general principles as specific learning objectives for the individual student. It is important that the field instructor discuss these objectives with the student at the beginning of the practicum and provide an opportunity to clarify concepts and meanings. Through this process, the student will become familiar with learning expectations and can thereby participate more actively in his or her own learning. In particular, by referring to these objectives throughout the field instruction process, the student is enabled to make changes in his or her professional practice.

Objectives also provide the conceptual framework for students to link practice behaviours to a social work knowledge base. The phase of linkage in the ITP Loop Model includes articulating the connections between concepts and the associated professional responses. For example, a field instructor might develop learning objectives for interviewing behaviour such as the following: acknowledge and clarify verbal messages accurately; reflect affective information appropriately; clarify underlying or implied subjective meanings of the client's communication. These behaviours are associated with theoretical formulations and empirical findings about factors which lead to effective helping relationships and which facilitate self-disclosure on the part of the client. By drawing the connections between these professional behaviours, expressed as learning objectives, and the social work concepts they represent, the field instructor reinforces the integration of theory and practice.

At the beginning of the practicum, students vary in their skill and knowledge levels. Therefore, it is likely that they will vary in the extent to which they achieve objectives at the end. Change and individual development are central values in social work practice and influence field instruction. If students who began with little or no experience, knowledge, and skill begin to make positive changes, field instructors value that gain. However, development alone is not sufficient. A student must reach a minimum level of competence in order to achieve a passing grade. This often presents a dilemma for a field instructor when a student has not quite met expectations. Since movement has been demonstrated there is a desire to reward that gain. Field instructors may hope that if the student continues his or her education, through a second-level practicum, an advanced degree program, or supervised employment, further growth will occur, and a satisfactory performance level will ultimately be reached. However, passing the student ahead, based on this hope, may leave the student struggling in each successive experience to 'catch up' to ever-increasing expectations. Field instructors may find they need instead to recommend an extension or repeat of the practicum, so that the student who has begun to develop necessary knowledge and skill is given additional time to meet the standards of the current level of education.

Maintaining Objectivity

The position of the field instructor as teacher and socializing agent, and the intensity of teaching in a dyad, may compromise the field instructor's objectivity in evaluation. A period of critical reflection may help field instructors prepare for the evaluation. As a first step, field instructors may wish to use the ITP Loop Model and retrieve their own experience as students during mid-term and final evaluations. Through reflection about the events and feelings recalled, they may identify effective as well as problematic approaches. It may also be useful for instructors to think about evaluation and appraisals in general, and about writing the current evaluation by committing their thoughts regarding the student to paper. Wilson (1981) suggests reviewing the current practicum experience, recalling the beginning, highlights along the way, what is important for the next field instructor or job supervisor to know about the student, and feelings the field instructor has about the student that have never been shared. The purpose of this critical reflection phase is to identify positive or negative biases that may act as obstacles to objectivity and to provide some guidelines about how the field instructor wishes to conduct the evaluation.

While reviewing the student's practice, it is important to differentiate between knowledge and skill and the student's personality. Assessments of the student's personality are not an appropriate part of educational evaluations. However, when the student's personality interferes with effective practice performance, this should be addressed by using a practice example to demonstrate the issues of concern. For example, it is not appropriate to label a student as aggressive and hostile. Rather, persistent inability to establish cooperative relationships with colleagues, angry outbursts, or attacking others' intentions are concrete demonstrations of how a personality difficulty interferes in practice.

Objectivity is enhanced when learning objectives are specific. Brennan (1982) notes that the more general the guideline for evaluation, the more opportunity for subjectivity. Time spent in contracting and re-contracting so that outcome behaviours are clearly understood facilitates student learning and final evaluation.

Objectivity is enhanced by using accurate information to form a judgment. In chapter 5 a variety of methods for teaching and learning are presented as well as a consideration of the strengths and weaknesses of methods that provide direct access to practice data and methods that provide indirect access to practice data. Direct data is likely to be more accurate than verbal or written reports for assessing students' knowledge of and skill in interactional processes, although written reports are useful in evaluating conceptual and writing skills. Since it is not unusual for student performance to be inconsistent, according to the nature of the practice task and as a result of various idiosyncratic factors, multiple observations of the student's work may provide a more adequate data base on which to make accurate judgments. Multiple reviewers can also add to objectivity in evaluation. Some field instructors contract for other social workers in the setting to participate in aspects of the evaluation. In some schools, the faculty-field liaison or other field instructors will also review samples of the student's practice.

Kadushin (1985) describes some classic pitfalls supervisors experience in evaluating workers which are similar to those facing field instructors when they evaluate students. He refers to the 'error of central tendency,' which occurs when supervisors are in doubt. They tend to rate specific aspects of the worker's performance as fair or average. Another common error is referred to as the 'halo effect.' In this instance, the supervisor tends to make a global judgment about the worker's performance and then to perceive all aspects of her or his performance as consistent with that general judgment. Another common error occurs when the supervisor tends to evaluate the worker using him- or herself as a standard. The 'leniency bias' involves a reluctance to evaluate works of students negatively or critically. Finally there is the 'recency error,' by which a recent particular incident over-influences the evaluation. A particularly dramatic incident might also have too great an effect on evaluation. Others have noted that evaluation judgments can be confused when effort and motivation are equated with competence (AASWWE 1991).

Links to the Learning Contract

Contracting involves setting individualized objectives for a particular student. Very often, despite considerable energy having been devoted to constructing the learning contract, it is not used in evaluation. A structured educational approach to field instruction, as presented in this book, builds on and uses the contract as a plan to guide the educational activities and as a standard against which to evaluate progress. A baseline assessment of the student's level of knowledge and skill is formulated at the beginning of the practicum. By comparing this assessment to the practicum objectives, a determination of what needs to be learned is made. The contract also states what learning activities, resources, and techniques will be used so that the learning objectives can be achieved. In this way, the contract provides the framework to evaluate the effectiveness of the setting, the staff, and the field instructor in their educational roles. Finally, the method of evaluation is also clearly indicated in the contract at the beginning, including which persons other than the field instructor will be consulted and what concrete data and evidence will be used, such as tapes or reports.

The Final or Summative Evaluation

Preparing for and Managing the Evaluation Conference

The final evaluation conference takes on great significance for students since it summarizes their learning and progress, documents areas for future development, and can serve as an important source of information for employment references. Even when regular feedback has been a feature of the practicum, the formality of a final and written evaluation marks this conference as an important event. The quality of the evaluation is enhanced through advanced planning. Both the student and the field instructor will find it useful to prepare for the conference by clarifying all aspects of format in advance, such as the length of the conference and the procedures they will follow, so that each is clear about expectations and responsibilities. Agreement can be reached about who will prepare and review which materials.

   As stated above, the learning contract is the logical place to begin, as it represents the initial assessment of the student, the learning goals agreed upon, and the educational plan. Additional agreements arrived at through re-contracting further clarify the range of outcome objectives. It is likely that the student and the field instructor will be aware of the objectives and forms for evaluation provided by the educational program. It is helpful for both to review them in advance of the conference to become familiar with the terms used. If a rating scale is to be used, the definitions and guidelines for rating should be clear and understood by both the student and the field instructor. The faculty-field liaison can be called upon for information and clarification. Data on which to base judgments should be accessible to both participants. If other personnel from the setting or the school are to be involved in evaluation, both the student and the field instructor should choose a sample of materials to be reviewed. It is useful for both the student and the field instructor to prepare by reviewing, in advance of the conference, the objectives and the practice material, perhaps making rough notes and highlighting conclusions so that the conference can be used for discussion.

As the student is likely to be anxious about the final evaluation, Kadushin (1985) suggests opening the conference by presenting a general evaluation of performance in simple, clear, and unambiguous terms. Discussion is then held regarding the achievement of objectives, and specific practice illustrations are used by the field instructor and the student to support the judgments. Gitterman and Gitterman (1979) suggest the field instructor focus the discussion, emphasizing the details of the student's practice and learning. Themes will be identified, and areas of mastery highlighted, as well as problem areas and areas for further growth. The field instructor offers explicit feedback and helps the student to actively participate, to offer self-appraisal, and to raise any differences with the field instructor's perceptions and assessment.

The ITP Loop Model implies that students' work is influenced by contextual issues, such as organizational pressures and by the appropriateness and aptness of practice assignments. The evaluation should include sufficient attention to these often overlooked issues. For example, a student practicum in a policy development unit constrained by current political pressures did not provide the opportunity for the student to develop committee leadership skills. The field instructor was aware of these limitations and provided this explanation in the evaluation. Since student evaluation is also based on the nature of the practice assignments, it is important to highlight the constraints affecting the student's learning. For example, if many of the clients assigned were unable to converse in depth because of physical injury which impairs speech or lack of facility in a common language, then the student will have limited opportunity to develop in-depth counselling skills, if that was a goal.

Field instructors are generally sensitive to students' reactions and attempt to openly discuss issues and concerns. If the student and field instructor have been able to develop effective communication throughout the learning process, they will be able to deal with negative and positive reactions in evaluation. If the student and field instructor have experienced difficulty achieving open and direct feedback or in managing disagreements and conflict, then these problems are likely to appear again in the evaluation conference.

Forms of Evaluation and the Written Evaluation

A variety of formats are used for written evaluations in social work field practica and are described in the literature: the narrative form, a rating scale, or both (Wilson 1981). The narrative form may be more or less structured with designated headings to provide organization and focus for the evaluation. This format usually covers changes in performance over time, emphasizes strengths and weaknesses, highlights significant practice and learning issues that have arisen, and designates areas that need further work. Time is required by this format to review and analyse the student's practice and learning, and to describe clearly the student's knowledge, skill, and qualities. In addition to being time-consuming, its disadvantages are that it may tend to be subjective, and may produce a generalized and vague report.

Numerical rating scales consist of various knowledge and skill competencies, attitudes, and characteristics that are rated numerically to identify the level of the student's performance. For this approach to be useful in individualizing the student's evaluation, specificity is needed in two areas: the definition of the competencies and the definition of the points along the rating scale. Competencies may be defined in a general way (e.g., 'is able to establish purposeful relationships with clients'); or they may be defined more specifically, with the expected behaviours associated with each competency. For example, the general competency 'is able to establish purposeful relationships with clients' is further defined as 'communicates the worker role clearly; elicits the client's expectations about the help that can be received from the worker and the agency; develops a plan with the client, including the tasks for the client and the worker; is aware of and helps the client express feelings about the helping process,' and so on. This latter approach provides clarity and specificity but can also generate an extremely long list of behaviours, thereby making the evaluation process an onerous one. Rating scales also differ in clarity and specificity, depending on the definition of points along the scale. For example, in some instances the scale ranges from 1 (unsatisfactory) through to 5 (outstanding). The definitions of the points along the scale are left up to each individual evaluator, and thus a subjective rating results. A higher degree of inter-rater reliability is obtained when rating scales have behavioural indicators for each point along the scale. For example, using a three-point rating scale, for the competency 'ability to demonstrate support to clients' a rating of 1 is defined as 'generally does not convey interest, concern, or empathy; is silent when the client expresses difficult personal experiences'; a rating of 2 is defined as 'provides periodic support through positive comments; does not regularly recognize and respond to client distress'; and a rating of 3 is defined as 'frequently communicates genuine concern for client's situation and expressed feelings.' Examples of each of the rated skills help the field instructor and student arrive at better understandings of these ratings. The dilemma in choosing evaluation approaches centres around maximizing objectivity while at the same time developing a method that is efficient. As a general principle, the more general the competency definition is, the more likely it is that subjective factors will intrude into the evaluation. However, greater specificity in definitions of competency generates an enormous amount of material and results in a cumbersome evaluation tool and process.

A creative innovation for use in evaluation rating scales is the Practice Development Indicator (PDI) originated by McGoey-Smith (1995). This instrument incorporates the phases in the ITP Loop Model by evaluating practice using seven levels 'which progressively build one analytic learning strength upon another to reflect the thinking, knowing, doing and being of competent practice' (McGoey-Smith 1995, 250). The first level of practice evaluation is the student's ability to discern the practice knowledge needed to perform and corresponds to the phase of retrieval in the ITP Loop Model; the second level of practice evaluation is the student's ability to reflect on practice knowledge needed to perform and corresponds to the phase of reflection; and the third level of practice evaluation is the student's ability to formulate a knowledge-based plan for practice and corresponds to the phase of linkage. The next four levels of practice evaluation correspond to the phase of professional response in the ITP Loop Model and reflect the student's ability to progress along a continuum from reliance on the field instructor's support to autonomous practice competence. These four levels are the student's ability to initiate practice with support; perform adequately with support; perform competently with minimal support; and perform competently.

For each level of the Practice Development Indicator, an operational definition of the student's learning behaviours is provided. The student's learning behaviours are complementary to the teaching behaviours of the field instructor, discussed in chapter 5 on using the ITP Loop Model to guide the learning process. The first level concerns practice knowledge needed to perform, the phase of retrieval. The student is expected to recall the content of the practice experience as both a participant and observer, that is, describe what happened, the setting, and circumstances using a person-in-environment perspective. The second level reflects on practice knowledge needed to perform, the phase of reflection. The student is expected to reflect on the process and outcome of the retrieved practice; identify the feelings and reactions of all the participants, including the student's own feelings; and consider in what ways the practice was effective or ineffective. The third level formulates a knowledge-based plan for practice, the phase of linkage. The student is expected to explore and explain the process and outcomes of the practice experience in relation to theory; think about why the participants might have felt and reacted in the ways they did in relation to the chosen concepts and theory; and create a plan of action. For the remaining levels, the phase of professional response, four categories of increasing competence and autonomy in practice are described. The fourth level initiates practice with support. The student is expected to make an informed response to the practice situation and recognize the need to retrieve, reflect, and link practice experience. In the fifth level, the student is expected to perform adequately with support and is expected to provide evidence of performance through the methods for direct and indirect access to practice data; to demonstrate the ability to process and practise the first four items on the scale with support from the field instructor; and to recognize and seek constructive feedback. In the sixth level, the student is expected to perform competently with minimal support. The student is expected to provide evidence of performance; to demonstrate the ability to effectively process and practise the first four items on the scale with minimal support from the field instructor; to seek constructive feedback; and to contribute to the agenda for field instruction. In the seventh, and final level, the student is expected to perform competently. The student is expected to provide evidence of performance; to demonstrate the ability to effectively process and practise the first four items on the scale with independence from the field instructor; to seek consultation as needed; and to set most of the agenda for field instruction. McGoey-Smith's (1995) creativity in adapting the ITP Loop Model for use in evaluation further extends the use of the concept to this important aspect of the field instruction process.

Each school of social work has its own procedures for writing and submitting the final evaluation. In most schools, the field instructor takes responsibility for assembling the documentation and writing the final evaluation, following the school's guidelines. Field instructors generally recommend a grade, and the faculty-field liaison gives the grade based on the written evaluation. In some schools, the practicum is a credit/no credit course; in others there are numerical or letter grades.

Useful guidelines for the written document are provided by Wilson (1981). In narrative reports, a clear, factual, and specific description of the student's performance, in which significant comments are substantiated with brief practice examples, is most useful. The written evaluation aims to clearly identify areas of mastery, problem areas, and areas for further growth. If a rating scale is used, it is important that there be congruence between the narrative section and the final rating.

The written evaluation is best prepared as soon after the evaluation conference as possible. It is necessary for the student to have the opportunity to express any feelings about the written evaluation or to request changes in specific parts. If the field instructor does not agree, some schools suggest that the student attach her or his own written statement to the evaluation. If there is a concern, the faculty-field liaison should be consulted for specific assistance and clarification of procedures. Schools have grievance and appeal mechanisms, which the student may want to use to settle a major disagreement regarding evaluation. The student is expected to read the evaluation and sign it, thereby indicating that it has been read. If the student reads the evaluation and refuses to sign it, this should be documented.

The original written evaluation is the property of the student and is placed on the student's record. In most schools, the student and field instructor keep a copy. The evaluation is not subject to disclosure without the student's consent. Schools have policies regarding use of the evaluation for reference purposes. It is useful to be familiar with these policies.

The Marginal or Failing Student

The possession of a social work degree credits a graduate as a competent social work practitioner. Though most jurisdictions have enacted legislation regulating social work practice, for the most part, the schools of social work are the gatekeepers controlling entry into the profession. Most students admitted into a university program possess the necessary scholastic aptitude to successfully complete academic courses. This does not necessarily mean that they are suited for professional practice. Therefore the field instructor may be the first person to identify students who are not able to learn competent social work practice.

Social workers are trained to help, and believe in the potential for individuals to grow, develop, and change. When confronted with problematic behaviours on the part of a student, this orientation is likely to prevail. Field instructors tend to view problematic behaviour with equanimity, almost expecting lack of competence as typical of beginning students. They will encourage identification of issues and expect students to progress and regress, to struggle and accept, as they engage in learning in the field setting. However, when students are consistently unable to demonstrate enough learning through changed behaviour, then the field instructor must consider recommending a failing grade.

Many have noted that field instructors find it difficult to fail students (Hartman and Wills 1991; Rosenblum and Raphael 1987; Wilson 1981). Regardless of their level of experience, some field instructors tend to doubt themselves, questioning whether a student's failure is attributable to them. They may feel they were unable to teach the student as a result of differences in style, personality clashes, the nature of the practice assignments, the amount of time they gave, or the approaches they used. They may also question their own standards and wonder if their expectations are too high and whether another instructor would pass the student. They wonder if the faculty-field liaison will support them or see them as unrealistic in their expectations.

Some field instructors may have had equivocal experiences with their own field instructors, with supervisors, or with the particular school. This may lead to over-identification with the student and a wish to protect or rescue the student, and ultimately to a collusion to keep the faculty-field liaison uninformed about a failing performance.

Students will react to failing evaluations in a variety of ways. While some will agree with the evaluation, others may be quite upset and verbally hostile, forcing field instructors to deal with considerable anger

and conflict. Failing grades are often challenged by students in grievance or appeal hearings. Most often the student's case rests on a critique
of the field instruction. It takes strength, conviction, and commitment to
standards for a field instructor to take a stand regarding failure.

Importance of Documentation

Firm evidence must be available to substantiate the decision that a student does not meet the objectives of the program. Schools of social work
provide objectives for the practicum, which the field instructor and
student concretize and individualize through the mechanism of contracting. As discussed in chapter 3, the learning contract specifies the
learning resources to be used to help the student meet those objectives,
as well as the evidence to be examined to evaluate whether the learning
objectives have been attained. Discussions and decisions about passing
or failing take place within this framework.

When a field instructor has concerns about a student's performance,
these concerns should be documented and shared with the student as
soon as possible. In general, this will occur before or at the mid-way
point. Evidence to substantiate the concern must be available, such as
taped interviews, process records, reports, memos, and notes from field
instruction sessions which summarize issues discussed and the
student's responses. The faculty-field liaison should be consulted.
Schools have procedures which must be followed when there is a concern about a marginal or potentially failing student. These procedures
are designed to ensure fairness, to support the educational activities of
the student and the field instructor, and to provide every opportunity
for student learning to be successful. The faculty-field liaison can clarify
the expectations of student performance and the degree to which the
particular student is at risk of failing. Some schools have provided
opportunities for field instructors to meet together to assess the performance of students in difficulty. The faculty-field liaison can also help
the student and field instructor evaluate their field instruction sessions
and identify areas causing difficulty, such as different learning-style
needs, frequency of sessions, and whether feedback has been specific,
frequent, and understood.

The early identification of learning issues can help the field instructor
and student set concrete, clear, behavioural objectives for the student at
risk. Re-contracting may take place at this point, specifying the time
frame for the achievement of certain behaviours and the evidence to be

used to assess progress. This provides the student with the opportunity to demonstrate change. It is useful for the field instructor to keep notes of the field instruction sessions, highlighting the issues discussed and responses to feedback. Field instructors must enlist the active involvement of the faculty-field liaison to monitor the progress of a student in danger of failing. These reviews should be documented so that all partners are fully aware of concerns and plans. Though this structure may help the student to achieve a passing grade, this is not always possible. For some students, there is no way to prevent failure. The steps suggested above, however, should prepare the student for a negative evaluation and a recommendation to the school of a failing grade.

Students who are at risk of failing are likely to experience considerable anxiety about their performance. They may become so overwhelmed by their fear of failure that they become unable to learn. This is understandable and more than ever challenges the field instructor to try to maintain a professional relationship which provides both realistic support and encouragement. While it is helpful to discuss the student's feelings, a focus on the process of learning and the changed behaviour expected may help the student partialize the task and reduce anxiety.

Indicators

INDICATORS OF PROBLEMS IN LEARNING PRACTICE

Students fail the practicum because of the presence of dysfunctional behaviours which are inappropriate for the professional practice of social work, or because they have not been able to develop competence in professional practice, or any significant combination of the above. It is not to be assumed that marginal students can be allowed to pass because they will do no harm. Incompetent service given to a client in need is as harmful as a worker who is actively destructive. The presence of the indicators discussed here should alert field instructors to the existence of potential problems. These should be raised with the student, and if a satisfactory resolution cannot be found, field instructors should request the involvement of the faculty-field liaison.

A number of dysfunctional behaviours have been associated with unsatisfactory performance (Hartman and Wills 1991; Wilson 1981). The student who displays behaviours which are destructive to others, and which are clearly unprofessional, must be removed from the practicum setting. Examples would be physically injuring someone, appearing at the agency intoxicated or under the influence of drugs, having frequent temper outbursts, sexually seducing clients, stealing, or threatening to harm clients, staff, other students, or the field instructor. Such behaviour may indicate mental illness or extreme personality disorders. When confronted with this behaviour, the student may deny that it has occurred and blame the field instructor for causing the student difficulty with the school. In these situations, the field instructor and faculty-field liaison must use their professional judgment and terminate the practicum if clients and others are at risk. Appropriate educational review procedures should be used in such extreme situations.

Some dysfunctional behaviours may be sporadic, leaving the field instructor with concerns about the student's capacity to learn and perform appropriately. Examples are inconsistent attendance or lateness, or periodic lying about work done. While not as obviously indicative of personality problems as the earlier examples, the field instructor will be left feeling uncertain about the student's honesty, trustworthiness, and readiness to learn. In such situations, concerns should be documented and brought to the student's attention. The faculty-field liaison should be involved to help clarify appropriate expected behaviours and to determine whether the student is to continue in the setting.

For most students who fail the practicum, difficulties in learning will be expressed in practice with clients or project assignments. Evidence, on audio- or videotape, in written records or reports, or in memos describing the behaviour, must be available which demonstrates persistent problem areas. In general, students who fail have difficulty using social work theory in respect to purpose, role, function, and process to guide their behaviour in the practice assignments. They cannot develop purposeful collaborative relationships with clients or community groups that enable participation in assessment, planning, intervention, and evaluation of service. Some of the specific problems in this regard are discussed below. Most students manifest many of these behaviours early in the practicum. Field instructors should become concerned if these behaviours persist after they have directed the student's attention to their repeated use.

Some students have strong beliefs or values which they impose on their clients with conviction. They cannot accept the social work value of a non-judgmental, respectful attitude. They tend to be tenacious and dogmatic in their belief systems and attempt to convince the client to see things their way. They may be judgmental and critical of the client, harsh, angry, bullying, or subtly depreciating and condescending.

All students need to develop competence in the selective and differential use of non-directive and directive techniques. A student who is overly authoritarian, directive, and task-oriented may have difficulty forming working relationships with clients based on mutuality. Such a student may behave in a cold, aloof, businesslike manner and prescribe behaviour inappropriate to the client's needs. The student may lecture clients and try to convince them to adopt the student's plan of action. At the other extreme is the student who is unable to provide appropriate leadership and direction to the social work purpose. This student may be shy, ill at ease, overwhelmed by being a professional. These feelings may be seen in a lack of appropriate eye contact, uncomfortable and distancing body posture, a frightened or quiet voice tone, a tendency to be silent too often, an avoidance of regular meetings with the client, as well as in the absence of behaviours which focus the practice task.

A number of problematic behaviours arise when students overpersonalize the events in their interactions with clients or community groups. Such students are extremely preoccupied with themselves, their feelings, and their needs to feel comfortable. Mishne (1983) notes that many social work students are struggling with their own self-esteem and their needs to be liked and successful. The complexities and uncertainties of social work theory and practice create a conflict with these needs. This conflict will be seen in inappropriate reactions while delivering service, such as shock or disbelief regarding clients' lifestyles and choices, attempts to get clients to like the student, anger at clients, groups, or committees who do not comply with the student's wishes, inability to listen to client messages as the student attempts to do something for the client to reduce his or her own sense of helplessness, and refusal to work with client groups who make the student feel uncomfortable or upset.

Some students equate professional behaviour with a cold, aloof stance. They feel they must reject this stereotype by adopting a natural, spontaneous, and friendly relationship with the client. Self-disclosure is used inappropriately to meet the student's need for comfort, and the client is burdened with listening to the student's problems and experiences.

Some students have difficulty dealing with conflict and, uncertain about how to handle it, react by keeping their practice at a superficial level. They may engage in social conversations, not respond to negatives or conflict when these are brought up by the client, change the subject to a less conflictual one, and avoid clarifying underlying negative dynamics. Such students may actually avoid face-to-face contacts and report few meetings with clients or community groups.

INDICATORS OF PROBLEMS IN ORGANIZATIONAL BEHAVIOUR AND PROFESSIONAL COLLABORATION

All settings have policies, regulations, and practices which apply to students as well as staff. Though students should appropriately question organizational policy and practice, the failing student may unilaterally contravene agency policy, without first raising concerns with the field instructor. Such students may fail to meet agency recording requirements, disregard procedures about storage of clients' files, and may frequently arrive late at the agency.

Professional staff from other disciplines may find the failing student unwilling or unable to collaborate on behalf of the client. The student may act mistrustfully, withholding important information or being destructively critical of other staff to the client. The student may behave inappropriately with other professional staff, treating them in a depreciating manner, giving orders, or embarrassing them in team meetings.

Students need to learn to give feedback to others that will be accepted and used. It is expected that in learning these skills students may be too passive or too aggressive. It is also expected that students use field instruction to retrieve these situations, and reflect on the impact of their behaviours on others. Failing students are unable to appreciate the effect of their actions and continue to repeat them despite considerable discussion in field instruction.

INDICATORS OF PROBLEMS IN THE USE OF FIELD INSTRUCTION

Students who demonstrate problematic behaviours in practice and in collaboration with other staff generally have difficulty in using field instruction productively. Failing students often do not understand what social work theory and practice actually mean. These students may have learned theory presented in academic courses; however, they cannot use these concepts in their practice. They rely heavily on the field instructor to tell them what to do, and they do not necessarily learn from concrete experience. Each situation feels new, and they ask repeatedly for the same direction and structure. Incremental gains in learning are not seen. Confusion and mistakes appear again and again.

Some students, for a variety of personal reasons related to trust and risk, cannot be open with their field instructor. They avoid exposing their behaviour in practice situations; they do not ask for help with issues they are uncertain about; and they do not admit to mistakes or problems. These students are usually very uncomfortable in any discussion about their own reactions and may respond with silence or cautious minimal comments. As they cannot engage in discussion about what is happening to them, they are greatly hindered in developing self-awareness and tend to act without adequate reflection.

Some students attempt to use field instruction for personal therapy, bringing their problems to instruction and seeking help. Field instructors may notice that these students are overly concerned about their own reactions in a professional exchange and tend to omit any reflection of how others may be feeling.

Some students overly personalize feedback and experience it as a validation of or an attack on their self-esteem and personal worth. They may focus considerable attention on trying to please the instructor, always agreeing with the feedback, but not changing in any significant way. Alternatively, a tenuous sense of self-worth may permit only negative feedback to be heard, while positive comments are screened. Students can become so concerned with the quality of their performance, that they have difficulty connecting to the needs of the practice situation. They can become immobilized and unable to learn.

Students who experience negative feedback as a blow to their self-esteem may not hear what the field instructor is saying. Their energy may go into defending their actions by giving explanations and blaming others or the situation for their lack of competence. Such students, at some point, may project blame for their poor performance onto the field instructor. Some recriminations expressed by students include personality incompatibility, insufficient support and direction, allegations of bias or racial discrimination, and unrealistic expectations of the student. These negative perceptions may be indicative of a failing student or may be an accurate reflection of the interaction between student and field instructor. When serious disagreements cannot be resolved, the faculty-field liaison should be alerted as soon as possible. The school has a responsibility to assist both student and field instructor to mediate and seek a fair solution to problems.

Appeal of a Failing Grade

Most schools have formal grievance or appeal procedures for students to challenge academic decisions, including practicum grades. Before reaching the appeal stage, efforts are generally made to resolve disagreements through regular procedures, such as review meetings with the faculty-field liaison and the field coordinator. If these methods are unsuccessful, the student may, during a specific time period, present a written request for an appeal hearing. A designated person or committee, usually the chairperson or members of the appeal committee, decides whether there are sufficient grounds to hold a formal appeal. The appeal committee usually consists of faculty members and students. Since field-related issues are often heard before the school's appeal committee, it is critical that field instructors also comprise part of the membership of an appeal committee.

In preparation for the appeal, the student gathers support for his or her case, may contact witnesses to appear at the hearing, and may bring an advocate, such as another student, a faculty member, or a lawyer. The field instructor and faculty-field liaison should be aware of the issues that the student is challenging, so that they too can prepare their position and present evidence to support it. The field instructor and faculty-field liaison may present the case, or they may be assisted by the field coordinator, or the school may engage a lawyer.

The appeal committee hears the case and communicates its decision in writing to all participants within a set period of time. If the student is not satisfied with the outcome of the appeal, there may be a higher level of appeal within the university or the student may seek a hearing in a court of law.

The following are some recurring issues that have been raised at appeals of field grades.

1. Is there sufficient evidence to support a failing grade? Written process records, project reports, audio- or videotapes, and written documentation of observed student behaviours are necessary to provide examples of the lack of appropriate performance behaviours or the presence of harmful or inappropriate behaviours. Evaluation of these materials must be in relation to the objectives of the practicum. There is thus a need for clearly defined behavioural objectives against which judgments can be made about the student's learning and practice performance. Even in the case of bizarre or inappropriate student behaviour, it is advisable to document the incident at the time it occurs and to share this notation with the student. If other personnel were involved, they should be asked to document their observations, and these individuals may be called as witnesses.

2. Is there agreement that the student's performance warrants a failing grade? When a failing grade is considered, the field instructor and the faculty-field liaison are expected to review the student's work. In some schools, a 'second reader,' a faculty member or field instructor who does not know the student, is asked to review a selection of the student's work and provide an evaluation.

3. Were regular procedures followed in field instruction that conform to the school's expectations? Was the educational contract or agreement met? That is, did the field instructor carry out the activities and tasks in his or her role related to student teaching? Did the student have enough learning opportunities to master the required skills? Did the student have field instruction sessions as contracted? Was the procedure in field instruction fair? That is, was the student given feedback, was the student informed of problem behaviours, were the objectives for change specified, was the student given sufficient time to make changes? Was the student informed of the possibility of failure? Was the faculty-field liaison involved? Were the outcomes of meetings with the faculty-field liaison clearly conveyed to the student? It is very helpful for field instructors to have notes summarizing field instruction sessions, highlighting when the field instructor and the student met, what was discussed, and what issues for change were identified. In some schools, the faculty-field liaison is responsible for documenting minutes of meetings. These written materials may be used in an appeal as evidence to demonstrate that the student experienced fair and regular field instruction which attempted to assist the student in achieving practice competence.

Evaluation of the Field Instructor and the Setting

Discussion of the dynamics of teaching and learning as they relate to the particular student and field instructor is an important part of evaluation. The student's learning style and pace, the field instructor's educational approaches, and the interactions between the two are subject to evaluation. Students should be encouraged to evaluate the educational effectiveness of the field setting, the assignments carried, the activities attended, and the process of field instruction itself. As most students are fearful that a critical evaluation will negatively affect their grade, it is advisable that the evaluation of students' performance be submitted to the school prior to students' evaluation of their field instructors and field setting. In most instances, students' evaluation of the setting and the field instructor will be constructive and demonstrate the students' ability to give balanced feedback to those with the power to grade them. In some instances, students who have been dissatisfied with their field instructors or other aspects of their practicum, but have not chosen to raise the issue directly during the year, will take this opportunity to express their negative feelings. It is disheartening for field instructors to learn, after the fact, what the student was thinking, feeling, and experiencing and not have had the opportunity to attempt to change their interaction. Throughout this book, we have advocated for field instructors to take the lead in eliciting ongoing feedback and demonstrating to the student that it is safe to be critical. In most instances, this teaching approach, while it does not necessarily uncover all issues all the time, does increase the likelihood that students will share their concerns to some extent.

Student feedback to the field instructor has been discussed throughout as a feature of constructing and maintaining an educational partnership. Since this process is analagous to activities used in societal and organizational change, some of the skills of advocacy can be learned. In all of these instances, the fact of the field instructor's authority and evaluator role has been noted, as well as the dynamics of power, its use and misuse, and the student's experience of vulnerability. Educational workshops given by schools of social work to students and field instructors to focus on these dynamics are viewed as an important factor in facilitating ongoing as well as final feedback to field instructors (Bogo 1993; Johnston, Rooney, and Reitmeir 1991).

Many schools of social work have formal procedures to evaluate field instructors. Some of these procedures are compulsory and some are voluntary. It is essential for students and field instructors to be familiar with the guidelines and criteria for this evaluation at the outset of the practicum. As indicated, formal evaluation is usually done after the student's evaluation and grades have been submitted. It is recommended that field instructors have a copy of any written evaluation of their work.

The Importance of Endings

The ending of the practicum is built into its beginning. The contract made with the school and the student specifies the length of the practicum. Separations will occur at the scheduled time, but, as in all relationships, such knowledge is generally denied by all parties until the actual time of parting has arrived. As the ending approaches, it is not unusual for a kind of mourning process to take over. This can be manifested by apathy in field instruction sessions, or apprehension on the part of the student at contemplating having to face the real world of employment.

If the practicum has been a satisfying experience for both student and field instructor, it is not unusual for a field instructor to wish that the practicum was a little longer so that new learnings can be reinforced. Both the student and the field instructor are likely to feel some ambivalence about ending. There is pleasure in the successful outcome of having established a good teaching and learning relationship, and sadness that this relationship must now end. It is relatively easy for the field instructor to acknowledge this ambivalence. In some instances, separation is postponed because students remain in the agency as short-term employees or may be employed on an ongoing basis. Some students and field instructors avoid separation when each has received such gratification from the relationship that they become lifelong friends and colleagues. A different and troubling situation occurs, however, when only the student wishes to continue the relationship and the field instructor does not share this need. Phone calls and lunch invitations need sensitive but honest responses. It is certainly true that field instructors can become lifetime models for students, who do incorporate large parts of the professional behaviour of their field instructor.

Similarly, if the practicum has been perceived as more positive by either the student or the field instructor, the acknowledgment of feelings is more difficult. Either may feel great relief that the practicum is ending and be unaware that the other is feeling the loss of an important relationship. It is helpful to review the events of field instruction sessions together, and to recall the successful and difficult experiences of the work. This process should be initiated by the field instructor in order to give the student permission to express feelings about the experience and about separation and ending.

It is possible for a practicum to end with the student receiving a passing grade, yet the general tone of the field instruction relationship has been unsatisfying and troubled. In this instance, the field instructor may feel guilty about his or her part in contributing to the difficulty and may also feel some anger and resentment toward the student and the school. These feelings are more difficult to express, but they should not be glossed over in an attempt to put a neutral closure on the experience. It may be a helpful process to review the events and to identify whatever can be learned that might be helpful to the student and to the field instructor in working with students in the future. Both parties may feel guilty and angry, and these feelings need to be explored and expressed. Field instructors should express any dissatisfaction about the role of the school to the faculty-field liaison, the practicum coordinator, or the dean or director of the school.

By initiating the review of the practicum experience, the field instructor is modelling appropriate behaviour for the student to employ in helping clients, colleagues, or staff whose work with that student is also ending. The analogous nature of these processes provides the field instructor with the opportunity to demonstrate the very skills the student needs to use with clients. The student needs to be encouraged to set the ending process in motion with clients well in advance of the actual ending date.

Ritual is frequently employed to mark the rites of separation. The field instructor can facilitate the expression of feelings about the end of the practicum not only by initiating the review of events with the student but also by noting the ending date in a meeting with other staff so that the ending phase is formally acknowledged. Staff lunches, parties, or small gift exchanges are rites that provide students with a feeling of having been a valued part of an organization. Ritual alone, however, tends to focus on the positive and superficial, and if this is all that marks the end of the practicum there may be an unsatisfied feeling of unfinished business. A farewell event alone cannot take the place of a careful discussion and review of the whole practicum experience.

This book will end with a look at the reader's future as a field instructor. To learn the skills of field instruction takes a significant investment of time and energy on the part of field instructors and the schools. It is clear that continued use of the skills of field instruction will refine and sharpen them and can only ensure a more effective practicum and students better prepared to enter the profession. Schools have an interest, therefore, in retaining field instructors who have acquired these skills. In a study to investigate the factors that lead field instructors to continue in this role, Bogo and Power (1992) found that intrinsic rewards, the enjoyment field instructors experienced from teaching students and contributing to the profession, and realistic expectations about the increased workload of field instruction were important factors associated with a desire and intent to continue in the role. Since being able to offer quality field instruction gives personal and professional satisfaction to social workers, it is important that field instruction be recognized as a distinct professional practice skill by both the agency and the educational institution.

Field instructors may choose from among several options to ensure that field instruction becomes a part of their professional careers. These options include ongoing association as a master field instructor or adjunct professor with one school; alternating between two or more schools in a community as a field instructor; taking a student periodically rather than consecutively; or recruiting and training agency colleagues to become field instructors. Many field instructors have found it challenging to participate with university-based faculty in developing field education policy, planning continuing education activities to enhance quality field education, and conducting joint research projects on the practicum. Schools of social work need to acknowledge the effort expended by field instructors and the importance of their contribution to social work education. Schools might consider inviting field instructors to lecture to practice classes and to participate on school committees which set educational policy; they might also consider awarding adjunct faculty appointments to field instructors. Recognizing and honouring field instructors who demonstrate leadership, innovation, and commitment is another way for the university to give tribute to those who make such an important contribution to the quality of social work education.

A final word of reassurance. Field instruction is only a part of a long and demanding working day. This book has focused on field education which can be folded into your workload through flexibility and the knowledge that learning is slow, incremental, and hard to trace by the day, but suddenly visible by the month.

Field learning is a crucial component of social work education, the aim of which is to prepare creative, competent, and ethical social work practitioners. Field instructors are the key to the success of the experience. In this book, the Integration of Theory and Practice (ITP) Loop Model has been presented to provide a framework and a process to facilitate the important educational practice of field instruction. Faced with challenging and ever-changing social issues, the profession of social work searches for new knowledge and effective practices, programs, and policies. It requires the cooperation of academic and field educators to produce social workers who will enhance professional knowledge and practice, and address real societal needs. Integration of theory and practice can serve, not just students, but also field and school educators.

A Teaching Guide

Aim

This appendix is a guide for teaching the Integration of Theory and Practice (ITP) Loop Model of field instruction. The generic concepts which have been presented in this book are framed in a series of teaching modules which can be used by those responsible for the orientation and professional development of field instructors. The aim of this section is to provide a comprehensive curriculum which can be used flexibly. Field coordinators can adapt the content to meet local needs and ensure that educational experiences are relevant to their local context. Although we have developed a teaching module for each chapter in the book, instructors who offer seminars, workshops, or courses may use the material in any order that best fits the purpose of their training and the specific group's needs. Field instructors who do not have access to a formal university-sponsored group-training program may find they can use some of the educational activities on their own or informally with colleagues in their setting.

The curriculum can provide the foundation for the development and implementation of a formal certificate program in field instruction. Such a certificate program could be administered in a variety of ways. The professional association of social workers may offer such programs in conjunction with the university; the continuing education program in a university may offer such courses in conjunction with the social work program; government or a consortium of agencies may sponsor such a program. Wherever the program is located, it should reflect the reciprocity between the academic and practice settings which come together for field education.

Educational Methods

In this appendix, a module is presented which corresponds to each chapter of the book. Broad objectives are provided for each module, along with a variety of suggested educational methods and teaching points. Methods include those for presentation of content and experiential activities. Participants are involved directly in learning the concepts of field instruction through discussion, role play, analysis of field instruction situations, and applying their knowledge and experience. Adult educators have demonstrated the usefulness of such approaches in teaching adults (Knowles 1980).

A growing body of research has identified a number of approaches to field instructor training that produce positive results. Rogers and Mac-Donald (1992), in a study of experienced field instructors enrolled in a course focused on developing a critically reflective approach to their social work and field instruction practice, found that participants differed from the control group in their overall ability to think critically. A particularly effective educational strategy was an assignment that required field instructors to infer students' learning styles, stages, and needs from dialogue with students and observations of students' work. Another strategy was the presentation of a portion of a videotape of participants' field instruction with their students demonstrating a skill, a problem, a stage in learning, or an issue. The group viewed the tape and used it to promote discussion and give feedback to the presenter.

Abramson and Fortune (1990) found that students reported that trained field instructors demonstrated expected supervisory behaviours more often than did untrained field instructors for 75 per cent of the activities studied. The field instructors in the training sessions rated the following educational activities and processes in the seminar program highly: doing process recordings of their own field instruction sessions with their students; and having content in the seminar which was intellectually stimulating, relevant to their learning needs, clear, and presented in depth. The seminar leaders encouraged group problem-solving and discussion of common issues. Respondents identified the learning environment and group process as important to the success of the program.

A model for training new field instructors using small groups led by the faculty-field liaison has been developed, based on principles of adult education and group learning (Bogo 1981). The field instructors are actively involved in identifying the content of the course and the timing of presentation of topics, so that the material covered is relevant to understanding and to solving the immediate problems, tasks, and issues they face with their students. The experiential educational activities that are used include the following: discussion of students' practice with clients and projects; review of students' process recordings; audio- and videotapes of their practice; and presentation and discussion of audio- and videotapes of the participants' field instruction sessions. The small group is designed so that members assume responsibility for developing their teaching effectiveness in a mutually supportive environment. The intention is to stimulate critical self-examination and mutual feedback about field instructors' assumptions and practice with their students. In an exploratory study, Bogo and Power (1994) found support for this approach. Group members reported that the most helpful learning activities were those which addressed their immediate learning needs, specifically the tasks and issues of field instruction. The respondents emphasized the importance of a supportive collegial learning group in which the participants felt comfortable enough to expose their concerns and work on common issues in field instruction. The realization that others share similar concerns, uncertainties, and educational needs was helpful in assuming a new role. With this foundation, not only were strengths reinforced, but members also offered suggestions for responding to problems and confronted each other's blocks, obstacles, and difficulties in role performance. The importance of effective faculty seminar leaders was emphasized. Effectiveness included a balance between direction, structure, and focus, on the one hand, and responsiveness to members' current issues and needs, on the other hand. Direction was defined as giving information in the expert role, developing an agenda for the training session, structuring the work of the group, and ensuring equal participation of group members. Responsiveness included involving the participants in deciding the content and timing of the training topics, as well as being supportive, approachable, and available. Leadership skills also included the ability to develop a learning environment that encouraged problem-sharing and giving useful feedback. Learning was enhanced when participants felt comfortable to express opinions and free to voice ideas without fear of criticism.

Role play, process recording, and group problem-solving are experiential activities used in field instructor training offered in a concentrated format of several full days, rather than in an ongoing seminar series (Cohen and Ruff 1995). The same situation – for example, a process recording of a field instruction session – can be used as a stimulus for a role play demonstrating other ways of handling the situation and for a group discussion that might result in joint problem-solving. Participants reported that role play helped them empathize with students, experience and examine different approaches to field instruction, and understand better the roles of faculty, student, and field instructor; as well, it provided an opportunity for discussion and problem-solving about field education. In summary, the above training approaches and empirical studies support the effectiveness of group-training formats for new field instructors. A variety of creative educational methodologies have been used which can be incorporated with the material in this training guide, or seminar leaders can develop their own variations and training activities.

The composition of new field instructor groups merits some consideration. Social workers practise in a range of specialized service fields, with diverse population groups, and perform a range of practice interventions, from direct intervention, to community practice, administration, planning, and policy development. The focus of field instructor training is on educational processes to help students learn professional social work practice. The ITP Loop Model begins with retrieval of practice data, and all stages in the process return and re-examine retrieved data through new understandings and hypotheses. It is understandable therefore that participants in the learning group will sometimes become caught up in the retrieved practice situation and give each other advice about how to handle a case, a team, a project, or an organizational issue, in the process losing the focus on education. Then, too, some field instructors may feel they have little to contribute to a discussion of field instruction for a community practice issue if their own practice is, for example, in a clinical practice setting. As the research demonstrates, a sense of group commonality promotes learning. The task for the group facilitator, therefore, is to use retrieved data about a specific practice situation as a springboard for highlighting the common field education issues to be addressed by the group. The task for group members is to extend themselves beyond their own practice expertise. As mutuality in the learning group develops, members are able to give and accept useful feedback from each other about their performance in their educational roles. The successful group will evolve as members see their commonality as social work practice educators with a shared nomenclature and expertise in the practice of field instruction.

The Integration of Theory and Practice: The ITP Loop Model

Objective

Field instructors will learn how to provide a conceptual bridge that will link classroom theory discussion and reading to actual practice application. This bridge will help students navigate between the class and the field.

Educational Activities

1. *The ITP Loop Model*

The essential differences between academic learning and practical application can be outlined and presented:

Classroom	Field
Presentation and integration of historical antecedents to a special theoretical approach	Complex human situations
Conceptual application taught through use of case examples in which facts remain as presented	Each situation is ongoing, progressive, changing.
Limited classroom practice of theoretical principles	Analysis is tentative, needs constant checking for re-analysis.

Rational, linear approach   Uncertainty is always present in
                                 all aspects of interaction between
                                 worker, clients, and relevant
                                 systems.

The Integration of Theory and Practice (ITP) Loop Model is the bridge
that can help students to transfer classroom knowledge to practice by
separating and labelling the elements of practice as a constantly moving
and cumulative process; that is, it moves forward slowly and tentatively
with many returns, repetitions, and corrections, diagrammed as a looping process.

SUGGESTIONS FOR TEACHING/LEARNING ACTIVITIES

a. Present the ITP Loop Model using the material in chapter 1. Figure 1
can be made into an overhead and distributed as a hand-out.
b. Provide an opportunity for group members to try to superimpose the
ITP Loop Model on their practice using the guidelines below.

Exercise: The ITP Loop Model and Your Practice

- Group members work individually and write out their thoughts as
  they progress through each stage of the loop.
- In debriefing, participants can present this written material to each
  other.
- An alternative approach is to divide the group into dyads. In turn,
  each member of the dyad will begin with retrieval and describe a situation from his or her practice to the partner. Both participants will
  then try to move through the loop, and the partner may probe, asking
  questions on specifics or for clarification to assist the individual who
  is using the loop to analyse her or his own practice.

Guidelines for Using the ITP Loop Model Independently or in Dyads

Retrieval
- Recall the salient facts of a recent practice experience. Choose a situation that you felt went well or one that is troubling.

- Examples: work with a client or group, supervision of a staff member, your role in a team meeting, chairing a committee meeting, writing a draft of a policy

Reflection
- Recall your thoughts and feelings about the situation.
- Focus on subjective beliefs and attitudes, personal life experiences, and cultural world-views that are relevant to the situation.
- Identify how these factors influenced your interaction.

Linkage
- Identify the key actions you took.
- Explain how you chose those actions. Did you consider:
- concepts from a model or models of practice;
- principles learned through your career (practice wisdom);
- techniques or skills learned from others (who and what has influenced these ideas);
- internal contradictions in an 'eclectic approach'?

Professional Response
- Think about the example again.
- Consider whether your response was selected through deliberate or intuitive use of reflection and linkage?
- At the time of the next contact, did you feel your response was effective, appropriate, sufficient?

Debriefing Teaching Points

Use of the ITP Loop Model
The ITP Loop Model provides a process for social workers to deconstruct their practice and break it down into its component parts. Practice is an amalgam of listening, feeling, thinking, and acting in which all these processes occur simultaneously. What appears at first glance holistic and intuitive can be unravelled. Most social workers are likely to listen, think about what they are hearing, react to the situation and form impressions about it, link the current experience to pieces of knowledge, and take some action, usually without labelling each of these components. The articulation of these parts is necessary to prepare for the role of field educator because students need to experience this partialization

of practice process. Group leaders can ask the participants whether these exercises and using the ITP Loop Model as a guide helped them unravel their intuitive practice.

Practitioner as Field Instructor
To function as effective field instructors, social workers need to be able to unravel and articulate the underlying assumptions of their practice. This analysis and articulation of practice is one of the unique features of field instruction as a form of social work practice and is common to field education in all settings and at all levels of intervention. It is the generic and universal base of field instruction and provides a shared purpose for working and learning together as a group of social work field instructors.

c. Present the examples below for group discussion of the application of the ITP Loop Model to student practice.
d. Suggest that group members present examples of students' work.

Debriefing Teaching Points

- The loop model helps to identify the component processes of practice.
- The loop model is a generic critical reflective process that can be applied in all settings and at all levels of professional practice.

EXAMPLE OF STUDENT PRACTICE: INTERPROFESSIONAL PRACTICE

Retrieval

The student's practicum is in a home for elderly persons, where he is involved in a plan to bring together elementary schoolchildren and some residents of the home in a grandparent-tutorial program. The student had asked the school principal and the director of nursing to meet with him to discuss the plan. At the meeting, the student stated that he would organize and manage the program for four months, until his practicum was completed. The nursing director said, 'I don't think we do our residents any service by getting them into something and then just dropping them.' Though the student and the school principal continued to talk with enthusiasm about the project, the nursing director's resistance resulted in no further action, and the meeting ended on an indecisive note.

Reflection

The field instructor recognized the student's confusion and disappointment that the program seemed to be at a dead end. The student admitted that he felt that the nursing director's comment seemed to be a 'put
down' of him as just a student. Since he felt belittled by her comment, he
had difficulty taking leadership in the meeting. On further reflection,
the student said that he really had assumed that the nursing director
would approve of the plan, on the basis of a casual and informal interchange he had with her. He had set up the meeting with the school principal without a prior formal meeting with the nursing director to
explore the possible program in depth.

Linkage

The student and field instructor reviewed what they each knew about
organizational theory and program development, noting important
aspects that the student had ignored in this practice situation. The field
instructor reviewed with the student preliminary steps that should have
occurred before the meeting he described took place. These steps might
have included recognition of the need to discuss his proposal more thoroughly with the nursing director, in order to draw out her concerns and
gain her support. The field instructor also drew attention to the importance of program continuity and suggested that the student had to give
some thought to who would be responsible for the program after he left.

Professional Response

The student decided that he would meet with the nursing director and
ask if she thought the program had merit; he would also solicit her suggestions about how the program might be implemented and then how it
might be continued after he had left.

EXAMPLE OF STUDENT PRACTICE: CHILD PROTECTION

Retrieval

The student's practicum is in a child protection agency, and the student
has been assigned to investigate a complaint that children are being left
unattended. Unable to reach the mother by telephone, the student went

directly to the apartment. There was no response when the student knocked on the door. A neighbour opened her door in response to the noise and peered at the student. The student could hear a child crying in the apartment, but it took five minutes before the door was finally opened abruptly by a woman who appeared quite angry. The student said, 'I am Sara Brown from the Children's Aid Society. We have received a complaint that your children are being left unattended.' The woman looked as if she might explode and shouted, 'Lies!' The student asked if she could come in to talk about it, but the woman slammed the door in her face.

Reflection

The student was encouraged by the field instructor to reflect on the effect her unannounced arrival might have had on the client's reaction. The student also speculated on whether the neighbour had heard what she said about the children being neglected and what effect this might have had in the matter. She realized that as she had waited for the door to open, she had become more and more uncomfortable. The field instructor suggested that she try to reflect on that uncomfortable feeling and speculate on its source. The student was able to talk about her distaste at having to confront the mother, using the authority of the Children's Aid Society, when she really wanted to establish a trusting relationship.

Linkage

The student is struggling with the role of authority vested in the child protection mandate and worker role, and the apparent contradiction with social work relationship theory. The field instructor must identify the student's conflict in these terms and help the student to seek a way to reconcile the contradiction. This might be accomplished by looking for the positive aspects of authority, as a means to engage that part of the parent that desires to protect and provide for her child. This process is derived from linkage with concepts such as reframing and establishing a working alliance.

Professional Response

The field instructor suggested that she and the student role play the next encounter with the mother. This would provide the student an opportunity to try out alternative responses that incorporate her understanding of the conflict she feels between authority and helping.

2. The Ecological Framework for Social Work Practice

SUGGESTIONS FOR TEACHING/LEARNING ACTIVITIES

a. Present the content framework of the ITP Loop Model using material in chapter 1. Figure 2 can be made into an overhead and distributed as a hand-out. Tables 1 to 3 can also be used.
• Note that all social work practice situations contain elements of the following four factors: psycho-social, interactive, societal or contextual, and organizational.
• Point out that while the framework and dimensions in the tables attempt to be comprehensive, the setting's mandate and the purpose of intervention guide the choice of those factors that are relevant to the specific practice situation at a particular point in time. *Though a holistic overview is necessary, actual work can only be responsive to selected elements of any situation at given points in time.*
b. Provide an opportunity for group members to apply the content framework of the ITP Loop Model.

Exercise: The Content Framework of the ITP Loop Model

• Break the seminar group into small groups of three or four field instructors according to similarity of setting, practice approach, or level of intervention.
• Instruct field instructors in each group to present a practice situation of their own that illustrates how retrieval can be accomplished in their setting.
• Instruct the groups to analyse whether the data retrieved can be categorized according to psycho-social, interactive, contextual, and organizational factors.

Debriefing Teaching Points

• Examine how much similarity of opinion there was in each group regarding psycho-social, interactive, contextual, and organizational factors connected to the retrieved situation.

- Examine how much similarity and difference there was between groups in the factors deemed important.

c. Conduct the same exercise as above, but instead divide the seminar group into small groups with a mix of field instructors from a variety of settings, practising a range of interventions, and using a variety of models.

Debriefing Teaching Points

- Identify the extent to which setting, methods, and models predominate in choosing relevant and priority content factors.
- Consider whether generic social work values and principles emerged to the point where a shared overarching social work metaphor or framework is evident, though emphases differ.

d. Present the following example for group discussion of the application of the content framework of the ITP Loop Model.
e. Suggest that group members present examples of students' practice.

EXAMPLE OF STUDENT PRACTICE

The student's practicum is at an agency serving adolescents. Neighbourhood residents, angry about a proposed group home for 'street kids,' have invited the field instructor and the student to speak to them at a community meeting. It is expected that the following factors, and others, may emerge from the discussion:

Psycho-social Factors

- fear of drugs and crime, especially sexual assault
- fear of the effect on the safety of local institutions and facilities, such as schools and parks, because of street kids
- effect on property values

Interactive Factors

- effect on the student of the group's anger and the student's uncertainty and fear about how to present at the meeting

Contextual Factors

- knowledge about the population, its issues and needs; racial and ethnic bias
- failure of the educational and social service systems to provide for families and children
- societal attitudes toward shared responsibility for children and families
- the power of group action to effect changes in zoning laws

Organizational Factors

- degree of the agency's involvement with the community in needs identification and program planning
- extent to which the agency's funding depends on community support

3. The ITP Loop Model and Field Instruction

SUGGESTIONS FOR TEACHING/LEARNING ACTIVITIES

a. Prepare field instructors to orient students to the ITP Loop Model.
- Share the figures and tables in chapter 1 with students.
- Remind field instructors that students will likely need time and repetition to understand and master the use of the loop model.
- Review the following introductory exercise as a first step, noting the strength of using a shared practice experience as a basis for teaching students how to use the ITP Loop Model.

Exercise: Orienting the Student to Using the ITP Loop Model

- Have the student observe the field instructor in a practice situation, with the expectation that the student will use the ITP Loop Model after the session to reflect on and analyse this shared experience.
- Have the student submit a written analysis of the practice situation to the field instructor prior to the next field instruction conference, so that the conference can be used for discussion.
- The written analysis will include:
- retrieval of the relevant facts of the situation;

- reflection about the student's subjective reactions to the situation and the student's impressions of the effect of the field instructor's professional responses;
- linkage of ideas the student uses to understand the practice situation as well as concepts or theories the student is currently learning in academic courses which might be used to explain the practice situation;
- professional responses which the student thinks would be useful in the next practice session.

---

4. Using the ITP Loop Model with a Range of Retrieval Methods

In chapter 5, 'Guiding the Learning Process,' approaches to using the ITP Loop Model in field instruction with a range of retrieval methods are discussed. Group seminar leaders may wish to include that section at this point and will find teaching approaches for field instructors in module 5.

The World of Field Instruction: The School, the Student, and the Agency

Objective

Field instructors will learn about the organizational context of the practicum, namely, the interface between the university-based school and the community-based agency or department. They will learn how to link the school's program, curriculum, and practicum objectives with the learning opportunities in the practice setting.

Educational Activities

1. The School/Agency Interface

Field instructors, students, and faculty-field liaisons participate in an activity which takes place in 'two worlds.' Field instructors will need to learn enough about the particular school to represent its field program in their work with students.

SUGGESTIONS FOR TEACHING/LEARNING ACTIVITIES

a. Present 'The School and the Agency' using the material in chapter 2. Figure 3 can be made into an overhead.

Teaching Points for Presentation

The Nature of Professional Education
All professional education is dependent on creating opportunities for students to move beyond the classroom to the community, where they learn about provision of specific social work services.

Roles
- The school is represented in the field program through the faculty-field liaison, and the agency is represented by the field instructor.
- Have group members identify the respective responsibilities of each role.
- Review the faculty-field liaison model used in the program.

b. Present 'The School and the Field: Different Frames of Reference' using the material in chapter 2. Table 4 can be made into an overhead and distributed as a hand-out.
c. Present and distribute material about the school's program and field practicum; for example, the field practicum manual, the school calendar, and course outlines.

Teaching Points for Presentation

Specific Models
If the school has a specific model or approach to practice which it expects field instructors to use in the practicum, it is necessary that this expectation be made clear and a module provided for training in this approach.

Continuing Education Opportunities
As an adjunct to this training program and as continuing education for all field instructors, some schools offer seminars on new course content, current social problems and issues, and new knowledge emanating from faculty members' current research. In this way, field instructors are apprised of the current pertinent curriculum issues and knowledge-generating activities of the school.

Changing the Curriculum
- Review the way in which policy and curriculum are developed in the program and how field instructors can participate in that process. Most schools usually have a structure, such as a field education committee, an advisory board, or an association of field instructors, where such concerns are raised.
- It is useful for field instructors to share their views on curriculum content that would serve their special practice needs, such as knowledge about specific mental illnesses, knowledge about alcohol and substance abuse, or knowledge and skills required to identify children at risk.

- How can students learn to cope with emergency or crisis situations before they begin the practicum? Present the following example for discussion.

EXAMPLE: FRIDAY AFTERNOON CRISIS

The student has been in the practicum, a psychiatric service of a large hospital, for one week. She was preparing to leave on a Friday afternoon, having stayed behind to finish some dictation, when she received a call from the ward nurse, who told her that a depressed and suicidal woman had just been admitted. The woman had been accompanied by her two children, aged eight and ten, and they had no one to take them home or ensure their care once they arrived there. The eldest child had said that they just planned to go home by subway, a long journey to a deteriorated and unsafe part of the city.

- Pose the following questions in the discussion:
- Are students with minimal practice experience prepared to handle such situations, increasingly more common in this climate of reduced staff and growing workloads?
- Who has responsibility to train students for crisis situations in which immediate action is called for and analysis can only occur later?

2. Assessing the Fit between the Academic Courses and the Practicum

SUGGESTIONS FOR TEACHING/LEARNING ACTIVITIES

a. Provide the opportunity for group members to assess the quality of the fit between the students' knowledge base and the setting.

Exercise: Assessing the Fit

- Divide the seminar participants into small groups of field instructors on the basis of their sharing similar settings, practice approaches, or levels of intervention.
- Instruct each group to develop an inventory of concepts they deem important to support students' learning in the field.
- Have field instructors scan the school's curriculum and identify areas of overlap and fit, as well as gaps.

- Ask field instructors to identify literature and other educational resources that would help students address the gaps.

---

3. Practicum Objectives

a. Present the school's practicum objectives.

Teaching Points for Presentation

- Field education objectives are expressed in global terms and are intended as a framework and guide.
- Since social work is practised in settings that are problem or population specific, these general goals must be expressed as setting-specific knowledge and skill components that reflect the agency's mandate and practice approaches, as well as the needs of its clients and projects.

Exercise: Developing Practicum Objectives

- Return the seminar group to the earlier small groups of field instructors who share similarities of setting, practice approach, or level of intervention.
- Instruct participants to select two or three of the school's practicum objectives and, for each, to identify related specific objectives in their setting or field of practice. For example, for the general objective of understanding and using the organizational context in practice, field instructors in community settings serving the elderly might specify the following learning objectives:
- understanding the legislative policies which affect the population and programs offered in the setting
- learning how to participate in an inter-agency coalition to advocate for better seniors' housing
- learning how to present findings to lay people serving on board committees to influence policy formulation
- learning how to write program proposals for government and funding bodies

– understanding service team dynamics; and learning how to present in a team meeting with appropriate information that can influence decisions

---

Debriefing Teaching Points

- Have the entire seminar group examine the similarities and differences in the various sets of objectives created.
- Note how this activity begins to create a curriculum for each practicum. These specific objectives can be used in field instruction
  – in contracting and goal setting;
  – as a guide in selecting learning assignments;
  – as outcome measures in evaluation.

The Beginning Phase

Objective

Field instructors will learn how to prepare themselves and the organization for the field practicum. They will learn how to implement the tasks of the beginning phase, which are orientation of the student to the setting and to field education, development of a learning contract, and selection of learning assignments.

Educational Activities

1. The Phases of Field Instruction

Field education is composed of phases or stages with associated activities and tasks. The work of each phase will influence the effectiveness of subsequent phases.

SUGGESTIONS FOR TEACHING/LEARNING ACTIVITIES

a. Present an overview of the stages and tasks of field education using the material in chapter 3. The following table can be made into an overhead and distributed as a hand-out.
• Group seminar leaders can highlight specific issues that are important in their own programs and direct field instructors to relevant reading materials, manuals, and procedures.

Overview of Field Education

Stage	Tasks
Pre-practicum	• negotiation among the educational program, the agency, and the student • anticipation and preparation
Beginning	• relationship-building • orientation • educational assessment, objective setting, and contracting • selecting learning assignments
Middle	• relationship development • re-contracting • guiding the learning process
End	• evaluation • termination

2. Anticipation and Preparation of the Field Instructor and the Setting

It is useful for new field instructors to begin with themselves and reflect on their own feelings and expectations as they prepare for their new role as educators.

SUGGESTIONS FOR TEACHING/LEARNING ACTIVITIES

a. Ask participants to identify some of the issues they are concerned about as they anticipate the new role of field instructor. The material in chapter 3 can be included. Lead a group discussion of preparation strategies that can be used to deal with anticipated issues.
b. Suggest that participants, in dyads or individually, reflect on the following issues:
• What do you consider to be the ingredients of a successful practicum?

- Conversely, what would a difficult practicum be like?
- What are or what might be your strengths as a field instructor?
- What are or what might be your limitations?
- What do you need to do before the practicum begins to prepare yourself for a successful experience?

c. Prepare field instructors to orient students to the setting and to field instruction through the following exercise.

Exercise: Creating the Climate

- Break the seminar group into small groups of four to six participants. Appoint a recorder for each group.
- Ask participants to take a few minutes on their own to write a plan for the student for the first week at the agency, noting what they want to accomplish with the student as the field experience begins.
- Ask participants to share these ideas in the small groups.
- Reconvene the large group. Have each group's recorder summarize the activities and goals for the first week.

Debriefing Teaching Points

- As recorders report back, the seminar leader can note the main points on a flip chart or blackboard. The points can be grouped as follows:
- the agency context, including persons, space and equipment, required procedures
- the student and field instructor roles
- learning assignments
- Compare the activities proposed by the participants with the items in the following checklist.

Preparation and Orientation Activities

1. Prepare personnel in the organization.
- Discuss student field education with:
- administration;
- social work colleagues;
- members of various professions;
- team members;
- support staff.

2. Arrange physical aspects of the practicum.
- Obtain space for the student.
- Obtain equipment and supplies, such as audio- or videotape recorders, access to computer terminal, telephone, paper.
3. Prepare and clarify procedures and forms required by the agency.
- Obtain necessary documents, such as manuals, protocols, and forms.
- Arrange necessary procedures, such as obtaining a student identification card or taking a driver's test.
- Orient the student to risk management and personal safety.
- Arrange for the student to participate in agency-sponsored orientation sessions.
- Inform the student of the agency's requirements about attendance, recording, and confidentiality of records.
4. Structure and discuss the educational component of the field experience.
- Provide educational materials, such as a package of readings, a bibliography, unpublished papers of staff members, audio- or videotapes, a chart of the organizational structure, and reports on community characteristics and issues.
- Inform the student of the agency's educational activities for staff and students.
- Orient the student to the structure and process of field education, being sure to cover the following items:
  – the roles and responsibilities of the student and the field instructor, emphasizing participation and joint responsibility
  – the methods and data for field instruction sessions and agenda setting
  – the regular time for the field instruction conference
  – the use of the ITP Loop Model for field education
  – back-up arrangements for crises
- Provide opportunities for the student to observe the field instructor and other staff.
- Select and assign cases and/or projects.

3. Characteristics of a Learning Contract

SUGGESTIONS FOR TEACHING/LEARNING ACTIVITIES

a. Present the characteristics of a learning contract using the material in chapter 3. The following chart can be made into an overhead and distributed as a hand-out.

The Characteristics of a Learning Contract

A learning contract consists of:	• goals; • means to achieve goals; • evaluation criteria; • time frame.
Goals are based on:	• teaching capacity of field instructor and agency; • school's expectations or field education objectives; • student's interests.
Contracting is a process which:	• begins with assessment of student's competence; • involves mutual participation of student and field instructor; • promotes self-directed learning; • leads naturally into evaluation; • provides a stimulus for re-contracting.
Contracting is an analogous process to contracting in social work practice with clients, groups, and committees.	

Teaching Points for Presentation and Discussion

• The learning contract establishes clear goals, and it specifies the means to achieve those goals, the indicators of successful achievement, and a time frame.
• A learning contract is based on what the field instructor and the agency can teach, what the school expects the student to learn, and what the student wishes to learn.
• Contracting is based on an assessment of the student's practice competence at the beginning of the field practicum.
• Negotiating and developing the learning contract begins the process of collaboration, negotiation, and feedback between the field instructor and the student.

- The learning contract provides an opportunity for the student to learn how to become a more self-directed learner, an essential component of adult learning. Depending on the student's education level, however, more or less guidance is required so that the student can participate actively in the contracting process.
- The learning contract can be used regularly to determine progress and leads naturally into the evaluation process.
- The learning contract can serve as a road map for the field; to pursue this metaphor, it is expected that over time detours will occur and new roads will open.
- This process is analogous to contracting with clients, groups, and committees, and can serve as a model for teaching students this skill.

4. How to Develop a Learning Contract

It may be helpful to develop two levels of a learning contract:
- a working contract
- an educational contract

SUGGESTIONS FOR TEACHING/LEARNING ACTIVITIES

a. Present the components of a working contract using the material in chapter 3. The following chart can be made into an overhead and distributed as a hand-out.

A Working Contract

- Time expectations, field days and hours of attendance
- Agency policies and procedures
- Field instruction conference time
- Preparation expectations of the student and the field instructor
- Practice assignments
  - from the field instructor's practice
  - from agency activities supervised by agency personnel
  - from the student's interests

---

b. Present the components of an educational learning contract using the material in chapter 3. Group seminar leaders can use the examples of contracting learning objectives given in the text or develop their own examples. The following chart can be made into an overhead and distributed as a hand-out.

Educational Learning Contract

- Setting learning objectives
- Specifying learning experiences
- Establishing evaluation methods

Teaching Points for Presentation and Discussion

Setting Learning Objectives
- The educational assessment must be based on an assessment of the student's practice competence at the outset of the field assignment. The following are some suggested methods for assessment:
- The student is asked to observe the field instructor's practice and discuss her or his observations with the field instructor.
- The field instructor observes the student's practice.
- The field instructor and the student identify specific strengths and areas needing development.
- Through using the ITP Loop Model in contracting, useful concepts to link practice and theory can be identified as learning objectives. The exercise in module 1 on orienting students to the use of the loop model in field instruction can be reviewed.
- Through using the ITP Loop Model in contracting, learning objectives will include psycho-social, interactive, contextual, and organizational components as indicated by the practice situations.
- The educational contract should change over time as competence grows and new areas for development emerge.

Specifying Learning Experiences
- The learning experiences are derived from the learning objectives and include assignments and methods for teaching and learning.
- Clients, tasks, and projects are selected that will provide the opportunity for the student to learn the knowledge and skills specified in the objectives.
- The educational methods incorporate all aspects of the ITP loop; for

example, written records and discussion promote retrieval, reflection, and linkage, while observation, co-leadership, and live supervision promote learning professional responses and skills.
   – Educational resources in the setting and in the community which support achieving the learning objectives are identified, such as case conferences, seminars, policy submissions, professional meetings, and library and videotape collections.
 • The learning experiences should incorporate the student's preferred learning style and should also include a variety of teaching approaches.

Establishing Evaluation Methods
 • The contract will specify the type of practice data needed to guide and evaluate student learning, such as tapes, process records, and reports.
 • Decisions will be made about how, when, and where the student will receive feedback about his or her practice and learning. When staff other than the field instructor are involved in student teaching, the contract should specify their role in evaluation.
 • The ITP Loop Model can assist both the student and the field instructor to determine whether the student has achieved the stated learning objectives. Reflection, linkage, and professional response contain the psycho-social, interactive, contextual, and organizational elements which must be demonstrated in discussion and performance.

c. Provide an opportunity for group members to practise contracting through the following exercises.

Exercise: Developing Educational Contracts

 • Divide the seminar group into two. Each group will develop an educational contract for one of the following learning objectives:
   – To develop interviewing skills such as tuning-in to client feelings, observing non-verbal communication, clarifying, and summarizing. The learning objective includes mastering these skills with clients of similar ethnicity and race to that of the student as well as different ethnicity and race.
   – To gain an understanding and appreciation of the lifestyles, strengths, issues, and concerns of gay and lesbian adolescents in a suburban high school.

Exercise: Educational Contracts in the Field Instructor's Own Setting

• Divide the seminar group into dyads. In turn, have each member role play a student and a field instructor in a session the purpose of which is to develop an educational contract.
• Instruct participants to select learning objectives which are important for practice in the field instructor's setting for the role play.
• Have participants conclude with a written statement of a learning objective, the related learning activities, and the evaluation method.
• Reconvene the group and share the written statements and the experiences of contracting.

---

5. Selecting Assignments

When field instructors select learning assignments for students, they report the following concerns:

• workload: what is an appropriate number of clients, projects, or tasks?
• complexity: how are practice situations to be selected that are challenging enough to provide learning opportunities, but not so complex that the student cannot offer effective service?
• accountability: how closely do field instructors have to supervise the student's work so that the agency can be assured that the client is receiving appropriate and responsible service or the project is being conducted in a successful way?

SUGGESTIONS FOR TEACHING/LEARNING ACTIVITIES

a. Engage the group members in a discussion about these issues and any others they consider when they select learning assignments. Summarize criteria and guidelines for selecting learning assignments that emerge from this discussion. The material in chapter 3 can also be integrated.

The Instructional Relationship

Objective

Field instructors will learn how to develop and maintain productive and effective student–field instructor relationships. The important factors and challenges associated with field instruction relationships will be identified, and practice strategies to address these will be studied.

Educational Activities

1. *The Importance of Relationship*

Field instructors' beliefs about effective field instruction are likely to be influenced by their own experiences as students.

SUGGESTIONS FOR TEACHING/LEARNING ACTIVITIES

a. Provide an opportunity for group members to identify their beliefs about the components of effective field education.

Exercise: Effective Field Education

- Form the seminar group into small groups. Appoint a recorder for each small group.
- Instruct each group member to recall her or his own experience as a student in the field.
- Reflect on the positive and negative elements that affected learning.

- Share these experiences with the small group.
- Reconvene in the large group to report back.

Debriefing Teaching Points

- As recorders report back, the seminar leader can note the main points on a flip chart or blackboard. The points can be grouped as follows:
- student–field instructor relationship
- organizational climate, mandate, and assignments
- faculty–field liaison and the school's involvement
- student characteristics (e.g., experienced student, young student)
- methods of field instruction (e.g., observation, process recording)
- Discuss the influence of each instructor's own student experience as he or she prepares to become a field instructor.
- Emphasize the importance of separating each field instructor's unique learning needs, styles, and reactions from those of her or his present student.
- Encourage reflection on what it is like to be a student in the field, including the normal expectations, anxieties, and concerns about such issues as the following:
- whether social work will be a satisfying career
- whether employment will be available
- whether the student will develop enough competence to be effective
- self-esteem and adequacy when confronted with learning and the need for personal change
- the power differential with the field instructor
- Note that students make very strong identifications with field instructors, perceiving them as role models. Empirical studies report that the most important influence on the development of the student's practice is the field instructor's orientation (Baker and Smith 1987; Tolson and Kopp 1988).

2. *Qualities of an Effective Student–Field Instructor Relationship*

SUGGESTIONS FOR TEACHING/LEARNING ACTIVITIES

a. Summarize, from the earlier group reports and from the literature presented in chapter 4, the key components associated with effective

student–field instructor relationships. These are likely to include the following:
• availability
• emotional support
• structure
• promoting student autonomy
• feedback and evaluation
• linking theory and practice
Note that these qualities and behaviours are an 'ideal' and that each student–field instructor dyad will reflect the unique needs and characteristics of the participants.

3. Learning and Teaching Styles

Introduce this topic by noting that problems in relationship can often be a function of lack of match or fit between the student and the field instructor.

SUGGESTIONS FOR TEACHING/LEARNING ACTIVITIES

a. Present the concept of learning and teaching styles using the material in chapter 4.
b. Provide group members with a tool for use in assessing their own styles. A number of inventories exist which field instructors and students can use to assess their respective learning and teaching styles:
• Davenport and Davenport (1988) have designed a questionnaire to assess preference for andragogical styles in teaching.
• Kolb (1985) has designed a questionnaire to assess learning styles according to his theory of experiential learning.
• Middleman and Rhodes (1985) present a number of tools to assess orientation to supervision which can be transferred to field instruction.
• Myers (1980) has designed a questionnaire which is widely used in counselling, education, and business to assess personality type and learning style.

Teaching Points for Presentation and Discussion

• Present the concepts which each inventory measures and the characteristics of each style.
• Note that it is important to identify the learning style of both the field

instructor and the student, and that similarities and differences should be acknowledged.

- Note that inventories identify predominant styles; social work practice may benefit from all learning strategies at different times.

c. Lead the group through the following exercise.

Exercise: Learning and Teaching Styles

- Have the group members complete one of the inventories.
- Divide into small groups according to the participants' preferred learning styles.
- Assign each group the task of preparing a student who has a different preferred learning style for her or his first client or project meeting. For example, if using the Kolb Learning Style Inventory, have the group whose members score highest on concrete experience plan for a student whose predominant style is abstract conceptualization.
- Have small groups report back to demonstrate the complexity of the issue.

---

4. Challenges to Effective Relationships

Despite the recognition that positive relationships are central to both social work practice and to teaching and learning, many field instructor–student relationships are difficult, and can actually sometimes be unproductive, interfering with student learning and causing stress for both participants.

SUGGESTIONS FOR TEACHING/LEARNING ACTIVITIES

a. Ask the group to speculate about the reasons for relationship difficulties. Such issues as the following are likely to be raised:

- lack of trust and fear of openly expressing concerns and differences
- need for approval and difficulty accepting and using negative feedback
- crossing boundaries between professional and personal issues
- issues of ethnicity, race, and diversity
- pressures created by the organization

b. Present the following examples for the group members to discuss and analyse, and then have them role play alternative responses. Additional vignettes can be found in Cohen and Ruff 1995.

- Suggest that group members present their own current experiences with their students verbally, in written form, or through audio- or videotapes of the field instruction sessions.
- For each topic:
- present the field instruction issue to be addressed using the material in chapter 4;
- present the vignette or have group members present current field instruction examples;
- instruct the group members to identify:
  1) the crucial practice issue;
  2) the educational issue;
  3) possible strategies to address the educational issue;
- ask for volunteers to role play alternative strategies in front of the entire group or structure role plays in dyads;
- debrief role play and identify generic principles of field instruction.

1. Lack of Trust and Fear of Openly Expressing Concerns and Differences

Introduce this topic, noting that:
- in these situations, field instructors will not likely learn directly of student concerns;
- field instructors may infer a problem exists from indirect cues; for example: a student not submitting data about his practice, substantial absence from the field, passivity in field instruction sessions.

Example: Indirect Cues about a Student's Concern
The student's practicum is in a children's mental health centre. The student has returned to school for graduate education, and a primary learning objective is to learn family therapy. He has a degree in an allied profession and considerable experience in individual counselling. He has always received positive job evaluations and has found individual counselling challenging. He feels, however, that it is important to learn family therapy and chooses to do his practicum where he can be observed and receive direct supervision.

His field instructor uses direct supervision with a one-way mirror and telephone. The field instructor has been surprised at the student's passivity in family interviews. Given his experience level, he had expected the student to learn more quickly. In debriefing sessions, the student asks questions but rarely offers his own opinions about the family dynamics or interventions.

In a recent session, the field instructor was observing the student's second interview with a blended family which consists of mother, stepfather, and two teenaged boys. The instructor and student had planned the goals and interventions for this session. The major issue was that the student would join with the stepfather and then give him a task to do with the identified patient. As the field instructor watched the interview, he was dismayed to see the student assuming a passive stance, allowing the teenagers to dominate the interview. On three occasions, the instructor telephoned to the student and told him to engage the stepfather. The student either did not follow through or made one comment and then again allowed the teenagers to dominate the interview. Finally, the instructor entered the room and took over the interview.

During the debriefing session, the instructor spoke at length about the concepts of blended families and building alliances, and referred to the literature and research. He pointed out how he had suggested various techniques to join with the stepfather. He also mentioned that when he telephoned in to the interview, it was at moments when he thought the student could have joined with the client. The student listened quietly and attentively to the field instructor's explanations. He avoided eye contact with the field instructor and stated that he felt he was finally understanding the approach to working with families. A few days later, the student asked to terminate his practicum at the agency. One-way mirror supervision, he said, was too stressful for him.

2. Need for Approval and Difficulty Accepting and Using Negative Feedback

Introduce this topic, noting that although students ask for direct feedback about their practice from field instructors, receiving negative feedback may result in misunderstanding, demoralization, or anger, as well as in a rupture in the collaborative nature of the student–field instructor relationship.

Example: Negative Feedback Resulting in Misunderstandings
The student's practicum is in a small agency which aims to help women return to the workforce. The agency uses a feminist approach to practice. The client, an unmarried mother with two children under the age of five, has requested help in 'getting her life together.' The student is a

beginning student with limited life experience. She has met weekly for six sessions with the client and developed a friendly relationship. The interviews tend to last for two hours. The instructor has commented that this seems lengthy but has not pursued the issue. The student's focus with the client is on daily issues regarding her children, some consciousness raising about the position of a young single mother in society, and preparing for job training. The student has gathered considerable information about training programs, has shared this with the client, and recently has helped her prepare an application for a government-supported training program in computer skills. Arrangements for child-care have been discussed at length.

The session under consideration was audiotaped for field instruction. The client begins by excitedly telling the student about a new boyfriend, who has been mentioned occasionally in the past interviews, and informs her that she is pregnant. She then talks about little babies and how much she enjoys taking care of them. The student remains silent. The client says to the student, 'Don't you think it's nice that I'm going to have a baby?' The student says, 'What ... you're not serious ... you're not planning to have this baby?' The discussion continues with the client telling the student about her plans to have the child. The student vacillates between comments which reveal her negativity about the client's intention to drop her plans for training and have another child, and comments which reveal her attempt to listen in an empathetic way. The discussion ends with the client reassuring the student that she can always take a training course when the next child is older.

In the field instruction session, the instructor and student discuss the student's reactions to the client's plans. The field instructor empathizes with the student's disappointment that the client is dropping the plan they had worked on for weeks. She notes that since both she and the student identify with a feminist perspective, it would be important to have explored with the client the dominant societal messages that women should equate their self-worth with mothering. The field instructor says, 'It seems that you had already made the decision that continuing the pregnancy at this time would not serve the client's best interests.' The student responds, 'Well, that's what I believe. I think professionals are often dishonest with clients and do not tell them how they really feel.' The student continues and challenges the instructor, saying, 'I thought feminist therapists were different ... open and honest with their clients. I thought you were like that, but now it sounds as if you are suggesting that I lie to the client. I wonder if you've been truthful with me about other situations.'

Example: Negative Feedback Resulting in Demoralization
The student's practicum is at a multi-service centre in a low-income neighbourhood which provides a range of programs to children and families, mainly immigrant families. The field setting adopts a generalist practice perspective, and thus far the student's assignments have been with groups and community action committees. The student has performed well and is feeling very positive about her practice. The executive director requests the student be assigned to him to help develop a confidentiality policy for the agency. The student reluctantly agrees to this, noting that she is really not interested in administration.

The student spends considerable time researching the literature and relevant legislation, interviews directors of some community centres, and prepares a report. The executive director invites the student to present the report at a staff meeting.

The first item on the agenda takes twice as long as anticipated. The executive director comments to the staff that they are running late and asks the student to summarize her report. The student appears tense, blushes, stammers, ruffles through her papers, and speaks in a strained and quiet voice. The field instructor sees that staff are impatient and not interested in the presentation. When the student is finished, the executive director asks if there are any questions. A question is raised, and the student gives the information, which was not mentioned in her summary, but which nevertheless was in the report. This occurs a few more times. Finally the student's primary field instructor, appearing annoyed, says, 'Well this is a complicated issue and somehow this report, instead of helping us, seems to have created more confusion. We had better study the issue further.' After the meeting, the student comments to the field instructor, 'I better stick to working with people and groups and avoid this more complicated stuff.'

3. Crossing Boundaries between Professional and Personal Issues

Introduce this topic, noting that:
• reflection for educational purposes and therapeutic purposes differ;
  In reflection in the ITP loop, as discussed in chapter 1, students are helped to explore how their personal values, beliefs, and attitudes affect their assessments and interventions in practice. The goal of such exploration is to promote critical thinking and enhance professional behaviour. It is not for therapeutic purposes.
• dual relationships are to be avoided;

If the student and field instructor cross the boundary between an educational and a therapeutic relationship, they enter into a dual relationship. As in social work practice, dual relationships create ethical and practical conflicts and should be avoided.

- options for therapy with students can be discussed as seems appropriate.

If current personal or unresolved developmental issues are identified as an issue for a student, then field instructors can helpfully discuss options for appropriate counselling or therapy.

Example: Professional and Personal Issues

The student's practicum is in a general hospital setting. She has been assigned to a middle-age male client who has kidney disease. The student has met with this client weekly over the past three weeks, developed a positive working relationship, and helped him organize community resources needed to cope with discharge. At a recent case conference, the student learned that her client's medical condition is rapidly deteriorating and is expected to end in fatal kidney failure.

In her field instruction session, the student tells her instructor about the conference and asks her how she should deal with this information when talking with her client. Her instructor asks her if she has had any personal experience with death. The student tells her instructor about the death of a close uncle many years ago. Her instructor probes for the reactions of the student and her family to this loss. The student shares her personal reactions and those of her family members. The instructor makes supportive and interpretative comments about the student's reactions. The student appears uncomfortable during the discussion. The instructor then asks the student to use this past experience with loss to understand what she might be reacting to with the client. The student says that she sees no parallels and states that she would like the instructor to tell her how to talk to the client about his future. The session continues with the instructor urging the student to make linkages between her own experience and the experience of the client. The student continues to state that she sees no connections, and that she wants techniques and suggestions to deal with the topic. The field instructor comments on her perception that the student appears reluctant to recognize the link between her own experience and reactions and those of the client and offers: 'Because you are not in touch with your own feelings, you are struggling with how to handle the client's feelings.'

Example: Crossing Boundaries
The student's field setting is in a school social work unit. During the second month, the student tells her field instructor that she is having serious marital problems. The field instructor sympathetically explores the circumstances of the marital difficulty. The student eagerly elaborates and tells her that her husband was not in agreement with her proposal to return to school to complete her undergraduate degree in social work. She continued with her plan despite his opposition, but he has become increasingly dissatisfied and is threatening to leave the relationship. The student confides that she has been unable to fully concentrate on her field assignments and is worried about her progress. The field instructor says she understands, and subsequent field instruction conferences contain much discussion of the student's personal and marital problems.

4. Issues of Ethnicity, Race, and Diversity

- Introduce this topic, noting the necessity for attending to issues of diversity in the field instructor–student relationship.
- Discuss the relationship between diversity and power in field education as it reflects societal issues, and as it relates to the organization, the student's practice assignments, and the field instructor–student relationship.

Example: Gender Differences
Two students, one male and one female, are assigned to a male field instructor in a family practice unit. A one-way mirror is used for teaching interviewing skills to students from multiple professions. The male student is to interview a new family for the first time. Prior to the interview, he meets with the instructor to plan the session. During the session, the field instructor supervises from behind the mirror, with the other student (the female student) observing. After the session, they all meet to review the interview. The female student is critical of how much her fellow student structured the interview. A lively discussion about the approach ensues. The instructor intervenes and reviews the concepts and empirical research that support the need for structure and direction in beginnings.

After the debriefing session, in a casual conversation with her fellow student, the female student becomes aware that the instructor and male student had pre-planned the interview. At her next instruction session, the field instructor begins to discuss the student's opinions about the interview. The student becomes very upset and tells the instructor that she feels he and the other student have 'ganged up against her,' and she wonders if the instructor favours working with male students.

Example: Racial Issues
The student, age thirty-two, a Canadian Jamaican, is doing her final practicum in a family service agency in an urban area. She had immigrated to Canada six years ago to join her husband, from whom she is now separated. She lives with her five-year-old daughter but has no other family in Canada. In the second week of her practicum, her field instructor, a first-generation immigrant of Italian descent, comes to the student office and asks the student to accompany an adolescent Canadian-Jamaican girl, age fifteen, a client of hers, to a hospital clinic appointment. The field instructor shares with the student her worry that the adolescent is pregnant.

In the field instruction conference the following day, the student angrily confronts the field instructor. She says she has worked very hard to get this far in her social work program. She expects this practicum to prepare her for a good social work job, and she needs to be assigned to cases if she is going to learn anything. Asking her to take a Canadian-Jamaican girl to keep an appointment is not going to teach her to be a social worker. She adds that she knows that the other students in the agency have already been assigned cases.

Example: A Native Student
The student is a thirty-two-year-old native woman in a part-time graduate social work program. Her current field experience is her final one, and upon completion she will graduate. Her learning objectives focus on practice with divorced women, support groups for women, and mediation. Early in the year, as the learning contract is discussed, the student expresses some criticism of her previous field instructor. She suggests that he held her back from learning, treated her 'like a beginner,' and insisted that she prepare a plan before she saw a client. She maintains that the hours spent in preparing and discussing process records at length would have been better spent in more direct practice. She learns by 'getting in there' and working with people. She is an active member of a native support group for single mothers and feels that her previous field instructor did not understand her very well or take her personal experiences enough into account. She did enjoy the rare times when they met with clients together and then reviewed their

sessions. She hopes that her experience this year will better prepare her for practice in her own native community, to which she plans to return upon finishing the practicum.

5. Pressures Created by the Organization

Ask group members to identify organizational issues that are having an impact on their current field instruction. The following are some possible issues:

- downsizing and reorganization
- increased workload and less time for field instruction
- inappropriate assignments and expectations of too heavy a workload for students
- interprofessional dynamics

Example: Inappropriate Workload Expectations for Student
The student's practicum is in a general hospital where a new cost accounting system for all professional services has just been introduced. The hospital administration has made it clear that since the time taken up for student field instruction is not reimbursable, students' workloads must be increased so that they, in part, offset the funding lost as a result of the time social workers spend in student education. The administration has also suggested that group supervision led by only one field instructor replace one-on-one supervision. Individual field instructors would only be concerned with case management. The hospital has an affiliation agreement with the university, and the social workers in the hospital wonder whether the school can help them with this matter.

MODULE 5

Guiding the Learning Process

Objective

Field instructors will learn how to use a variety of teaching and learning methods with the ITP Loop Model to guide student learning and monitor student progress.

Educational Activities

1. Developing a Strategy for Guiding and Monitoring Learning

Field instructors consider a variety of factors as they develop a teaching plan or strategy. A plan will include the identification of two components:
• the modes of presentation students will use to present their practice
• the teaching approaches that will be used

SUGGESTIONS FOR TEACHING/LEARNING ACTIVITIES

a. Review the modes of presentation and teaching approaches available using the material in chapter 5. The following tables can be made into overheads and distributed as hand-outs.

Modes of Presentation	
Direct Access to Student Practice • observation • audiotape • videotape	Indirect Access to Student Practice • written reports • process records • verbal reports

---

Teaching Approaches

direct observation/modelling
co-working
live supervision
audiotape review
videotape review
process recording
summary recording
verbal recording
role play

Teaching Points for Presentation

- Multiple methods for retrieval and teaching enhance learning.
- Teaching can focus on segments of the student's practice as well as on the totality of the case, task, or project. Through use of the ITP Loop Model, the student will consider all factors: psycho-social, interactive, contextual, and organizational.
- Research studies (Barth and Gambrill 1984; Larsen and Hepworth 1980; Sowers-Hoag and Thyer 1985) consistently find that social work students prefer to learn through observation of others; as well as through observation of student practice by the field instructor, followed by immediate feedback and discussion. It is useful to provide early and ongoing opportunities for students to observe and comment on the field instructor's work and that of others. This provides modelling and establishes a safer climate in which students can allow their own work to be observed or presented on audio- or videotape.

b. Review the guidelines presented in chapter 5 for using audio- and videotapes. Demonstrate the use of the ITP Loop Model for tape analysis using a four-column written format as illustrated below.

The ITP Loop Model for Tape Analysis			
Retrieval	Reflection	Linkage	Professional Response
Key words in the dialogue	Student's subjective thoughts and feeling	Concepts, themes, issues	Evaluate the response and provide alternative responses.
Client: 'let go from work and feeling lousy...' Student: 'how will you support yourself?'	I felt her sadness and fear; I was also anxious about how she would support herself and her children.	Loss of work has an impact on client's financial resources, selfesteem, and energy level.	I asked about concrete issues and could have also said, 'It's been a real blow to you losing such an important part of your life.'

c. Review the various formats for process recordings presented in chapter 5.

d. Engage the participants in a discussion of the methods they plan to select for use with their students. Help participants identify the factors they take into consideration when choosing retrieval methods and teaching approaches. The following factors are presented in chapter 5:

agency context

- type of practice (e.g., individual, community, administration)
- sensitivity of practice issues (e.g., palliative work, forensic settings)
- availability of technology (e.g., audio and video machines)
- location of practice (e.g., office, hospital room, facility, home, community)

	• agency-required data (e.g., records, research protocols)
learning and teaching styles	• preferred style of student
	• preferred style of field instructor
	• Research finds that social work students prefer observation and feedback.
educational objectives	• Select methods most likely to promote a specific set of learning goals.
	• As objectives change, retrieval and teaching methods will vary.
service needs	• immediate needs of clients or committees
	• response to crises

2. Giving and Receiving Effective Feedback

SUGGESTIONS FOR TEACHING/LEARNING ACTIVITIES

a. Present and discuss the components of effective feedback using the material in chapter 5. The following chart, 'Components of Effective Feedback,' can be made into an overhead and distributed as a handout.
b. Practise giving and receiving effective feedback.

Exercise: Feedback

• Have the seminar participants supply examples of students' practice through audio- or videotape, written process records, or by presenting students' practice verbally.
• Organize role plays by dividing the seminar group into threes, or work with the entire group. One participant plays the student, one the field instructor, and one is the observer with the role of giving feedback.
• The purpose of the role play is to practise giving and receiving feedback.

Components of Effective Feedback

- stated in behavioural terms and based on learning objectives
- based on data accessible to both student and field instructor
- timely: ongoing, regular, and as close to the event as possible
- clearly stated in a concise and direct manner
- clearly stated in a respectful manner
- Feedback is specific, defined by examples.
- Feedback is balanced, including positive and critical comments.
- Clearly identify strengths.
- Clearly identify skills that need to be developed.
- Clearly identify 'ineffective' behaviours.
- Clearly identify alternative helpful behaviours.
- Feedback is understood and invites discussion.
- Feedback is reciprocal and mutual.
- Follow up on use of feedback.

---

3. Using the ITP Loop Model

The ITP Loop Model is a field education model which is used in conjunction with a variety of educational methods to promote student learning.

SUGGESTIONS FOR TEACHING/LEARNING ACTIVITIES

a. Review the ITP Loop Model using the teaching activities presented in module 1. Participants will:
- understand the two dimensions of the model:
- the phases of retrieval, reflection, linkage, and professional response;
- the framework of psycho-social, interactive, contextual, and organizational factors;
- understand how to use the model in field instruction, having discussed examples of its application;
- know how to orient students to the use of the model in field instruction.

b. Present the steps in the ITP Loop Model for field instruction. The following outline is reproduced from chapter 5 and can be used in the presentation as an overhead and a hand-out.

The ITP Loop Model and Field Instruction

Retrieval
Select methods of retrieval.

Reflection
1. Start with students' life experience associations when these associations occur spontaneously, and help students to compare and contrast their personal experience with that of the situation, using psycho-social, interactive, contextual, and organizational perspectives.
2. Encourage students to identify their feelings, thoughts, and assumptions regarding the practice data.
3. Encourage students to consider their behaviour as a factor that affects the practice situation.
4. Give feedback regarding students' behaviour as it affects the practice situation.

Linkage
1. Start with the students' cognitive associations and understanding of the practice situation, considering psycho-social, interactive, contextual, and organizational factors.
2. Give your own cognitive associations. You can identify the theoretical concepts you are using to explain, examine, and analyse practice phenomena.
3. Encourage students to look for the fit or lack of fit between the theory and the specific practice situation.

Professional Response
1. Field instructors and students use the insights uncovered in reflection to plan the next professional response.
2. Field instructors and students use the relevant theories discussed in linkage to form the next professional response, by setting priorities demanded by a particular situation and selecting appropriate responses.
3. Field instructors and students contrast approaches to anticipate the possible effect of a specific intervention. Field instructors and students can examine possible responses at psycho-social, interactive, contextual, and organizational levels, and consider the relative effects of actions directed at one, several, or all levels as appropriate to the situation.
4. Field instructors prepare students, as needed, to carry out the plan through such methods as observation, role playing, co-working, live supervision, and assigning reading materials.

c. Practice using the ITP Loop Model and the components of effective feedback with a variety of teaching methods.

Exercise: Using the ITP Loop Model to Identify Teaching Issues and Give Feedback

Part One
- Have the seminar participants present examples of students' practice or use the following example.
- Organize the presentation as follows:
- Provide brief information about the student, such as age, experience, learning style, and learning objectives.
- Present brief background data about the client, task, or project.
- Present a segment of the student's work, using any of the data retrieval methods discussed above.
- Ask participants to identify reflection issues and linkage concepts relevant for teaching.

Part Two
- Have the seminar participants present examples of their field instruction sessions with students.
- Invite the presenting field instructor to ask the group members for feedback about specific teaching and learning issues.
- Discuss possible teaching approaches to facilitate the student's learning.
- Have the group members analyse the session in the following terms:
- Did it achieve the goals of reflection, linkage, and professional response?
- How effective was the feedback?
- Discuss and role play alternative approaches.
- Identify general principles of field instruction from the examples presented.

EXAMPLE: PREPARING A STUDENT FOR AN INTERVIEW

The student, age twenty-one, is in her first year in a masters program, has little social work experience, is open to learning, and readily asks the field instructor for direction and guidance. Her learning objectives include learning how to practise with clients from diverse cultural and racial backgrounds, and learning how to work with adolescents and families. Her field setting is in a social work unit in a high school. The student has met with the client, Joyce, age fifteen, who was referred to the social work unit because she has been missing classes and has failed to turn in assignments. In the first interview, the student learned that Joyce's parents have remained in Hong Kong and she has been living with her elderly grandparents for the past year. Joyce feels that her grandparents are old-fashioned and do not at all understand life in their new country. The student and field instructor are meeting to prepare the student for an interview with the client, the teacher, and Joyce's grandparents.

Possible Reflection Issues

- attitudes toward immigrants
- assumptions about Chinese culture
- feelings about adolescents being separated from their parents
- feelings about living with elderly grandparents
- feelings about the relevance of high-school education
- assumptions about racism in the high school

Possible Linkage Issues

- culture shock
- racial discrimination
- adolescent developmental issues
- separation from parents
- generational conflict
- educational resources for students whose first language is not English

Special Situations

Objective

Field instructors will explore the issues involved in working with students who differ from the average student. The ITP Loop Model may be a useful instrument to assist field instructors in assessing and effectively managing atypical students.

Educational Activities

Factors that may present a particular challenge to the student, the field instructor, the agency, and the school are the following:
- age, such as a large difference in age between student and field instructor
- work experience as a social worker prior to current student status
- racial, ethnic, or cultural differences
- students with disabilities

Present the following descriptive issues with regard to atypical students using the material in chapter 6. Ask the group members to comment on and add to the issues.

1. Age as an Issue

Teaching Points for Presentation

- How might a significant age difference affect the learning/teaching relationship between student and field instructor?
- perceptions of authority and power
- perceptions of expertise

- perceptions of life knowledge
- transference–counter-transference
- peer age competitiveness
- collusion to make few demands

Exercise: Age as an Issue

- Ask the group participants to share their own experiences when age discrepancy made a difference.
- Describe the situation.
- Was the issue of age identified?
- How did the situation evolve?
- Could it have been handled differently?

---

2. The Student with Prior Social Work Experience

Teaching Points for Presentation

Positive Effects
- Can identify and build on prior skills and knowledge; and set new learning objectives.

Negative Effects
- Students may be unwilling to reveal ongoing actual work; attempt to keep supervision vague and unfocused.
- Students may assess their competence, knowledge, and skills at a higher level than their performance would support.

Exercise: Experience as an Issue

- Ask the group participants to share their own experiences when prior social work experience was an issue.
- Describe the situation.
- Was the issue of prior experience identified?
- How did the situation evolve?
- Could it have been handled differently?

---

3. The Exceptionally Good Student

Teaching Points for Presentation

Positive Effects
- stimulating student, both a challenge and a joy
- mutuality in learning and teaching in which both parties are enriched

Negative Effects
- tendency for the field instructor to relax; to spend supervision time in collegial conversation or to shorten the time because only case management issues are discussed
- resentment of the student felt or expressed by other students in the practicum
- tendency for the agency's management to expect the exceptionally good student to carry a larger case-load, particularly given staff cutbacks and increasing pressure for service

---

Exercise: An Exceptionally Good Student

- Ask the group participants to share their own experiences with exceptionally good students.
- – Describe the situation.
- – Was the issue of exceptional performance identified?
- – How did the situation evolve?
- – Could it have been handled differently?

---

4. The Resistant Student

Teaching Points for Presentation

Identifying Characteristics
- student who is insecure; fearful that he or she possesses insufficient knowledge of theory and few skills; wishes to avoid exposure
- student who has always just scraped by through using a pleasant façade; clients may like this student because no demands are made
- student who wishes to operate as a 'loner'; misperceives the role of a student as one who must be dependent on the field instructor; inde-

pendence is maintained by withholding evidence of practice transactions insofar as possible

---

Exercise: Resistance as an Issue

• Ask the group participants to share their own experiences when resistance was an issue.
– Describe the situation.
– Was the issue of resistance identified?
– How did the situation evolve?
– Could it have been handled differently?

---

5. Students with Disabilities

Teaching Points for Presentation

Disabilities may include:
• learning disabilities; visual or auditory impairments; speech dysfunctions; limitations on mobility, including dependence on a wheelchair.
Concerns may include:
• capacity and willingness of the agency to make requisite accommodations to the physical needs of the person with the disability;
• the information provided by the school to help the field instructor prepare for an initial interview;
• the time required to prepare agency staff for the accommodations that may be required by the student;
• anticipation of whether extra work will be required of the field instructor in order to accommodate to the special needs of the student;
• anticipation regarding whether the work of the agency may be negatively affected by the accommodations required.
– Considerations include the need to separate bias or unproved assumptions about client reactions from the reality that may exist.
– Factors such as the personality of the student, the student's level of comfort with the disability, and the student's competence may be more important indicators than the fact of the disability.
– Should this student do a practicum in a setting that serves persons with similar disabilities? Some students believe their disability gives

them specific insight into other disabled persons and want to select this setting as preparation for professional goals. Other students may perceive such a setting as limiting their potential as social workers. Accommodations are only necessary to compensate for the student's specific disability or limitation. They might include phone attachments that enhance hearing capacity; doorways wide enough to accommodate a wheelchair; elevators to ensure mobility; accommodation to a seeing-eye dog; dictation of all records; accommodation to capacity for oral or written reports; accommodation to the use of a person as aide.

Exercise: Disability as an Issue

- Ask the group participants to share their own experiences when disability made a difference.
- Describe the situation.
- Was the issue of disability identified?
- How did the situation evolve?
- Could it have been handled differently?

Present the examples below for the group to discuss and role play.
- For each example, instruct the group to identify:
- the crucial practice issues;
- the educational issue;
- possible strategies to address the identified issues.
- Ask for volunteers to role play strategies for intervention in front of the entire group, or structure role plays in dyads.
- It may be instructive to suggest that role players select a special cultural, racial, or ethnic identity for the student or the field instructor to experience, in order to explore whether this factor influences their approach or attitude to the given situation.
- Debrief the role play and identify generic principles of field instruction.

Example: Mature Student
The student, age forty-four, had worked at a child protection agency for ten years as a case aide and community outreach worker. She had now returned to school to earn her first-level degree in social work in a program designed for part-time students. The practicum coordinator had

agreed to permit the student to do her practicum in her employing agency, under an experienced MSW field instructor who headed a counselling team new to the student. The agency's director had agreed to permit the student to take fourteen hours per week from her regular job to complete her practicum requirement.

The student's immediate supervisor, who had been informed of the final arrangement, agreed to the plan without enthusiasm. After the first month, the student complained that she was feeling pressured and as if she had to do a full-time job plus the practicum. She was a competent, experienced, action-oriented worker, but her competent manner kept her at a superficial concrete level with her practicum clients. She had difficulty understanding what it was that her field instructor seemed to be wanting of her when she was told to take a less active role and to learn to attend to process issues.

Example: Resistant Student
The student, age thirty-one, was doing his practicum in a junior high school. While he seemed pleasant and polite, he also seemed to hold himself aloof in field instruction and resisted all attempts of the field instructor to obtain some evidence of his actual work. He reported that parents were sometimes not at home when he called to make an appointment, that his tape recorder malfunctioned during an interview, or that students were absent on the day he planned to see them. This evasive behaviour continued for the first month of his practicum. He was not forthcoming in debriefing an interview that he had observed the field instructor conduct. When the field instructor pointed out his frustration about how learning could take place without any performance data, the student remained silent for a short time. Then he said that he had always worked alone in his former job as a computer programmer. He had made a decision to change careers because he felt he could work with people. He admitted that he felt uneasy and uncertain about how successful he could be with people.

Example: Students with Disabilities
A student who was confined to a wheelchair as a result of spina bifida was doing a practicum in a setting that provides treatment of alcohol and drug abusers, working mainly with groups and doing some individual work as required. The agency was large, with meeting rooms, conference rooms, library, and cafeteria located on various floors. The student frequently arrived late for group meetings and appointments.

The field instructor learned that the bus transporting her to the agency was not always on time. In addition, once in the building, the student seemed unsure of the elevators and would wait until someone came to assist her to get on and off the elevator. One staff member complained of this to the field instructor, commenting that the student seemed to want special consideration. The student had done well academically and had requested that she be given this particular practicum.

Legal Aspects of Field Instruction

Objective

Field instructors will learn basic legal principles governing their professional responsibilities as field instructors. Though legislation differs from province to province in Canada and within the United States, the principles presented are generally applicable.

Educational Activities

Present the following legal issues using the material in chapter 7.

1. Liability Issues

Student-client situations that have the potential basis for criminal or civic action include the following:
- failure to inform the client of student status
- providing treatment without proper consent
- keeping inadequate or inaccurate records
- administering inappropriate treatment
- failing to consult with or refer to a specialist
- failing to seek proper supervision
- failing to take action to prevent a client's suicide
- failure to warn third parties of potential harm
- breaching confidentiality
- professional misconduct, such as engaging in sexual relations with clients, abandoning clients, or failing to be available when needed

2. Informed Consent

Teaching Points for Presentation

- Required by law in most jurisdictions
- What constitutes informed consent?
- full disclosure
- ascertaining that the client truly comprehends what is being asked and what will occur if permission is not given
- time limits, if any, attached to consent
- disclosure of other persons who might be involved in the matter

3. Privileged Communication and Confidentiality

Teaching Points for Presentation

- Clients hold the privilege; only clients can waive that privilege.
- No privilege attaches to a communication made by a client to a social worker.
- A social worker can be subpoenaed to testify in court, though laws differ from jurisdiction to jurisdiction.
- Clients have a right to be informed that what they say to a social worker may not be confidential if the social worker is compelled to give evidence in court.

4. Students in Potentially Dangerous Situations

Teaching Points for Presentation

- Practicum settings that may be dangerous include the following:
- mental health facilities
- corrections and after-care facilities
- family court settings
- social assistance settings
- child protection
- danger in permitting students to use their personal cars to transport clients; liability attaches to student, field instructor, and agency management
- liability of field instructor for student's involvement with clients

Provide an opportunity for participants, in the whole group or in dyads, to present situations involving legal aspects of practice and field instruction that have arisen in their own experience.

• Does their practice require that they carry malpractice insurance?
• Is their practice governed by a professional body, such as a college, with power to hear complaints and to discipline members?

Present the following example situations.

• For each situation, instruct the group to identify:
  – the crucial practice issues;
  – the educational issue;
  – possible strategies to address the identified issues.
• Ask for volunteers to role play strategies for intervention in front of the entire group, or structure role plays in dyads.
• Debrief the role play and identify generic principles of field instruction.

Example: Confidentiality
The student, doing a practicum in a women's counselling centre, received a telephone call from a lawyer involved with one of her clients in a custody and access matter concerning the client's four-year-old daughter. The lawyer told her that a crucial hearing had been moved ahead and he needed some information from her in order to prepare for the hearing. The student gave him the information he requested over the telephone. The next week, in supervision, her field instructor told her that she had just received a call from the agency's director informing her that the student's client was threatening to sue the agency for giving out information about her without her knowledge or permission.

Example: Informed Consent
The student was doing a practicum in a child and family centre serving a population that faced multiple problems associated with low income and racial and cultural barriers. A well-known family therapist had been asked to do a teaching session for the staff with a family just assigned to the student. The student was asked to get permission from the family, a mother and two children aged eleven and seven. The eleven-year-old was the identified patient and had been involved in a serious assault on a child in the school playground.

    The student obtained the mother's signature on the consent forms, having explained their purpose. During the interview with the family therapist, which took place in a large room with many observers, the mother said that she gave consent because she was afraid to say no because the police had told her she needed to attend this clinic to get help. She was really not comfortable about being interviewed in front of so many people.

Example: Sexual Harassment
The student, age twenty-five, was doing her practicum in a mental health centre. One day she complained to her field instructor that she felt that the chief social work supervisor was making sexual advances to her. He frequently asked her to come to his office, where she felt intimidated by sexually suggestive remarks about how she looked and by inappropriate touching, such as his putting his arm around her or standing very close. The field instructor was relatively new to the setting, and she had been hired by the chief supervisor. This was her first experience as a field instructor, and, after expressing shock and disbelief, she told the student that though she could file a formal complaint in compliance with agency procedure, she thought maybe the student should think about this carefully before taking any action. When the student left her office, the field instructor immediately informed the chief supervisor about what the student had told her.

Evaluation

Objective

Field instructors will learn how to evaluate student learning and progress during the term and at the end of the field practicum. They will learn about the indicators that alert field instructors to a marginal or problematic situation.

Educational Activities

1. Formative or Ongoing Evaluation

Evaluation is the determination of the extent to which a student has achieved the objectives of a particular learning activity. Formative evaluations are held throughout the practicum.

SUGGESTIONS FOR TEACHING/LEARNING ACTIVITIES

a. Present the concept of evaluation as ongoing feedback using the material in chapter 8. The chart on page 251 can be made into an overhead and distributed as a hand-out.

2. Evaluation of Competence

Field instructors are concerned about what the school expects students to learn in order to pass; students are concerned about what they have to do in order to pass. The field practicum still serves a 'gatekeeping' function as entrance to the social work profession.

Evaluation as Ongoing Feedback

- Is dependent on ongoing feedback to the student.
- Will focus on psycho-social, interactive, contextual, and organizational factors through use of the ITP Loop Model.
- Begins with the educational contract (review module 3).
- Encourages re-contracting and setting new learning objectives.
- Occurs through guiding the learning process (review module 5).
- Provides feedback to the field instructor about the effectiveness of the teaching.
- Requires active participation of the student, who learns how to self-evaluate.
- Relieves the student's performance anxiety.
- Provides direction, so that students can continually work on needed competencies.
- Provides a data base for summative evaluation.

SUGGESTIONS FOR TEACHING/LEARNING ACTIVITIES

a. Provide the opportunity for participants to review the concept of defining agency-specific competence (see 'Practicum Objectives' in module 2).

Teaching Points for Presentation

- Knowledge and skill competencies are usually expressed by the school practicum manual as field education objectives in general terms applicable to the wide range of social work practice and settings.
- Each field instructor must adapt these competencies and specify learning objectives that reflect knowledge and practice approaches in the particular setting. This activity is part of linkage in the ITP Loop Model.

b. Practise developing agency specific competencies from global objectives.

Exercise: Specifying Competencies

- Divide the seminar participants into small groups of field instructors on the basis of their sharing similar settings, practice approaches, or levels of intervention.
- – Instruct each group to develop a list of some of the core competencies that a student must master to successfully complete a practicum in such a setting.
- – Have each group report and share their list of competencies, noting similarities and differences.

---

c. Suggest that, in preparing for the final evaluation, some field instructors have found it helpful to ask themselves a global question: 'Would I hire this student as a beginning worker?'
- The field instructor might bear in mind two desirable characteristics of a beginning worker: (1) ability to work autonomously on certain tasks; and (2) ability to ask for and use supervision when appropriate.
- In considering this question, if the answer is negative, the field instructor might speculate on what is problematic.
- Feedback may then be given to the student with respect to these issues.
d. Have the seminar participants practise using the school's competency rating measures.

Exercise: Evaluating Competence

- Identify the relevant competency on the school's evaluation form.
- Have the seminar participants present samples of students' practice to each other on audio- or videotape, or through process records or reports.
- Ask each field instructor to independently rate the sample.
- Have participants share their ratings and discuss their reasons for differences.

---

3. Maintaining Objectivity

SUGGESTIONS FOR TEACHING/LEARNING ACTIVITIES

a. Ask participants to use the ITP Loop Model to recall from their own experience as student, social worker, or supervisor factors that promote or interfere with maintaining objectivity in evaluation. The following factors are presented in chapter 8:

- issues in the field instructor–student relationship
- conflict about valuing development and progress even if competency is not yet achieved
- differences between knowledge and skill and the student's personality
- clarity and specificity of learning objectives
- availability of multiple samples of student's practice data to form a judgment
- equating effort and motivation with competence
- using one's own performance as the standard
- reluctance to evaluate students negatively or critically

4. The Final or Summative Evaluation

Summative evaluations are conducted at specific points in time, such as mid-term and the conclusion of the field experience.

SUGGESTIONS FOR TEACHING/LEARNING ACTIVITIES

a. Present and thoroughly explain the materials and procedures the school expects the field instructor to use in conducting the final evaluation.
b. Using the material in chapter 8, discuss the general points about final evaluation listed in the chart on page 254. (The chart can be made into an overhead.)

5. The Marginal or Failing Student

When the field instructor is concerned that the student may be experiencing difficulties early involvement of the faculty-field liaison is strongly recommended. Early recognition of potential problems is encouraged, and they should be shared with the student so that the opportunity for change is available in advance of summative evaluation.

Summative Evaluation

- Builds on and uses the learning contract.
  - The learning objectives are a standard against which to evaluate progress.
  - The learning activities and resources are a framework to evaluate the effectiveness of the setting and the field instructor.
  - The methods of evaluation indicate what data are to be assessed and who will make evaluation judgments.
- Incorporates objectives from re-contracting and ongoing evaluation.
- Assesses where the student is in relation to an externally set standard.
- Is past and present oriented and indicates the level of growth.
- Requires the active participation of the student.

SUGGESTIONS FOR TEACHING/LEARNING ACTIVITIES

a. Present and discuss the following indicators of the marginal or failing student using the material in chapter 8. (See charts on pages 255–6.) Give examples, or encourage the participants to give examples.

Teaching Points for Presentation

- Documentation of behaviours that seem problematic and that continue in spite of discussion with the student is important. Documentation may include written notes of field instruction sessions, memos to the student, or tapes and records of the student's practice.
- Since field instructors respond to aspects of the student's personality, it is useful to separate objective factors from subjective reactions. To clarify this issue, field instructors may ask themselves the following question: 'Is this student's problem peculiar to this setting, a unique reaction to my field instruction approach or personality, to the kind of clients we serve, or is it something that will go with him/her wherever s/he goes?' (Wilson 1981, 197).

The Marginal or Failing Student
Indicators of Problems in Practice

The student is *consistently* unable to demonstrate sufficient learning through changed behaviour; there is little evidence of growth toward achieving core competence.

The student displays behaviours which are destructive to others (e.g., physically injuring someone, appearing at the agency intoxicated or drugged, or displaying frequent outbursts of temper).

The student demonstrates untrustworthiness or dishonesty.

The student is judgmental and critical of clients; attempts to impose his or her belief system; is consistently harsh, angry, bullying, or subtly depreciating.

The student is overly authoritarian, directive, and task-oriented to the extent that a working relationship based on mutuality cannot be established.

The student is unable to provide appropriate leadership and direction with clients.

The student *consistently* avoids responding to the client's strong affect and keeps interactions superficial and/or social.

---

6. Evaluation of the Field Instructor and the Setting

Field instructors will encourage ongoing feedback from students throughout the field experience regarding field instructors' ability to communicate clearly and to provide effective and helpful instruction.

SUGGESTIONS FOR TEACHING/LEARNING ACTIVITIES

a. Present and thoroughly explain the materials and procedures the

**The Marginal or Failing Student
Indicators of Problems in Organizational Behaviour
and Professional Collaboration**

The student unilaterally contravenes agency policy without prior discussion with the field instructor.

The student is unable or unwilling to work collaboratively with other staff.

The student consistently behaves inappropriately with other staff.

The student is unable to appreciate her or his effect on others and continues to repeat inappropriate behaviour despite considerable discussion in field instruction.

**The Marginal or Failing Student
Indicators of Problems in the Use of Field Instruction**

The student is unable to integrate theory and practice, and needs constant direction and structure.

The student is consistently unable to expose or discuss practice behaviour; for example, he or she rarely submits evidence of practice in the form of tapes or reports and avoids attempts to promote reflection.

The student is consistently unable to hear negative feedback and interprets criticism as a personal attack. The student remains defensive and unable to modify her or his practice.

school expects the student to use to give feedback. Students are more likely to give feedback to field instructors after their own evaluations are completed.

b. If the school does not provide a systematic form, field instructors can elicit feedback about the educational effectiveness of the following:
- the field setting
- the assignments carried
- the activities attended
- the process of field instruction

7. Evaluation of the Seminar

SUGGESTIONS FOR TEACHING/LEARNING ACTIVITIES

a. Lead a group discussion which evaluates the training seminars by focusing on the following:
- content addressed
- learning/teaching methods used
- the leadership provided by the faculty facilitator
- the effectiveness of the group process

A written evaluation form is also useful for gathering data for use in refining the teaching program. Ask participants to identify their own further learning needs as well as the potential organizational supports that would enhance their professional development in this role and make it more likely that they continue as field instructors.

References

Abels, P. 1977. Group supervision of students and staff. In F.W. Kaslow, ed., *Supervision, consultation, and staff training in the helping professions*, 175–98. San Francisco: Jossey-Bass.

Abramson, J.S., and A.E. Fortune. 1990. Improving field instruction: An evaluation of a seminar for new field instructors. *Journal of Social Work Education* 26(3), 273–86.

Allen, H.S., and A.E. Shragge. 1995. Community-based field placements: Recent innovations. In G. Rogers, ed., *Social work field education: Views and visions*, 92–105. Dubuque, Iowa: Kendall/Hunt.

Alperin, D.E. 1988. The physically disabled BSW student: Implications for field education. *Journal of Teaching in Social Work* 2(2), 99–110.

– 1989. Confidentialty and the BSW field work placement process. *Journal of Social Work Education* 25(2), 98–108.

– 1996. Empirical research on student assessment in field education: What have we learned? *Clinical Supervisor* 14(1), 149–61.

Amacher, K.A. 1976. Explorations into the dynamics of learning in field work. *Smith College Studies in Social Work* 46(3), 163–217.

Anderson, T. 1987. The reflecting team: Dialogue and meta-dialogue in clinical work. *Family Process* 26(4), 415–28.

Arkava, M.L., and E.C. Brennan, eds. 1976. *Competency-based education for social work: Evaluation and curriculum issues*. New York: Council on Social Work Education.

Australian Association for Social Work and Welfare Education (AASWWE). 1991. *A handbook for field educators in social work and social welfare*. Riverina, Australia: Charles Sturt University.

Baker, D.R., and S.L. Smith. 1987. A comparison of field faculty and field student perceptions of selected aspects of supervision. *Clinical Supervisor* 5(4), 31–42.

Bandura, A. 1969. *Principles of Behavior Modification.* New York: Holt, Rinehart and Winston.

Barth, R., and E. Gambrill. 1984. Learning to interview: The quality of training opportunities. *Clinical Supervisor* 2(1), 3–14.

Bernstein, B.E. 1977. Privileged communications to the social worker. *Social Work* 22(4), 264–8.

Besharov, D.J., and S.H. Besharov. 1987. Teaching about liability. *Social Work* 32(6), 517–22.

Bogo, M. 1981. An educationally focused faculty/field liaison program for first-time field instructors. *Journal of Education for Social Work* 17(3), 59–65.

– 1993. The student/field instructor relationship: The critical factor in field education. *Clinical Supervisor* 11(2), 23–36.

Bogo, M., and J. Globerman. 1995. Creating effective university-field partnerships: An analysis of two inter-organization models. *Journal of Teaching in Social Work* 11(1/2), 177–92.

Bogo, M., and R. Power. 1992. New field instructors' perceptions of institutional supports for their roles. *Journal of Social Work Education* 28(2), 178–89.

– 1994. Educational methodologies and group elements in field instructor training. *Clinical Supervisor* 12(2), 9–25.

Bogo, M., and E. Vayda. 1987. *The practice of field instruction in social work: Theory and process.* Toronto: University of Toronto Press.

– 1991. Developing a process model for field instruction. In D. Schneck, B. Grossman, and U. Glassman, eds, *Field education in social work: Contemporary issues and trends*, 59–66. Dubuque, Iowa: Kendall/Hunt.

Bonosky, N. 1995. Boundary violations in social work supervision: Clinical, educational and legal implications. *Clinical Supervisor*, 13(2), 79–95.

Bot, A., J. Lackstrom, J. McNamee, S. Urman, and M. Hutson. 1995. The teaching centre model of field education. In G. Rogers, ed., *Social work field education: Views and visions*, 30–7. Dubuque, Iowa: Kendall/Hunt.

Brennan, E.C. 1982. Evaluation of field teaching and learning. In B.W. Sheafor and L.E. Jenkins, eds., *Quality field instruction in social work*, 76–97. New York: Longman.

Brundage, D., and D. MacKeracher. 1980. *Adult learning principles and their application to program planning.* Toronto: Ontario Ministry of Education.

Claxton, C.S., and Y. Ralston. 1978. *Learning styles: Their impact on teaching and administration.* Washington, D.C.: American Association for Higher Education.

Cobb, N.H. 1994. Court-recommended guidelines for managing unethical students and working with university lawyers. *Journal of Social Work Education* 30(1), 18–31.

Cohen, J. 1977. Selected constraints in the relationship between social work education and practice. *Journal of Education for Social Work* 13(1), 3–7.

Cohen, M. 1988. Suggested outline for process recordings. Unpublished manuscript.

Cohen, M.B., and E. Ruff. 1995. The use of role play in field instructor training. *Journal of Teaching in Social Work* 11(1/2), 85–100.

Cole, B.S., and M.W. Cain. 1996. Social work students with disabilities: A proactive approach to accommodation. *Journal of Social Work Education*, 32(3), 339–49.

Collins, D., and M. Bogo. 1986. Competency based field instruction: Bridging the gap between laboratory and field learning. *Clinical Supervisor*, 4(3), 39–52.

Cowan, B., R. Dastyk, and E.R. Wickham. 1972. Group supervision as a teaching/learning modality in social work. *The Social Worker/Le Travailleur Social* 40(4), 256–61.

Crist, P.A., and V.C. Stoffel. 1992. The Americans with disabilities act of 1990 and employees with mental impairments: Personal efficacy and the environment. *American Journal of Occupational Therapy* 46(5), 434–43.

Davenport, J.A., and J. Davenport, III. 1988. Individualizing student supervision: The use of andragogical-pedagogical orientation questionnaires. *Journal of Teaching in Social Work* 2(2), 83–97.

Dore, M.M., B.N. Epstein, and C. Herrerias. 1992. Evaluating students' micro practice field performance: Do universal learning objectives exist? *Journal of Social Work Education* 28(3), 353–62.

Dwyer, M., and M. Urbanowski. 1965. Student process recording: A plea for structure. *Social Casework* 46(5), 282–6.

England, H. 1986. *Social work as art*. London: Allen and Unwin.

Feiner, H.A., and E.H. Couch. 1985. I've got a secret: The student in the agency. *Social Casework* 66(5), 268–74.

Feld, S. 1988. The academic marketplace in social work. *Journal of Social Work Education* 24(3), 201–10.

Fellin, P.A. 1982. Responsibilities of the school: Administrative support of field instruction. In B.W. Sheafor and L.E. Jenkins, eds, *Quality field instruction in social work* 37–59. New York: Longman.

Fortune, A.E. 1994. Field education. In F.J. Reamer, ed., *The foundations of social work knowledge*, 151–94. New York: Columbia University Press.

Fortune, A.E., and J.S. Abramson. 1993. Predictors of satisfaction with field practicum among social work students. *Clinical Supervisor* 11(1), 95–110.

Fortune, A.E., C.E. Feathers, S.R. Rook, R.M. Scrimenti, P. Smollen, P. Stemerman, and E.L. Tucker. 1985. Student satisfaction with field placement. *Journal of Social Work Education* 21(3), 92–104.

Fortune, A.E., J. Miller, A.F. Rosenblum, B.M. Sanchez, C. Smith, and W.J. Reid. 1995. Further explorations of the liaison role: A view from the field. In G. Rogers, ed., *Social work field education: Views and visions*, 273–93. Dubuque, Iowa: Kendall/Hunt.

Freeman, E. 1985. The importance of feedback in clinical supervision: Implications for direct practice. *Clinical Supervisor* 3(1), 5–26.

Frumkin, M. 1980. Social work education and the professional commitment fallacy: A practical guide to field-school relations. *Journal of Education for Social Work* 16(2), 91–9.

Gelman, S.R., D. Pollack, and C. Auerbach. 1996. Liability issues in social work education. *Journal of Social Work Education* 32(3), 351–61.

Gelman, S.R., and P.J. Wardell. 1988. Who's responsible? The field liability dilemma. *Journal of Social Work Education* 24(1), 70–8.

George, A. 1982. A history of social work field instruction. In B.W. Sheafor and L.E. Jenkins, eds, *Quality field instruction in social work*, 37–59. New York: Longman.

Gerhart, J.C., and A.D. Brooks. 1985. Social workers and malpractice: Law, attitudes, and knowledge. *Social Casework* 66, 411–16.

Gibbs, P., and B. Locke. 1989. Tenure and promotion in accredited graduate social work programs. *Journal of Social Work Education* 25(2), 126–33.

Gitterman, A. 1989. Field instruction in social work education: Issues, tasks and skills. *Clinical Supervisor* 7(4), 77–91.

Gitterman, A., and N.P. Gitterman. 1979. Social work student evaluation: Format and method. *Journal of Education for Social Work* 15(3), 103–8.

Gladstein, M., and M. Mailick. 1986. An affirmative approach to ethnic diversity in field work. *Journal of Social Work Education* 22(1), 41–9.

Globerman, J., and M. Bogo. 1996. Strengthening the integration of research, teaching, and practice in graduate programs: An academic field partnership model. Paper presented at Social Work Field Education for a New Generation conference. McMaster University, Hamilton, Ont.

Goldberg, D.A. 1985. Process notes, audio and videotape: Modes of presentation in psychotherapy training. *Clinical Supervisor* 3(3), 3–13.

Goodman, R.W. 1985. The live supervision model in clinical training. *Clinical Supervisor*, 3(3), 43–9.

Gray, S.W., D.E. Alperin, and R. Wik. 1989. Multidimensional expectations of student supervision in social work. *Clinical Supervisor* 7(1), 89–102.

Graybeal, C., and E. Ruff. 1995. Process recording: It's more than you think. *Journal of Social Work Education* 31(2), 169–81.

Gross, G.M. 1981. Instructional design: Bridge to competence. *Journal of Education for Social Work*, 17(3), 66–74.

Grossman, B., N. Levine-Jordano, and P. Shearer. 1990. Working with students' emotional reactions in the field: An educational framework. *Clinical Supervisor* 8(1), 23–39.

Hagen, B.J.H. 1989. The practicum instructor: A study of role expectations. In M. Raskin, ed., *Empirical studies in field instruction*, 219–35. New York: The Haworth Press.

Hamilton, G. (1954). Self-awareness in professional education. *Social Casework* 35(9), 371–9.

Hamilton, N., and J.F. Else. 1983. *Designing field education: Philosophy, structure and process*. Springfield, Ill.: Charles C. Thomas.

Hanson, P.B. 1975. Giving feedback: An interpersonal skill. *The 1975 Annual Handbook for Group Facililtators*.

Hartman, A. 1990a. Many ways of knowing. *Social Work* 35(3), 3–4.

– 1990b. Education for direct practice. *Families in Society* 71(1), 44–50.

– 1994. Social work practice. In F.J. Reamer, ed., *The foundations of social work knowledge*, 13–50. New York: Columbia University Press.

Hartman, C., and R.M. Wills. 1991. The gatekeeper role in social work: A survey. In D. Schneck, B. Grossman, and U. Glassman, eds, *Field education in social work: Contemporary issues and trends*, 310–19. Dubuque, Iowa: Kendall/Hunt.

Hawthorne, L. 1975. Games supervisors play. *Social Work* 29(3), 179–83.

– 1985. How can we provide field instruction for handicapped students. Paper presented at the Council on Social Work Education, Washington, D.C.

– 1987. Teaching from recordings in field instruction. *Clinical Supervisor* 5(2), 7–22.

Horner, A.J. 1988. Developmental aspects of psychodynamic supervision: Parallel process of separation and individuation. *Clinical Supervisor* 6(2), 3–12.

Hughes, L., and K. Heycox. 1996. Three perspectives on assessment in practice learning. In M. Doel and S. Shardlow, eds, *Social work in a changing world: An international perspective on practice learning*, 85–102. Aldershot, England: Arena.

Hunt, D. 1970. *Matching models in education: The co-ordination of teaching methods with student characteristics*. Toronto: Ontario Institute for Studies in Education.

– 1987. *Beginning with ourselves in practice, theory, and human affairs*. Cambridge, Mass.: Brookline Books.

Johnston, N., R. Rooney, and M.A. Reitmeir. 1991. Sharing power: Student feedback to field supervisors. In D. Schneck, B. Grossman, and U. Glassman, eds, *Field education in social work: Contemporary issues and trends*, 198–204. Dubuque, Iowa: Kendall/ Hunt.

Kadushin, A. 1968. Games people play in supervision. *Social Work* 13(3), 23–32.

– 1985. *Supervision in social work*. 2nd ed. New York: Columbia University Press.

– 1991. Introduction. In D. Schneck, B. Grossman, and U. Glassman, eds, *Field education in social work: Contemporary issues and trends*, 11–12. Dubuque, Iowa: Kendall/Hunt.

Kahn, S.L. 1981. An analysis of the relationship between social work schools and field placement agencies in their joint task of educating social workers. PHD diss., Columbia University.

Kaplan, T. [1991a]. Reducing student anxiety in field work: Exploratory research and implications. *Clinical Supervisor* 9(2), 105–17.

– 1991b. A model for group supervision for social work: Implications for the profession. In D. Schneck, B. Grossman, and U. Glassman, eds, *Field education in social work*, 141–8. Dubuque, Iowa: Kendall/Hunt.

Kapp, M.B. 1984. Supervising professional trainees: Legal implications for mental health institutions. *Hospital and Community Psychiatry*, 35(2), 143–7.

Kilpatrick, A.C., J. Turner, and T.P. Holland, 1994. Quality control in field education: Monitoring students' performance. *Journal of Teaching in Social Work* 9(1/2), 107–20.

Knight, C. 1996. A study of MSW and BSW students' perceptions of their field instructors. *Journal of Social Work Education* 32(3), 399–414.

Knowles, M.S. 1972. Innovations in teaching styles and approaches based upon adult learning. *Journal of Education for Social Work* 8(2), 32–9.

– 1980. *The modern practice of adult education*. Chicago: Association Press / Follett.

Kolb, D.A. 1984. *Experiential learning: Experience as the source of learning and development*. Englewood Cliffs, N.J.: Prentice Hall.

– 1985. *The learning style inventory*. Boston: McBer & Company.

Kolevzon, M. 1992. Should we support the continuum in social work education? No. *Journal of Social Work Education* 28(1), 10–14.

Koopmans, J. 1995. The use of the reflecting team to enhance student learning. In G. Rogers, ed., *Social work field education: Views and visions*, 229–33. Dubuque, Iowa: Kendall/Hunt.

Kruzich, J., B. Friesen, and D.V. Soest. 1986. Assessment of student and faculty learning styles: Research and application. *Journal of Social Work Education* 22(3), 22–30.

Kurland, P. 1989. Viewpoint: Process recording – an anachronism. *Social Casework* 70(5), 310–14.

Lacerte, J., J. Ray, and L. Irwin. 1989. Recognizing the educational contributions of field instructors. *Journal of Teaching in Social Work* 3(2), 99–113.

Larsen, J., and D. Hepworth. 1980. Enhancing the effectiveness of practicum instruction: An empirical study. *Journal of Education for Social Work* 18(2), 50–8.

Lemberger, J., and E.F. Marshack. 1991. Educational assessment in the field: An opportunity for teacher-learner mutuality. In D. Schneck, B. Grossman, and

U. Glassman, eds, *Field education in social work: Contemporary issues and trends,* 187–97. Dubuque, Iowa: Kendall/Hunt.

Liddle, H.A. 1991. Training and supervision in family therapy: A comprehensive and critical analysis. In A.S. Gurman and D.P. Kniskern, eds, *Handbook of family therapy,* 638–97. 2nd ed. New York: Brunner/Mazel.

Liddle, H.A., and R.C. Schwartz. 1983. Live supervision/consultation: Conceptual and pragmatic guidelines for family therapy trainers. *Family Process* 22(4), 477–90.

Loewenberg, F.M., and R. Dolgoff. 1992. *Ethical decisions for social work practice.* 4th ed. Itasca, Ill.: Peacock.

Magill, J., and A. Werk. 1985. Classroom training as preparation for the social work practicum: An evaluation of a skills laboratory training program. *Clinical Supervisor* 3(3), 69–76.

Marshack, E.F., C.O. Hendricks, and M. Gladstein. 1994. The commonality of difference: Teaching about diversity in field instruction. *Journal of Multicultural Social Work* 3(1), 77–89.

Marshall, C. 1982. Social work students' perceptions of their practicum experience: A study of learning by doing. PHD diss., University of Toronto.

Matorin, S. 1979. Dimensions of student supervision: A point of view. *Social Casework* 60(3), 150–6.

Mayadas, N.S., and W.D. Duehn. 1977. The effects of training formats and interpersonal discriminations in the education for clinical social work practice. *Journal of Social Service Research* 1(2), 147–61.

Mayers, F. 1970. Differential use of group teaching in first year field work. *Social Service Review* 44(1), 63–70.

McCollum, E.E., and J.L. Wetchler. 1995. In defense of case consultation: Maybe 'dead' supervision isn't dead after all. *Journal of Marital and Family Therapy* 21(2), 155–66.

McGoey-Smith, K. 1995. Building on strengths: Reconceptualizing evaluating student performance in the field practicum. In G. Rogers, ed., *Social work field education: Views and visions,* 245–55. Dubuque, Iowa: Kendall/Hunt.

Middleman, R., and G. Rhodes. 1985. *Competent supervision: Making imaginative judgments.* Englewood Cliffs, N.J.: Prentice Hall.

Miller, C.W., and W.R. Kennedy. 1979. *The effects of work experience and undergraduate education on the learning style and career development of technical professionals.* Washington, D.C.: Department of Education, Educational Resources Center.

Mishne, J. 1983. Narcissistic vulnerability of the younger student: The need for non-confrontive empathic supervision. *Clinical Supervisor* 1(2), 3–12.

Montalvo, B. 1973. Aspects of live supervision. *Family Process* 12(4), 343–60.

Myers, I.B. 1980. *Gifts differing*. Palo Alto, Calif.: Consulting Psychologists Press, Inc.

Prosser, W. 1971. *Handbook of torts*. St Paul, Minn.: West Publishing Co.

Raphael, F.B., and A.F. Rosenblum. 1987. An operational guide to the faculty field liaison role. *Social Casework* 68(3), 156–63.

– 1989. The open expression of differences in the field practicum: Report of a pilot study. *Journal of Social Work Education* 25(2), 109–16.

Raskin, M.S. 1983. A delphi study in field instruction: Identification of issues and research priorities by experts. *Arete* 8(2), 38–48.

– 1989. Factors associated with student satisfaction in undergraduate social work field placements. In M. Raskin, ed., *Empirical studies in field instruction*, 321–35. New York: The Haworth Press.

– 1994. The delphi study in field instruction revisited: Expert consensus on issues and research priorities. *Journal of Social Work Education* 30(1), 75–88.

Raymond, G.T., R. Teare, and C. Atherton. 1996. Is 'field of practice' a relevant organizing principle for the MSW curriculum? *Journal of Social Work Education* 32(1), 19–30.

Reamer, F.G. 1994. The evolution of social work knowledge. In F.G. Reamer, ed., *The foundations of social work knowledge*, 1–12. New York: Columbia University Press.

Reeser, L.C. 1992. Students with disabilities in practicum: What is reasonable accommodation? *Journal of Social Work Education* 28(1), 98–109.

Rhim, B. 1976. The use of videotapes in social work agencies. *Social Casework* 57(10), 644–50.

Richan, W.C. 1989. Empowering students to empower others: A community-based field practicum. *Journal of Social Work Education* 25(3), 276–83.

Rogers, C. 1951. *On becoming a person*. Boston: Houghton Mifflin.

Rogers, G., and L. MacDonald. 1992. Thinking critically: An approach to field instructor training. *Journal of Social Work Education* 28(2), 166–77.

Rogers, G., and P.L. McDonald. 1995. Expedience over education: Teaching methods used by field instructors. *Clinical Supervisor* 13(2), 41–65.

Romano, M. 1981. Social worker's role in rehabilitation: A review of the literature. In K. Browne and S. Watt, eds, *Rehabilitation services and the social work role: Challenge for change*. Baltimore: Williams and Wilkins.

Rosenblatt, A., and J.E. Mayer. 1975. Objectionable supervisory styles: Students' views. *Social Work* 20(3), 184–9.

Rosenblum, A.F. 1997. Developing partnerships between social work programs and the professional community: An exploratory study of field advisory groups. *Journal of Teaching in Social Work* 14(1/2), 111–25.

Rosenblum, A.F., and F.B. Raphael. 1983. The role and function of the faculty field liaison. *Journal of Education for Social Work* 19(1), 67–73.

- 1987. Students at risk in the field practicum and implications for field teaching. *Clinical Supervisor* 5(3), 53–63.
- 1991. Balancing students' rights to privacy with the need for self-disclosure in field education. *Journal of Teaching in Social Work* 5(1), 7–20.

Rosenfeld, D.J. 1989. Field instructor turnover. In M. Raskin, ed., *Empirical studies in field instruction*, 187–218. New York: The Haworth Press.

Rotholz, T., and A. Werk. 1984. Student supervision: An educational process. *Clinical Supervisor* 2(1), 14–27.

Ruffolo, M.C., and P. Miller. 1994. An advocacy/empowerment model of organizing: Developing university-agency partnerships. *Journal of Social Work Education* 30(3), 310–16.

Saleebey, D. 1994. Culture, theory, and narrative: The intersection of meanings in practice. *Social Work* 39(4), 351–9.

Schinke, S.P., B.J. Blythe, L.D. Gilchrist, and T.E. Smith, 1980. Developing intake interviewing skills. *Social Work Research and Abstracts* 16(10), 29–34.

Schlenoff, M.L., and S.H. Busa. 1981. Student and field instructor as group cotherapists: Equalizing an unequal relationship. *Journal of Education for Social Work* 17(1), 29–35.

Schon, D. 1987. *Educating the reflective practitioner*. San Francisco: Jossey-Bass.
- 1995. Reflective inquiry in social work practice. In P.M. Hess and E.J. Mullen, eds, *Practitioner-researcher partnerships: Building knowledge from, in, and for practice*, 31–55. Washington, D.C.: NASW Press.

Schur, E.L. 1979. The use of the coworker approach as a teaching model in graduate student field education. *Journal of Education for Social Work* 15(1), 72–9.

Seabury, B.A. 1976. The contract: Uses, abuses, and limitations. *Social Work* 21(1), 16–21.

Showers, N. 1990. Hospital graduate social work field programs: A study in New York City. *Health and Social Work* 15(2), 55–63.

Shulman, L. 1982. *Skills of supervision and staff management*. Itasca, Ill.: F.E. Peacock.

Siporin, M. 1981. Teaching family and marriage therapy. *Social Casework* 62(1), 20–9.

Skolnick, L. 1989. Field instruction in the 1980s – realities, issues and problem-solving strategies. In M. Raskin, ed., *Empirical studies in field instruction*, 47–75. New York: The Haworth Press.

Smith, H.Y., G. Faria, and C. Brownstein. 1986. Social work faculty in the role of liaison: A field study. *Journal of Social Work Education* 22(3), 68–78.

Smith-Bell, M., and J.W. Winslade. 1994. Privacy, confidentiality, and privilege in psychotherapeutic relationships. *American Journal of Orthopsychiatry* 64(2), 180–93.

Solomon, R. 1997. Legal survival for counselors and therapists. Seminar, Toronto, Ontario.

Sowers-Hoag, K., and B.A. Thyer. 1985. Teaching social work practice: A review and analysis of empirical research. *Journal of Social Work Education* 21(3), 5–15.

Star, B. 1979. Exploring the boundaries of videotape self-confrontation. *Journal of Education for Social Work* 15(1), 87–94.

Sterling, M.M. 1990. The use of role-play in psychotherapeutic training. In *Practical Applications in Supervision*, 373–84. San Diego: California Association of Marriage and Family Therapists.

Tebb, S., D.W. Manning, and T.K. Klaumann. 1996. A renaissance of group supervision. *Clinical Supervisor* 14(2), 39–51.

Thelen, H. 1960. *Education and the human quest.* New York: Harper and Row.

Thomlison, B. 1995. Student perceptions of reflective team supervision. In G. Rogers, ed., *Social work field education: Views and visions*, 234–44. Dubuque, Iowa: Kendall/Hunt.

Thompson, A.R., and K.D. Dickey. 1994. Self-perceived job search skills of college students with disabilities. *Rehabilitation Counselling Bulletin* 37, 358–70.

Tolson, E.R., and J. Kopp. 1988. The practicum: Clients, problems, interventions and influences on student practice. *Journal of Social Work Education* 24(2), 123–34.

Tourse, R.W.C. 1994. Completing the process tapestry. *Journal of Teaching in Social Work* 9(1/2), 155–67.

Towle, C. 1954. *The learner in education for the professions.* Chicago: University of Chicago Press.

Tropman, E.J. 1980. Agency constraints affecting links between practice and education. *Journal of Education for Social Work* 13(1), 8–14.

Tully, C.T., N.P. Kropf, and J.L. Price. 1993. Is field a hard hat area? A study of violence in field placements. *Journal of Social Work Education* 29(2), 191–9.

Urbanowski, M., and M. Dwyer. 1988. *Learning through field instruction: A guide for teachers and students.* Milwaukee: Family Service Association.

Urdang, E. 1979. On defense of process recording. *Smith College Studies in Social Work* 50(1), 1–15.

van Soest, D., & Kruzich, J. (1994). The influence of learning styles on student and field instructor perceptions of field placement success. *Journal of Teaching in Social Work* 9(1/2), 49–69.

Vayda, E. 1980. Educating for radical practice. *Canadian Journal of Education for Social Work* 6 (2), 102–6.

– 1981. The mature learner in field practice. Paper presented at the Canadian Association of Schools of Social Work Annual Conference, Halifax, Nova Scotia.

Vayda, E., and M. Bogo. 1991. A teaching model to unite classroom and field. *Journal of Social Work Education* 27(3), 271–8.

Vayda, E., and M. Satterfield. 1989. *Law for social workers: A Canadian guide.* 2nd ed. Toronto: Carswell.

Videka-Sherman, L., and W.J. Reid. 1985. The structured clinical record: A clinical education tool. *Clinical Supervisor* 3(1), 45–62.

Vinton, L., and B. White. 1995. The 'boutique effect' in graduate social work education. *Journal of Teaching in Social Work* 11(1/2), 3–13.

Wark, L. 1995. Defining the territory of live supervision in family therapy training: A qualitative study and theoretical discussion. *Clinical Supervisor* 13(1), 145–62.

Weinberg, L.K. 1978. Unique learning needs of physically handicapped social work students. *Journal of Education for Social Work* 14(1), 110–17.

Wigmore, J.H. 1961. *Evidence.* 3rd ed. New York: Little, Brown & Co.

Wilson, S.J. 1981. *Field instruction: Techniques for supervision.* New York: Macmillan.

Winter, M., and E.L. Holloway. 1991. Relation of trainee experience, conceptual level, and supervisor approach to selection of audiotaped counseling passages. *Clinical Supervisor* 9(2), 87–103.

Witkin, S. 1982. Cognitive processes in clinical practice. *Social Work* 27, 389–96.

Yalom, J. 1969. *The theory and practice of group psychotherapy.* New York: Basic Books.

Younghusband, E. 1967. The teacher in education for social work. *Social Service Review* 41(4), 359–70.

Zakutansky, T.J., and E. Sirles. 1993. Ethical and legal issues in field education: Shared responsibility and risk. *Journal of Social Work Education* 29(3), 338–47.